Betrayal of Too Trusting a People

The UN, the UK and the Trust Territory of the Southern Cameroons

Carlson Anyangwe

Langaa Research & Publishing CIG
Mankon, Bamenda

Publisher:
Langaa RPCIG
Langaa Research & Publishing Common Initiative Group
P.O. Box 902 Mankon
Bamenda
North West Region
Cameroon
Langaagrp@gmail.com
www.langaa-rpcig.net

Distributed outside N. America by African Books Collective
orders@africanbookscollective.com
www.africanbookscollective.com

Distributed in N. America by Michigan State University Press
msupress@msu.edu
www.msupress.msu.edu

ISBN: 9956-558-81-8

©Carlson Anyangwe 2009

DISCLAIMER

All views expressed in this publication are those of the author and do not necessarily reflect the views of Langaa RPCIG.

Other Titles by *Langaa* RPCIG

Francis B. Nyamnjoh
Stories from Abakwa
Mind Searching
The Disillusioned African
The Convert
Souls Forgotten
Married But Available

Dibussi Tande
No Turning Back: Poems of Freedom 1990-1993
Scribbles from the Den: Essays on Politics and Collective Memory in Cameroon

Kangsen Feka Wakai
Fragmented Melodies

Ntemfac Ofege
Namondo: Child of the Water Spirits
Hot Water for the Famous Seven

Emmanuel Fru Doh
Not Yet Damascus
The Fire Within
Africa's Political Wastelands: The Bastardization of Cameroon
Oriki'badan
Wading the Tide

Thomas Jing
Tale of an African Woman

Peter Wuteh Vakunta
Grassfields Stories from Cameroon
Green Rape: Poetry for the Environment
Majunga Tok: Poems in Pidgin English
Cry, My Beloved Africa
No Love Lost
Straddling The Mungo: A Book of Poems in English & French

Ba'bila Mutia
Coils of Mortal Flesh

Kehbuma Langmia
Titabet and the Takumbeng
An Evil Meal of Evil

Victor Elame Musinga
The Barn
The Tragedy of Mr. No Balance

Ngessimo Mathe Mutaka
Building Capacity: Using TEFL and African Languages as Development-oriented Literacy Tools

Milton Krieger
Cameroon's Social Democratic Front: Its History and Prospects as an Opposition Political Party, 1990-2011

Sammy Oke Akombi
The Raped Amulet
The Woman Who Ate Python
Beware the Drives: Book of Verse

Susan Nkwentie Nde
Precipice
Second Engagement

Francis B. Nyamnjoh & Richard Fonteh Akum
The Cameroon GCE Crisis: A Test of Anglophone Solidarity

Joyce Ashuntantang & Dibussi Tande
Their Champagne Party Will End! Poems in Honor of Bate Besong

Emmanuel Achu
Disturbing the Peace

Rosemary Ekosso
The House of Falling Women

Peterkins Manyong
God the Politician

George Ngwane
The Power in the Writer: Collected Essays on Culture, Democracy & Development in Africa

John Percival
The 1961 Cameroon Plebiscite: Choice or Betrayal

Albert Azeyeh
Réussite scolaire, faillite sociale : généalogie mentale de la crise de l'Afrique noire francophone

Aloysius Ajab Amin & Jean-Luc Dubois
Croissance et développement au Cameroun :
d'une croissance équilibrée à un développement équitable

Carlson Anyangwe
Imperialistic Politics in Cameroun:
Resistance & the Inception of the Restoration of the Statehood of Southern Cameroons
Betrayal of Too Trusting a People: The UN, the UK and the Trust Territory of the Southen Cameroons

Bill F. Ndi
K'Cracy, Trees in the Storm and Other Poems
Map: Musings On Ars Poetica
Thomas Lurting: The Fighting Sailor Turn'd Peaceable / Le marin combattant devenu paisible

Kathryn Toure, Therese Mungah Shalo Tchombe & Thierry Karsenti
ICT and Changing Mindsets in Education

Charles Alobwed'Epie
The Day God Blinked

G.D. Nyamndi
Babi Yar Symphony
Whether losing, Whether winning
Tussles: Collected Plays

Samuel Ebelle Kingue
Si Dieu était tout un chacun de nous ?

Ignasio Malizani Jimu
Urban Appropriation and Transformation: bicycle, taxi and handcart operators in Mzuzu, Malawi

Justice Nyo' Wakai
Under the Broken Scale of Justice: The Law and My Times

John Eyong Mengot
A Pact of Ages

Ignasio Malizani Jimu
Urban Appropriation and Transformation: Bicycle Taxi and Handcart Operators

Joyce B. Ashuntantang
Landscaping and Coloniality: The Dissemination of Cameroon Anglophone Literature

Jude Fokwang
Mediating Legitimacy: Chieftaincy and Democratisation in Two African Chiefdoms

Michael A. Yanou
Dispossession and Access to Land in South Africa: an African Perspevctive

Tikum Mbah Azonga
Cup Man and Other Stories

John Nkemngong Nkengasong
Letters to Marions (And the Coming Generations)

Amady Aly Dieng
Les étudiants africains et la littérature négro-africaine d'expression française

Tah Asongwed
Born to Rule: Autobiography of a life President

Frida Menkan Mbunda
Shadows From The Abyss

Bongasu Tanla Kishani
A Basket of Kola Nuts

Fo Angwafo III S.A.N of Mankon
Royalty and Politics: The Story of My Life

Basil Diki
The Lord of Anomy

Churchill Ewumbue-Monono
Youth and Nation-Building in Cameroon: A Study of National Youth Day Messages and Leadership Discourse (1949-2009)

Emmanuel N. Chia, Joseph C. Suh & Alexandre Ndeffo Tene
Perspectives on Translation and Interpretation in Cameroon

Linus T. Asong
The Crown of Thorns

Vivian Sihshu Yenika
Imitation Whiteman

Beatrice Fri Bime
Someplace, Somewhere
Mystique: A Collection of Lake Myths

Shadrach A. Ambanasom
Son of the Native Soil
The Cameroonian Novel of English Expression: An Introduction

Tangie Nsoh Fonchingong and Gemandze John Bobuin
Cameroon: The Stakes and Challenges of Governance and Development

Tatah Mentan
Democratizing or Reconfiguring Predatory Autocracy? Myths and Realities in Africa Today

Content

Preface vii

Chapter One
Historical Background 1

Chapter Two
Horse and Rider 15

Chapter Three
A Trust Betrayed by the United Nations 33

Chapter Four
A Trust Betrayed by the British Government 47

Chapter Five
A Black Colonialist Makes an Expansionist Claim 63

Chapter Six
Refutation of the 'History' Thesis 69

Chapter Seven
Refutation of the 'Consent to Incorporation' Thesis:
   The Plebiscite in 1961 85

Chapter Eight
Refutation of the "Consent to Incorporation" Thesis:
   The Pretended "Referendum" in 1972 103

Chapter Nine
The Bakassi Equation 129

Chapter Ten
The Matter of Secession 147

Chapter Eleven
Determination not by the "Self", but by the "Other" 169

Chapter Twelve
The 'Independence by Joining' Hoax 191

Chapter Thirteen
Was the Southern Cameroons Ever Decolonised? 217

Chapter Fourteen
A Historical Injustice Crying Out to be Set Right 243

Preface

As 'saltwater' or white colonisation in Africa was drawing to an end, sadly a new and dangerous situation of black-on-black colonisation was emerging in parts of the continent. Some states, themselves beneficiaries of the right to self-determination, soon became latter-day colonisers of less fortunate peoples in countries that happened to be their neighbours. Imperial Ethiopia laid claim to Eritrea, Morocco to Mauritania and Western Sahara, Cameroun Republic to the Southern British Cameroons, and apartheid South Africa to South West Africa (Namibia). Other states with expansionist ambitions also made legally indefensible territorial claims and grabbed vast border areas within neighbouring countries: the claim of Somalia to northern Kenya and to the Ogaden region in Ethiopia, of Libya to the Aouzou Strip in Chad, and of both Nigeria and Cameroun Republic to the Bakassi Peninsula in the Southern British Cameroons. The formal basis of these claims has always been a supposed ethnicity and/or historical connection. In truth, however, the primary reason for the claims is economic – a craving for access to critical resources such as minerals, oil, gas, cash crops, water, and the sea. But in international law, all these claims are expansionist and destabilising and have therefore never been accepted by the international community. Today, all but two of these claims have been abandoned. Cameroun Republic has still not ended its annexation of the Southern Cameroons and Morocco has also still not ended its annexation of the Western Sahara. By hopelessly continuing to hold on to their respective colonial pretensions, Cameroun Republic and Morocco have chosen the path of defiance and violent confrontation.

While Morocco's occupation of the Western Sahara has received extensive international attention, Cameroun Republic's annexation of the Southern Cameroons hasescaped international notice and therefore concern. Many reasons account for this. First, the United Nations (UN), creator and supervisor of the international trusteeship system, and the United Kingdom (UK), trustee power for the Southern Cameroons for almost half a century, aborted the process of decolonisation they had set in motion, denying the Southern

Cameroons sovereign statehood. Second, the colonial takeover of the Southern Cameroons was not as flamboyant and dramatic as Morocco's seizure of the Western Sahara. The takeover proceeded surreptitiously, through political subterfuge and in a creeping way. Third, Cameroun Republic, the new colonial authority in the Southern Cameroons, has over the years put in place strategies aimed at concealing its colonial occupation from the world, aware, as it must be, that colonialism is now perceived like rape and robbery combined and a contemporary form of slavery.

The strategies it has deployed are many: the international isolation of the Southern Cameroons so that few people are aware of the problems faced by its people; a policy of impoverishment of the territory and its population so that the people are unable to challenge the coloniser or fight back; a policy of terror towards the population carried out by an occupying army with licence to abduct, imprison, rape, torture, plunder and kill in order to secure submission and maintain the colonial occupation; a of sustained attack on the people's inherited educational and legal culture, denying them their right to to exist, their right to cultural development and destroying their identity, their specificity and their individuality as a distinct people with a well defined territory attested to by international boundary treaties.

Another of Cameroun Republic's egregious strategies consists in making token and decorative placements of a few citizens of the Southern Cameroons in its colonial administration (a leaf borrowed from French colonial practice). This serves Cameroun Republic strategically by assimilating the people of the Southern Cameroons, English-speaking, in the French world of Cameroun Republic, camouflaging the dependent status of the people of the Southern Cameroons, and pacifying the people of the Southern Cameroons lest they rise and revolt (as they are duty-bound to) against their colonial oppressors.

This book is a critical study of the colonial takeover of the territory and people of the Southern Cameroons by Cameroun Republic, highlighting the complicity of the UN and the Trustee Power, the UK Government. The book has twelve chapters. Chapter one gives a brief historical background of the Southern Cameroons from its colonisation by white foreign powers to the inception of its colonisation by a black alien state, Cameroun Republic, its eastern neighbour. Chapter 2 considers in the broadest outline the annexation of the Southern Cameroons by the said Cameroun Republic through duplicity, fraud and use of force. Chapters 3 and 4 broach the subject of a "conspiracy theory" at the UN by identifying conduct, statements and acts that form the bases of the reasonable inference of a conspiracy involving the UN and the UK Government to treat the Southern Cameroons and its people as expendable.

Chapters 5 to 8 examine and confute the arguments variously advanced by Cameroun Republic in support of its colonial claim to the territories of the Southern Cameroons. Chapter 9 critiques some of the assertions made by Cameroun Republic in the *Case Concerning the Land and Maritime Boundary between Cameroon and Nigeria* (Cameroon v. Nigeria: Equatorial Guinea Intervening, 2002), the so-called "Bakassi case". Chapter 10 gives an overview of the subject of secession from the perspectives of both international and municipal law. Chapters 11 and 12 revisit and consider in greater detail the claimed UN decolonisation of the Southern Cameroons. The book ends with a number of general concluding remarks.

Overall, it is the contention of this book, based on cogent evidence, that:

(i) the Southern Cameroons is not, has never been, and will never be, part of Cameroun Republic;
(ii) Cameroun Republic, by its annexation of the Southern Cameroons and its colonial domination and oppression of its people, is in breach of various legal norms under municipal and international law;
(iii) the people of the Southern Cameroons have an inalienable right under international human rights law and the law of nature to rid themselves of their humiliating status of a dependent people, and to establish a sovereign independent state as a guarantee of their right to exist as a people; they alone must take the responsibility for their own liberation and collective salvation;
(iv) the anti-colonial struggle in the Southern Cameroons is not a case of secession since it does not impair the territorial integrity of the colonising state of Cameroun

Republic, the lawful territorial framework of which ossified when it achieved independence on 1 January 1960, consistent with the customary international law principle of *uti possidetis juris* and Article 4(b) of the Constitutive Act of the African Union; and

(v) the colonial occupation of the Southern Cameroons by Cameroun Republic is an aggression and a vicious form of terrorism, and resistance to that violence (like resistance in occupied Europe and all colonial territories now decolonised) is legitimate under international law.

Indeed, Cameroun Republic's colonisation of the Southern Cameroons constitutes a threat to international peace and security in the Gulf of Guinea. By fighting to end that colonisation, the Southern Cameroons is acting consistently with international law and contributing to the maintenance of international peace and security in the Gulf of Guinea.

Chapter One
Historical Background

In the fifth century BC, a Carthaginian sailor called Hanno navigated the West African coast as far as the Gulf of Guinea where he witnessed on the mainland a volcanic eruption from a high hill that would later be known as Cameroons Mountain or Fako Mountain. He was so dazzled by the awesome sight that he named the mountain, *The Chariot of the Gods*. But the mountain remained unknown to geographers until 1472 when it was "discovered" by the Portuguese navigator Fernao do Poo. For that "discovery" cartographers honoured the navigator by naming the mountain after him.

Indeed, for most of the next four or five centuries the mountain would be known by Europeans and shown on their maps as *Serra de Fernao do Poo*.[1] Between the seventeenth and early nineteenth century Europeans sailed to Ambas Bay in the Gulf of Guinea mainly to trade in slaves, in ivory, and in palm oil and kernels. This was well before the British Government, filled with righteousness about combating slavery that rose to a crescendo in the 1860s, ended the transatlantic slave trade along the West African coast.

In the mid-nineteenth century, the Ambas Bay area, together with its hinterland, fell to the British thanks to the activities of a British Baptist missionary society. On 31 March 1843, a treaty abolishing the slave trade in return for a £1,200 subsidy was signed between Britain and Bimbia, a coastal chiefdom on the southern edge of Ambas Bay. 'I, King William and all the chiefs of Bimbia,' the treaty recited, 'do solemnly promise to do away with the abominable inhuman and unchristian-like custom of sacrificing human lives on account of death of any of the chiefs, or on account of any of their superstitious practices.'[2]

The following year, Joseph Merrick, a black Jamaican missionary of the English Baptist Mission set himself up at Bimbia, establishing a school, learning Isubu the local language, and engaging in a lot of preaching.[3] In 1853 Colonel Edward Nicolls, who had been the British Governor of the Island of Fernando Po from 1829-1834, obtained a voluntary cession from King William of Bimbia of all the lands from Bimbia to Rio del Rey.

Five years later, in August 1858, the Reverend Alfred Saker, head of an English Baptist mission community, moved from the Island of Fernando Po to Ambas Bay on the mainland opposite, after a visit to the place earlier in June.[4] In the words of the missionaries and their followers, the place was 'a land where freedom of conscience and civil liberty could be enjoyed.' Alfred Saker named the place Victoria in honour of Queen Victoria who was the reigning British Monarch at the time. On 23 August 1858, he executed a sale-of-land agreement with King William of Bimbia who claimed jurisdiction over the area as part of his kingdom.

The contract of sale is the prototype of many such contracts, also known as treaties of cession,[5] concluded between European traders, missionaries or explorers and African rulers in the years immediately before and after the beginning of the European scramble for Africa.

> I, William, Chief and the known King of Isubu, and sole and lawful owner of a district contiguous to Isubu and known as 'War Bay' and 'Ambas Bay' and Islands belonging thereto, declare, and by this act do make known, that I this day make over and give unto Alfred Saker [...] all my rights and title to the sovereignty and possession of the district therein specified [...] a coastline beginning at War Bay [...] continuing and embracing Fo'o Bay and thence onward to the highlands of Bobia (Bimbia) [sic] . Second, the interior line of this district shall be from the stream in War Bay onward N.E. [...] to join another line N.E. from the highlands beyond Bobia (Bimbia) [sic]. Third, this district with all that appertains thereto [...] I do this day make over and give unto Alfred Saker [...] and his assigns forever for the consideration herewith annexed. And I do hereby acknowledge to have received this day a note of hand and demand for payment of the consideration [...][6]

The piece of land thus sold to Alfred Saker was about 16 kilometres long and 8 kilometres wide along Ambas Bay and it fetched King William goods worth about £2,000. Oddly enough, Alfred Saker bought from the same King William land in the same area that in 1853 King William is said to have "voluntarily" ceded to Colonel Nicolls, presumably for Britain.

The 128 square kilometres district of Victoria became a small theocratic republic, interposed between the people of the Old Calabar, and the Wouri River Duala people. This loyal British Baptist colony was the first permanent European settlement at the foot of the Cameroons Mountain.[7]

That territory, from Bimbia through Victoria to Bakassi, forms the littoral district of what became the Southern Cameroons. It did not form part of the *Kamerun* territories that Germany took possession of by proclamation on 12 July 1884. In fact, a week after that proclamation, the British Government issued the Notification of 19 July 1884 by which it called attention to the fact that Ambas Bay remained a British possession. The notification was actually a proclamation in terms of which Britain formally took over Victoria as an integral part of Her Britannic Majesty's Dominion.

> I, Edward Hyde Hewett, Her Britannic Majesty's Consul for the Bights of Benin and Biafra, do hereby notify to all whom it may concern that, in compliance with the wishes of the inhabitants, the territory which has long been in the possession and occupation of certain British subjects, viz., the Baptist Missionary Society at Amboizes [*sic*] Bay, has now been taken over by Her Majesty the Queen of Great Britain and Ireland and forms an integral part of her Dominion. Given under my hand on board Her Britannic Majesty's Ship *Opal* anchored in Amboizes [*sic*] Bay this 19th day of July 1884.[8]

The territory remained a British possession and its hinterland a British sphere of influence for more than 30 years until 28 March 1887 when the area was ceded to Germany and was then incorporated into the *Kamerun* Protectorate.[9] But German efforts at effective occupation of the hinterland of Ambas Bay did not begin until about 1889 and dragged on until about 1902.[10] Wherever the Germans established a presence the area in question automatically became part of the German *Kamerun* protectorate.

The German proclamation of 12 July 1884 brought under German sphere of influence an ill-defined swathe of territory at the hinge of Africa,[11] covering the Duala mud-flat enclave and its hinterland.[12] The *Kamerun* Protectorate, originally a mud-flat estuary, consisted of the land of the Duala people at the mouth of the Wouri River. That river was first named *Rio dos Camarões* (River of Prawns) by its Portuguese "discoverers." The English alliteratively rendered the Portuguese appellation as "the Cameroons River," instead of a literal translation that would have been "River of Prawns" or "Prawns River." With time, the name of the area became identified with the river that ran through it. *"Camarões,"* the Portuguese word for prawns or shrimps (in singular, *camarão*), became an adaptable name: "Cameroons" in English, "Kamerun" in German (rather than *garnele*, the German word for prawn/shrimp), "Cameroun" in French (rather than *crevette*, the French word for prawn/shrimp), and "Camarón" in Spanish (the Spanish word for prawn/shrimp).

Germany eventually established effective control over the River Wouri estuary and its hinterland by a slow process of discovery and conquest that lasted some twenty-five years. It was not until 1907 that the whole massive area, from Duala to Lake Chad down to the Congo and Rio Muni, was completely pacified and boundary definition became possible.

In 1914, when effective and peaceful German occupation had lasted for less than a decade, *Kamerun* was wrested from Germany by Anglo-French forces at the very beginning of World War I. At the outset of the war, British-led forces from Nigeria captured territory that included the Victoria district previously ceded to Germany in 1887. Meanwhile, Germany held on to its original *Kamerun* territory until March 1916 when its forces were defeated by those of Britain and France. The 1916 Anglo-French Agreement signed by Viscount Milner and Monsieur Simon, plenipotentiaries of the two powers, partitioned the Germany colony according to the area under each power's military occupation.

The 1916 Anglo-French partition in fact carved out two separate territories of unequal size, delimiting the international frontiers between the two along what came to be known as the Simon-Milner Line.[13] The smaller territory, one fifth the size of the erstwhile protectorate, went to Britain.[14] It was the same territory on Ambas Bay together with a narrow strip of land stretching further northwards up to Lake Chad; it covered in effect the pre-1888 British possession and sphere of influence on Ambas Bay. It took the anglicised form, *the Cameroons*.

The larger territory went to France and took the gallicised form, *le Cameroun*. However, France quickly excised from it two huge chunks of territory known as the *Neue Kamerun*[15] and the "Duckbill." These were then incorporated into French Equatorial Africa. The remainder of the French Cameroun territory in fact consisted essentially of the Duala estuary district and its hinterland. In other words it consisted of all of the territory claimed by Germany in 1884 as the *Schutzgebiet von Kamerun*. The mandated/trust territory of French Cameroun did not, therefore, include the *Neue Kamerun* and the "Duckbill." These two areas had been acquired in 1911 by Germany from France in exchange for Germany's withdrawal from and recognition of French interests in Morocco.

By the British Cameroons Administration Ordinance in 1924, Britain divided the British Cameroons Territory into Northern and Southern Cameroons, following an arbitrary line rather than where the continuity of the the territory of the British Cameroons is broken by the projection of a piece of Nigeria territory known as the 'Yola arc.' Northern Cameroons was incorporated into the Northern Region of Nigeria, and the Southern Cameroons into the Eastern Region of that country. Both parts of British Cameroons were administered as an integral part of Nigeria. The British thus held their Cameroons Trust Territory as a dismembered, and not as a unitary, colonial territory.

From 1924 to 1960, the Southern Cameroons, though under international tutelage and thus possessed of international status, was nevertheless administered as an integral part of that country, under the thin disguise of "an administrative union." The Southern Cameroons thus came to share with Nigeria a common constitution, budget, administration, legal system and technical services.[16] Between 1954 and 1960, it was a self-governing territory within the Federation of Nigeria. It exercised a wide measure of regional autonomy along with basic self-governing institutions – an executive, a judiciary, a bi-cameral legislature, a civil service and a police force.

On 1 October 1960 the Southern Cameroons was separated from Nigeria and the Southern Cameroons Constitution Order in Council came into force.[17] From 1 October 1960 to 30 September 1961, the territory was fully self-governing. It was fully responsible for its internal affairs except for defence which, along with foreign affairs, came under Britain's jurisdiction[18] and was poised for sovereign statehood.

On 11 February 1961 a plebiscite, at the behest and under the auspices of the United Nations, was held in the territory. The United Nations asked the people of the territory to decide whether they wish "to achieve independence" by joining Nigeria or French-speaking Cameroun Republic.[19] The vote went in favour of "joining" Cameroun Republic. In terms of the signed pre-plebiscite agreements between the political leaders of the British Southern Cameroons nd those of Cameroun Republic, the term "join" was construed to mean "federate."

The British Southern Cameroons achieved independence, though not as a separate state, on 1 October 1961. The plebiscite question held out the promise of independence, and General Assembly Resolution 1608 endorsed the decision of the people of the territory to achieve independence.[20]

In 1960 the British Southern Cameroons and Cameroun Republic had agreed in writing to form a federation of two states, equal in status, in the event where the plebiscite vote went in favour of "joining" Cameroun Republic. Details of the envisaged federation were to be finalised, evidenced by a federal constitution, the fruit of common bargain, and submitted to the respective peoples or legislatures of the two countries for ratification before 1 October 1961. This did not happen.

Details on the federal association were never finalised. No constitutional text was adopted, nor signed by both parties and submitted to their respective peoples or parliaments for ratification. Cameroun Republic simply embarked on the path of lawlessness. In breach of the international law principle of territoriality, it drafted, enacted and promulgated on 1 September 1961 a so-called "federal constitution" and foisted it on the people of the Southern Cameroons. The document in question was in reality an annexation law (disguised as an "amending constitutional law") through which Cameroun Republic claimed the Southern Cameroons as part of its lost territory. In mid-September 1961, it moved its troops into the Southern Cameroons and occupied the territory. This event, together with the extraterritorial legislation by Cameroun Republic, took place even while the Southern Cameroons was still a UN trust territory under UK administration.

Then on 1 October the same year Cameroun Republic imposed, under article 59 of the September 1961 annexation law, the French language as *langue légitime*, and left English only a tolerated language. On the 15 October, it appointed one of its nationals as viceroy to the Southern Cameroons, under the official name of *inspecteur fédéral d'administration* (décret no. 61/DF). Two months later, the Southern Cameroons was brought under the jurisdiction of the military tribunal sitting in Yaounde (décret no. 61/DF/73), and on 7 July 1962 the Southern Cameroons was constituted a military command unit under a military officer answerable to Yaounde (décret no. 62/DF/239).

On 1 October 1961 no legally valid federation came into being; only a *de facto* federal situation came into existence.[21] In May 1972 Cameroun Republic staged what its political rulers confessed was a '*revolution.*'[22] It was, in fact, the overthrow of the informal federation under the thin disguise of a pretended referendum.[23] The consequences of that action were dire for the Southern Cameroons. Cameroun Republic dramatically increased the already high level of its military presence in the Southern Cameroons. Those forces, especially the *gendarmerie*, have never hesitated to maltreat the people of the territory. Southern Cameroons' legal personality, its unity as a polity and its territorial integrity were destroyed; its constitution was revoked; its police force was disbanded; its parliament was dissolved; its government institutions were abolished; and its politicians sacked. There was a massive take-over of the land and military control was tightened. The territory was cut up into two provinces. Direct rule from Cameroun Republic, previously disguised through the viceroy as *inspecteur fédéral d'administration*, was now openly imposed.

The two provinces into which the Southern Cameroons was split in 1972 were placed, and have since remained, under the administration of a hierarchy of officials from Cameroun Republic known as *sous-préfets, préfets, gouverneurs, commissaires de police*, and *commandants de legion militaire*. French was imposed as the language of governance and the French system of administration was extended to the territory. It is difficult to resist the conclusion that this was another phase in a vast and insidious policy of subjugation, terrorisation, and forcible assimilation of the already traumatised people of the Southern Cameroons.

Having overthrown the informal "Federal Republic of Cameroon," Cameroun Republic proclaimed a so-called "United Republic of Cameroun." Then in February 1984 the "United Republic of Cameroun" was in turn scrapped and the hitherto defunct Cameroun Republic was revived as a legal and political expression. Cameroun Republic is the name and style by which French Cameroun achieved independence from France on 1 January 1960 and was admitted, on 20 September 1960, to membership of the United Nations.[24]

In the view of the political rulers of Cameroun Republic their country took over the British Southern Cameroons as part of Cameroun Republic's territory returned to it. 'Federal Republic of Cameroon' and 'United Republic of Cameroun' were simply labelling tricks, mere internal name and structural changes, aimed at facilitating the integration of that "returned territory." Cameroun Republic, they argue, had all along continued its identity, notwithstanding any addition to its territory. On this reasoning, Cameroun Republic is a two-faced Janus, capable of being identical and non-identical at the same time, a Sphinx capable of undergoing a number of births and rebirths without death.

In reaction to Cameroun Republic's imperial appetite, the people of the Southern Cameroons have continued to send deputations and memoranda to the government of Cameroun Republic to rescind its expansionist policy, but to no avail. Organised peaceful protest marches calling for an end to colonial domination and oppression are always violently suppressed by the military using grenades and live bullets, resulting in many deaths. In fact, by all accounts systematic repression and gross human rights abuses in the Southern Cameroons have intensified in the last twenty years, a clear indication that there is no reasonable prospect Cameroun Republic will see reason and change its imperialistic policy.

Given this reality the Southern Cameroons National Council (SCNC), the national independence movement, proclaimed, in a Radio Broadcast in December 1999, the revival of the Southern Cameroons as a legal and political expression. The SCNC stated that the action was a historic and legal necessity to vindicate the right of self-determination in order to achieve a peaceful and lasting solution to the colonial seizure of the Southern Cameroons by

Cameroun Republic. The SCNC's mandate to make the proclamation was given to it by a Conference of the people of the Southern Cameroons held at Bamenda in April/May 1994. The Final Act of that Conference, *The Bamenda Proclamation*, stated unambiguously that should Cameroun Republic 'either persist in its refusal to engage in meaningful constitutional talks or fail to engage in such talks [with the Southern Cameroons] within a reasonable time', the SCNC 'shall so inform the [Southern Cameroons] people by all suitable means and shall thereupon proclaim the revival of the independence and sovereignty of the Anglophone territory of the Southern Cameroons and take all measures necessary to secure, defend and preserve the independence, sovereignty and integrity of the said Territory.'

Cameroun Republic responded to the proclamation by abducting and torturing scores of Southern Cameroons' citizens. It abducted and detained for years without charge key leaders of the SCNC (e.g. Justice Ebong, Pa Sabum, Chief Ayamba Otun and several others). It executed some SCNC members extra-judicially (e.g. Che Ngwa Ghandi, Amindou Bel Suika, Boniface Mbinso, Sela Nsaiwiybin, Olivier Nyuyki and a number of Youth League members, e.g. Emmanuel Konsek, Mathias Ngum, Joseph Ndifon, Richard Ngwa, Julius Ngwa, Samuel Tita, Mathias Gwei, Daniel Tita, Lawrence Fai and Patrick Timbu). It held scores of others for years without charge under atrocious conditions, including solitary confinement and imprisonment in chains.[25]

The only plank of Cameroun Republic's national policy of terrorisation is the averment that the Southern Cameroons' anti-colonial struggle is a secessionist bid, which it claims is impermissible under international law and gives it the right to suppress by force of arms.

The Southern Cameroons, 43,000 square kilometres in area, has a current population of about 6.5 million inhabitants and is blessed with huge natural resources.[26] It is strategically located in the "armpit" of Africa in the Gulf of Guinea, sandwiched between Nigeria and Cameroun Republic like a wedge between West Africa and what is still in effect French Equatorial Africa. It shares land and maritime boundaries with Nigeria to the west and with Cameroun Republic to the east, and a maritime boundary with Equatorial Guinea.

Notes

1. V Le Vine, *The Cameroons from Mandate to Independence*, University of California Press, Berkeley & Los Angeles, 1964, p. 16; A Debel, *Cameroon Today*, Editions Jeune Afrique, Paris, 1977, p. 94.

2. Between March 1843 and September 1884 several treaties were entered into between Great Britain and the Chiefs along the Southern Cameroons coast (Bimbia, Bota, Batoki, Isobe, Bakingi, etc.). Six of these treaties, especially the treaties with the Chief of Bimbia are reproduced in SG Ardener, *Eye-Witnesses to the Annexation of Cameroon 1883-1887*, Government Press, Buea, 1968, pp. 63-69.

3. P Verdzekov, 'Victoria, now known as Limbe, is 150 years old,' note written on 13 January 2008 and posted on the *Internet* by Viban Williamson on 18 February 2008. Joseph Merrick left Bimbia in 1849 to return to Jamaica but died at sea.

4. The Island of Fernando Po, originally a missionary-inspired British settlement since 1827 was ceded by Britain to Catholic Spain in 1855. In May 1858, Spain, through the Island's Governor, Don Carlos Chacon, promptly declared Roman Catholicism the only permissible religion in the Island. Alfred Saker, his fellow missionaries and their followers, Protestants, were therefore constrained to leave the Island. They relocated to Ambas Bay, at Victoria, twenty miles from Fernando Po. Alfred Saker's missionary work in Victoria is recounted in detail in EB Underhill, *Afred Saker: Missionary to Africa – A Biography*, London, Carey Kingsgate Press, 1884 (reprinted in 1958).

5. For example, the explorer Henry Morton Stanley obtained on behalf of King Leopold II of the Belgians no less than 450 "treaties" from the several chiefs of the Congo Basin. One of these "treaties" dated 1 April 1884 stated that in return for 'one piece of cloth per month to each of the undersigned chiefs, besides present of cloth in hand,' the said chiefs promised to: 'freely of their own accord, for themselves and their heirs and successors for ever... give up to the said Association [of the Congo] the sovereignty and all sovereign and governing rights to all their territories... and to assist by labour or otherwise, any works, improvements or expeditions which the said Association [of the Congo] shall cause at any time to be carried out in any part of these territories ... All roads and railways running through this country, the right of collecting tolls on the same, and all game, fishing, mining and forest rights, are to be the absolute property of the said Association.' See A Hochschild, *King Leopold's Ghost*, Pan Books, London, 1998, p. 72.

6. For the full text of this treaty see SG Ardener, op. cit., p. 53.

7. KO Dike, *Trade and Politics in the Niger Delta 1830-1885*, Clarendon Press, Oxford, 1956, p. 65; Victoria Centenary Committee, *Victoria – Southern Cameroons 1858-1958*, Ballatyne & Co., London, 1958, p. 102; T Lewis, *These Seventy Years*, [book

does not indicate publisher], London, 1930, p. 60; S Ardener (ed), *Kingdom on Mount Cameroon. Studies in the History of the Cameroon Coast: 1500-1997*, Berghahn Books, 1998, p. 268.

8. See SG Ardener, op. cit., p. 68; E Hertslet, *The Map of Africa by Treaty*, Frank Cass & Co., London, 1967, vol. II, p. 694.

9. E Hertslet, *The Map of Africa by Treaty*, Frank Cass & Co., London, 1967, vol. II, p. 694; K Roberts-Wray, *Commonwealth and Colonial Law*, Stevens & Sons, London, 1966, p. 122.

10. See, for example, EM Chilver, *Zintgraff's Explorations in Bamenda, Adamawa and the Benue Lands*, 1889-1892, Government Press, Buea, 1966.

11. HR Rudin, *Germans in the Cameroon 1884-1914: A Case Study in Modern Imperialism*, Jonathan Cape, London, 1938; S Ardener, *Eye-Witness to the Annexation of Cameroon*, Government Press, Buea, 1968; EM Chilver, *Zintgraff's Explorations in Bamenda, Adamawa, and Benue Lands 1889-1892*, Government Printer, Buea, 1966.

12. On the 12th of July 1884, a German Protectorate was proclaimed over what was styled the 'Kamerun District.' A week later, on the 19th July 1884 the British Government issued a Notification of the assumption of British sovereignty over Ambas Bay, including Victoria which had since 1858 been a Settlement of the English Mission Society. By Arrangement between Great Britain and Germany dated 29 April – 16 June 1885, relative to their respective Spheres of Action in portions of Africa, both Powers agreed to withdraw any Protectorates already established within the limits assigned to the other, a reservation being specially made as to the Settlement of Victoria, Ambas Bay, which continued to be a British possession. Following negotiations between Britain and Germany relative to the cession of Ambas Bay, Victoria was transferred to the sovereignty of Germany on 28 March 1887. See, E Hertslet, *The Map of Africa by Treaty, Vol. III*, Frank Cass & Co., London, 1967, pp. 694, 868 and 871.

13. On 4 March 1916, Viscount Milner, the British Secretary of State for the Colonies, and Monsieur Henry Simon, the French Minister for the Colonies, met in Paris and partitioned the jointly conquered territory along a Line that came to bear their two names. The two British and French military governors who had established an uneasy short-lived Anglo-French condominium over Douala initialled the Simon-Milner delimitation agreement three weeks later in that town.

14. Not wanting to incur more financial responsibilities over yet another colonial territory, Britain was concerned merely to secure what it perceived as better boundaries for its vast contiguous territory of Nigeria. It was therefore content

with a tiny strip of territory to serve as infilling at the eastern border of Nigeria. In the words of Viscount Milner: 'We shall not, indeed, have added much to our possessions in West Africa, either in the Cameroons or in Togo. But the additional territory we have gained, though not large in extent, has a certain value in giving us better boundaries.' In fact, however, Britain had a sense of history. The area it took included the territories it had acquired by 1858 but ceded to Germany in 1887.

15. The *Neue Kamerun* was a territory of 278,000 square kilometres. In 1911 France had ceded it to Germany in return for Germany's withdrawal from, and recognition of French interests in, Morocco.

16. Up to 1960 the Commissioner of the Southern Cameroons was responsible to the Lieutenant Governor of the Eastern Region of Nigeria for the administration of the Southern Cameroons and ultimately to the Governor General of Nigeria at Lagos.

17. The Constitution of the Southern Cameroons was provided for in the *Southern Cameroons (Constitution) Order in Council*, 1960. The Order revoked the Nigerian (Constitution) Orders in Council 1954 to 1960, in so far as they applied to the Southern Cameroons. The powers and functions of the Southern Cameroons Government, hitherto exercised by the Governor General and the Government of the Federation of Nigeria, were left unaltered but transferred to the Commissioner of the Southern Cameroons, Mr. JO Field appointed in 1960 under Her Majesty's sign manual and signet and holding office during Her Majesty's pleasure.

18. *Yearbook of the United Nations*, 1958, pp. 346-349.

19. UN General Assembly Resolution 1352 (XIV) of 16 October 1959.

20. UN General Assembly Resolution 1608 (xv) of 21 April 1961, operative paragraph 2 (b) declared the UN's endorsement of the results of the plebiscite "that the *people* of the Southern Cameroons have... decided to *achieve independence.*" (Emphasis added). The plebiscite, resolution 1608, Foumban, the 'federation', the 1972 so-called referendum and the revival of Cameroun Republic are discussed in detail in subsequent chapters of this book.

21. In the *de facto* federation Cameroun Republic became the federated state of East Cameroun and the Southern Cameroons became the federated state of West Cameroon, both states apparently falling under the sovereignty of the federal State.

22. See collection of Ahidjo's speeches in *Anthologie des Discours 1968-1978*, Les Nouvelles Editions, Paris, 1979.

23. It is well to remember that Cameroun Republic, demographically and spatially bigger than Southern Cameroons, heavily dominated and controlled this informal federal situation. Its military forces maintained a brutal and intimidating presence in the Southern Cameroons and its citizens monopolized every aspect of public life in the informal federation and conceded merely a token and decorative presence to citizens of Southern Cameroons.

24. The revival of that denomination meant the *formal* restoration of the legal personality of that country. But there continued to be used, for the self-serving purpose of creating confusion in the mind of the outside world, the abbreviated and less formal appellation 'Cameroun' (translated into English as 'Cameroon'). At the UN therefore the sitting position of Cameroun Republic has remained unchanged since becoming a member of the UN in September 1960, notwithstanding the *de facto* federation from 1961 to 1972 and the farcical *république unie du Cameroun* from 1972 to 1984. This has reinforced the fiction that Cameroun Republic, which achieved independence from France on 1 January 1960 under that name and style, continues irrespective of whatever changes, *de facto* or *de jure*, may have occurred regarding its status or name. On the Roster of UN Member States there is the intriguing non-committal entry 'Cameroon,' *tout court*, rather than 'Cameroun Republic'.

25. A list of over three hundred names of persons abducted, severely tortured, detained without charge, or executed extrajudicially is contained in a document entitled 'Savage Intimidation, Arrests, Tortures, Assassinations and Genocide visited on Southern Cameroonians by the Biya Regime,' issued in 2005 by an organisation, the Southern Cameroons Information Agency (SCIA).

26. The Southern Cameroons is more populated than at least 60 UN and 18 AU Member States, and larger in size than at least 30 UN and 12 AU Member States. It is self-sufficient in food. Its natural resources include crude oil, gas, coffee, cocoa, bananas, tea, pepper, palm oil and kernel, rubber, timber, salt and fish. There are very strong indications of bauxite, diamond, gold and uranium in the territory, though no serious prospecting for these minerals has yet been carried out.

Chapter Two

Horse and Rider

In 1958 the Southern Cameroons celebrated with pomp the centenary of the founding of Victoria.¹ That year the British Government certified at the UN that compared with Nigeria the Southern Cameroons had not been delayed in political evolution and was expected to achieve in 1960 the objectives set forth in Article 76b of the UN Charter, self-government or independence. There was much excitement in the territory and great expectations regarding its future. The territory was already self-governing and so it was expected that independence as a sovereign state was to be achieved in 1960. In its Resolution 1282 (XIII) of 5 December 1958 the General Assembly took note of the certification by the British Government. Then, as if the devil himself had taken control, things suddenly began to go wrong.²

On 13 March 1959, the Assembly adopted Resolution 1350 (XIII) recommending a plebiscite in the Southern Cameroons to ascertain the wishes of the people concerning their future. Another Assembly decision, resolution 1352 (XIV) of 16 October 1959, ordered that a plebiscite be held 'between 30 September 1960 and March 1961.' On 11 February 1961 a limited vote took place. The UN interpreted the result, correctly, as having gone in favour of achieving independence. It also went on to interpret the same result as having gone in favour of the "alternative" of "joining" Cameroun Republic. In reality, as will be shown in chapter seven, that result was a negative vote against Nigeria (because of fear of Ibo domination) rather than a positive vote in favour of "joining" Cameroun Republic.³ On 21 April 1961 the General Assembly voted on the independence of the Southern Cameroons and adopted resolution 1608 (XV) with 50 votes for, two against and nine abstentions.

Significantly, and this fact has important legal implications, Cameroun Republic was one of the few States that voted against Resolution 1608. Cameroun Republic's negative vote meant that: (i) it refused to recognise the independence of the Southern

Cameroons, a decision taken by the plebiscite and endorsed by the UN, (ii) it rejected the UN decision on the Southern Cameroons "joining" as an independent country, and (iii) it rejected the UN invitation for the finalisation of the arrangements by which the agreed and declared policies of both countries were to be implemented. Moreover, by that negative vote Cameroun Republic continued the international boundary between itself and the Southern Cameroons as unchanged in character, despite appearances to the contrary. This negative vote explains Cameroun Republic's subsequent systematic delinquent behaviour regarding the Southern Cameroons.

By resolution 1608 (XV) of 21 April 1961 the UN General Assembly (i) endorsed the results of the plebiscite that the people of the Southern Cameroons 'decided to achieve independence by joining the independent Republic of Cameroun' , (ii) decided that the Trusteeship Agreement concerning the British Cameroons 'shall be terminated in accordance with Article 76b of the Charter of the United Nations [...] on 1 October 1961, upon [the Southern Cameroons] joining the Republic of Cameroun' and (iii) invited Britain, the Southern Cameroons and Cameroun Republic 'to initiate urgent discussions with a view to finalizing before 1 October 1961, the arrangements by which the agreed and declared policies of the parties concerned will be implemented.'[4]

A constitutional meeting between delegations of the two countries was held in July 1961 in Foumban, a town in Cameroun Republic. The purpose of the meeting was to work out the details of the proposed federal constitution and have it adopted by both sides in time for it to enter into force on 1 October. It was common ground that the draft federal constitution that would be agreed upon by the conference delegates would be submitted to the governments of the two countries and to their respective peoples or parliaments for approval. Since the two countries as yet had no common parliament, the document would have to be endorsed by their respective peoples or parliaments in order to be an "Act of Union" capable of being registered with the UN as a treaty consistent with Article 102 of the Charter of the United Nations.

Mr. Ahidjo, the President of Cameroun Republic chaired the meeting. The meeting lasted a mere five days. Three of of those days were taken up with ceremonial opening and closing long-winded speeches and with various diversions in which the delegates indulged themselves. Ahidjo produced a document and gave the Southern Cameroons' delegation two days to go over it and suggest for his consideration what the delegation would like to see included in the document. The delegation was taken back by Ahidjo's dictatorial conduct but decided that in the circumstances it had better make the best of an awful situation.[5] It then poured through the document as best as it could, made suggestions and expressed the desire for another meeting to finalise an agreed text for submission to popular approval or to the respective parliaments of the two countries.

Ahidjo rejected the critical proposals made by the Southern Cameroons delegation, including robust states, a bill of rights, a bicameral legislature and location of the federal capital in Douala. He said they were 'matters of technical details' to be attended to 'when the proposals shall be put into proper form.' He then peremptorily adjourned the meeting *sine die* and refused to reconvene the same despite repeated reminders from the Prime Minister of the Southern Cameroons. He decided that Cameroun Republic would proceed unilaterally on this matter. The inconclusiveness of the Foumban meeting was raised by two members of parliament during the debates in the Southern Cameroons' House of Assembly in the third week of September 1961.

> Mr Speaker, Sir, at Foumban whereas there were about eight or nine chapters for us to grind through, we were able to cover four of the chapters we thought were most pressing. The other chapters [...] we felt it necessary to postpone [...] and seek expert advice [...] Mr Speaker, Sir, this was never done, and [...] the next thing we saw was what is being termed the Constitution of the Federal Republic of Cameroon, including those aspects to which we wanted to give second thought. (Hon. PN Motomby-Woleta, MHA)

> Mr Speaker, Sir, I ask members of both sides of the House whether they feel satisfied that the feelings of the Southern Cameroons people have been reflected fully in this draft constitution [...] Sir, in Article 1 the Southern Cameroons Delegation asked for a modification of the national flag and

motto. They suggested that the federal capital should be in Douala instead of Yaounde in order to avoid a feeling of inferiority, a feeling that we have integrated with the Cameroun Republic [...] This has not been reflected in the constitution. [...] We are therefore registering our dissatisfaction with this draft constitution. (Hon. FN Ajebe-Sone, MHA)

Mr Speaker, Sir, [...] We are going to tell Cameroun Republic, that we are small but we are sharp. [...] We are going to tell Cameroun Republic that quality is different from quantity.[6] (Hon. S Moffor, MHA)

After the inconclusive Foumban bipartite meeting, Ahidjo mandated his French technical adviser on institutional matters, a certain Mr. Jacques Rousseau, to draft a constitutional document for him. When the document was ready he sent it to the legislature of Cameroun Republic for adoption as a mere 'law amending the constitution of Cameroun Republic'. The document was dutifully adopted on 1 September 1961 not even as a "constitution" but merely as a "constitutional amendment law"[7] meant, in the words of the document itself, to facilitate the 'recovery of a separated part of our country.'

Inasmuch as that document claimed to be binding on the Southern Cameroons, it was legally ineffective in relation to the territory. In September 1961 the Southern Cameroons was still a UN Trust Territory under the UK Administration. Neither the President nor the Assembly of Cameroun Republic had jurisdiction over the trust territory. They could not exercise constituent powers in respect of the Southern Cameroons. They could therefore not validly adopt a constitution binding on the territory. The document was adopted by a foreign legislature and promulgated by a foreign prince and therefore in theory of law could not have legal validity in the Southern Cameroons. Territoriality is an elementary principle of international law. Municipal law has territorial limits; it does not extend beyond the geographical area of the state.

To add injury to insult the long title of the document adopted by Cameroun Republic proclaimed the annexationist pretensions of Cameroun Republic when it recited that the *loi constitutionnelle* adopted by its Assembly merely 'revised the Constitution of Cameroun Republic for the purpose of facilitating the constitutional accession of a returned part of its territory.' To the extent that Cameroun Republic purported to assert in that document a territorial claim to the Southern Cameroons as part of its territory, the document adopted by the legislature of Cameroun Republic was patently in the nature of an annexation law contrary to international law and therefore legally ineffectual on that account.[8]

The cumulative legal effect of the plebiscite result, UN Resolution 1608 (XV), and Article 76b of the UN Charter, is that the Southern Cameroons arguably "achieved independence" on 1 October 1961. On that same day a *de facto* two-state federal union came into being. Though bereft of any legally valid founding text, the informal federation was a political association of two independent and equal states. It could not have been anything else since independence was expressed by UN Resolution 1608(XV) as achieved *by*, and not *upon* or *after*, joining.[9]

As one of two federated states within an overarching federation, the Southern Cameroons enjoyed internal government. Its political status could be said to have been that of an independent half-sovereign state on account of its internal independence and autonomy. It continued to enjoy its distinct identity and individuality. It was a political unit. It was also a single territorial unit. It had legal personality under municipal law. It could sue and be sued. It controlled much of its internal affairs. It had authority over and enjoyed the allegiance of its citizens. It exercised a large measure of territorial competence within its colonial-defined boundaries as they stood on the date of its independence on 1 October 1961. By the principle of self-determination (restated in common article 1 of the International Covenant on Civil and Political Rights and the International Covenant on Economic Social and Cultural Rights 1966 as a matter of treaty law) a colonial or similar non-independent territory determines its political future within the limits of the principle of *uti possidetis*.

It had a constitution, a government, a parliament, a civil service, a police force, an administrative system, a common language of public administration (English), a distinct legal and judicial system (based on the Common Law system), and a distinct educational system (based on the British model). It operated a democratic system of government based on the Westminster-type parliamentary system. Its government was founded on principles of democracy, accountability, the rule of law and respect for human rights and fundamental freedoms.

Soon after the inception of the informal federation, the demographically and spatially bigger Cameroun Republic quickly forgot about the federation when the full implication of federalism dawned on it.[10] It forgot about equality of status and about union in diversity. It started promoting a "father state" or a "principal-state" concept. One political science writer and a citizen of Cameroun Republic canvasses the fantastic idea that any territory with the name 'Cameroun' (however spelt) appertains to Cameroun Republic because 'Cameroun' is a brand name over which it has an intellectual property right by dint of its independence and membership of the United Nations under that name.[11] If any such thing exists, it cannot be in respect to the appellation 'Cameroon', *tout court*, but only in respect of the denotation *'la République du Cameroun'*, which is the official name and style by which that country achieved independence from France on 1 January 1960 and was admitted to the United nations on 20 September of the same year.

Cameroun Republic embarked on domination and on systematic oppression and repression. The federation ceased to be a vehicle of voluntary and equal partnership. It ceased to be a vehicle for the pooling of sovereignty and resources. It took a dangerous path, sliding down a fast and perilous road, without compass and without hope. In May 1972 Ahidjo dictatorially decreed the federation out of existence and then formally effected the annexation of the Southern Cameroons to Cameroun Republic.[12] As noted in the overview in chapter one, the government and institutions of the Southern Cameroons were sacked. The territorial, political and legal integrity of the Southern Cameroons were impaired. The state's constitution was abolished. The state was dismembered, losing its legal personality, its political and territorial unity and Home Rule.

Direct rule was imposed from Cameroun Republic and more troops were poured into the territory to reinforce its occupation. This was done under the smokescreen of a pretended "referendum" stage-managed to hoodwink the world into believing that the people of the Southern Cameroons had consented to their own annexation, a political euthanasia.

The claim was then made that the annexed Southern Cameroons and the annexing state of Cameroun Republic had become conflated to constitute a conjoint mongrel country known as *'république unie du Cameroun'*. This was Ahidjo's version of Hitler's 1938 *Germano-Austrian Anschluss*. The bogus "referendum" and the sham *"république unie"* were impostures and were forced on the Southern Cameroons in violation of the right of self-determination and of the principle of equal rights of all peoples. The people of the Southern Cameroons did not, and have insisted over the years they will never, accept either the fake "referendum" or the *"république unie"* or any other form of colonialism by Cameroun Republic.

In 1982 Ahidjo resigned as President of his counterfeit *"république unie"* and, as directed by France through its oil company ELF, handed over power to Biya Paul who, in 1984, scrapped the sham *"république unie"* he and Ahidjo had manufactured and revived the hitherto extinct *'République du Cameroun'*, the former French territory that achieved independence from France on 1 January 1960. The revival of Cameroun Republic as a legal and political expression marked the final stage in Cameroun Republic's creeping annexation of the Southern Cameroons.

The claim by the revived *République du Cameroun* to the territories of the Southern Cameroons signifies its rejection of the principles of territorial integrity and *uti possidetis juris*, and attests to its espousal of imperialism long abandoned by the civilized world. Cameroun Republic thus became in effect an empire in relation to the Southern Cameroons and the people of the territory have become a captive people in the Cameroun Republic house of bondage.

The current dependent political status of the Southern Cameroons under Cameroun Republic colonial rule compares most unfavourably with its dependent status under British colonial rule. In 1954 the Southern Cameroons achieved a measure of self-government and by 1960 became a full self-governing country in all but name, except that it had no competence in defence and foreign affairs. Further, during the informal federation, the Southern Cameroons was independent as far as its internal competence reached. As before, it continued to enjoy its personality and its legal, political and territorial unity. It had its own Constitution. It ran its own affairs through its own Government. It exercised jurisdiction over and had the allegiance of its citizens. In short, it enjoyed a large measure of self-government and exercised, along with the Federal Government, control over its population and territory.

Following its formal annexation in 1972 the Southern Cameroons ceased to exist as a single legal, political and territorial unit running its own government. It was, and remains, cut in two, each part ruled directly by civilian and military viceroys from Cameroun Republic. The people of the Southern Cameroons are denied meaningful participation in the making of critical laws and international agreements that determine or affect their fate, their lives and the future of their territory. They neither control nor freely pursue their political, economic, social and cultural development. They are effectively under the colonial domination, oppression and exploitation of Cameroun Republic. They are abused in every conceivable way and denied basic human rights, including the right of existence as a people. The pattern of human rights abuse is gross, consistent, unremitting and well documented by local and foreign agencies and organisations.[13]

In the self-determination plebiscite in 1961, the people of the Southern Cameroons determined for themselves within the limits imposed on them, independence and continuing self-government within an overarching federal system. That political status has been forcibly and unlawfully suppressed by Cameroun Republic. The right to self-determination is a continuing human right.

> Self-determination is not a single event – one revolution or one election. It is not a single choice to be made in a single day. It is the right of a group to adapt their political position in a complicated world to reflect changing capabilities and changing opportunities. The continuing nature of this right is implicit in the Human Rights Committee's description of it as 'inalienable'. The right is not exhausted upon its first

exercise. For instance, it cannot be forfeited by a colonial people once they have chosen to end their state of political tutelage. Such people may subsequently wish to alter their political status [...] or they may need to exercise that right again if their territory is militarily occupied by another state.[14]

Self-determination is now so widely recognised in international and regional conventions that it is considered a general principle of international law, an absolute principle, a peremptory norm of international law, opposable to all states without exception. In common article 1 of the International Covenant on Civil and Political Rights and the International Covenant on Economic Social and Cultural Rights, both adopted in 1966, the right to self-determination is restated as a matter of treaty law. Furthermore, self-determination operates in conjunction with the principle of territorial integrity so as to protect the territorial framework of the colonial period. French Cameroun achieved independence on 1 January as Cameroun Republic, within its colonially defined boundaries and cannot legally claim more territory than it had as of that critical date. Any such claim is necessarily expansionist, an annexation of territory.

For some, the annexation of the Southern Cameroons took place when it was occupied by Cameroun Republic in September or, more precisely, on 1 October, 1961 when the trusteeship over the Southern Cameroons was terminated. In its judgment of 2 December 1963 in the *Northern Cameroons Case*, the International Court of Justice (ICJ) remarked, *obiter*, that '[o]n 1 October 1961, pursuant to the results of a plebiscite conducted under the auspices of the United Nations, the Southern Cameroons joined the Republic of Cameroon *within which it then became incorporated*'.[15] The judgment does not say how the term "join" in the plebiscite questions suddenly became "incorporation", nor how the "incorporation" was effected and by what authority. Nor is it suggested anywhere in the judgment that the Court construed "joined" to mean "incorporated."

Gaillard suggests that there was in fact no union on 1 October 1961 and that what took place was a mere border adjustment.[16] Stark casts serious doubts on whether a federation in the sense of a voluntary relationship between political units ever existed. He implies that there was no true and genuine federation and that the

Southern Cameroons was in reality incorporated into Cameroun Republic.[17] He, too, does not say how and by what authority the incorporation was effected. Nevertheless, his view is shared by Vanderlinden who points out that the federation was merely a smoke screen designed to enable the Southern Cameroons to swallow the bitter pill of its annexation by Cameroun Republic, as in the case of Eritrea annexed by Ethiopia.[18] Professor J. Crawford cites the Southern Cameroons as one of a number of former colonial territories "integrated in a state".[19] The author also does not say how the integration was done and by what authority.

Benjamin, however, canvasses the thesis of a creeping annexation, while Pierre Messmer, the last colonial Governor in French Cameroun, is in no doubt that in October 1961 Ahidjo effected the annexation of the Southern Cameroons to Cameroun Republic. The so-called federal constitution, he points out, provided for merely a 'sham federation, which was, except in appearance, an annexation of [the Southern Cameroons].'[20] Sindjoun, a citizen of Cameroun Republic, observes that the federation was a mere make-believe designed by Cameroun Republic to hoodwink the UN and the Southern Cameroons. The federation, he posits, was "a federalism of absorption of the Southern Cameroons by Cameroun Republic [...] a phagocytosis strategy."[21]

The UN itself maintains a conspiratorial silence on this matter. The official UN publication, *Basic Facts about the United Nations*, provides a list of "Dependent Territories that have become integrated or associated with independent states since the adoption of the 1960 Declaration." These territories are listed in the book under the chapter heading, "Decolonisation." The publication indicates clearly which of the following five political status options each of the listed territories (except one) emerged into upon being decolonised: "free association", "returned" (the only case being that of the tiny Spanish enclave of Ifni returned to Morocco in June 1969), "joined to form a federation", "nationally united", or "integration."

'Cameroons under British administration' is one of the nine listed territories. But the publication is silent on the political status into which the territory emerged after its purported decolonisation. The cryptic entry in regard to the British Cameroons is that the southern part of the territory "joined" (not "incorporated in" or "integrated with" or "returned to") Cameroun Republic and the northern part "joined" Nigeria. No explanation is given of the term "joined", which is strange especially when one compares this with the annotation concerning, for example, North Borneo or Sarawak where it is stated as follows, "joined to form a federation". Why did the UN not make a similar entry concerning the British Southern Cameroons?

One may hypothesise that this is probably an indication that the UN did not recognise the purported "joinder" of the Southern Cameroons and Cameroun Republic as it was in the nature of an annexation. Hypothesising further, one may say that although the UN did not recognise the purported "joinder" it turned a blind eye because the Southern Cameroons itself did nothing and appeared to be content with the situation, however bad it was; and to the extent that there appeared to be "peace" the UN did not want to muddy the waters by making any pronouncement regarding that issue.

The Trust Territory of the Cameroons under British administration indeed consisted of two parts, Northern Cameroons and Southern Cameroons. With regard to the Northern Cameroons, UN Resolution 1608 (XV) of 21 April 1961 stipulated its joinder, on 1 June 1961, to the Federation of Nigeria "as a separate province of the Northern Region of Nigeria". It was therefore clear that the Northern Cameroons was to be integrated into, and to become part of, Nigeria. With regard to the Southern Cameroons, however, there was no similar stipulation.

The Resolution called for the finalisation, before 1 October 1961, of the "agreed and published policies of the parties". That was an obvious reference to the pre-plebiscite agreement between the Southern Cameroons and Cameroun Republic to form a two-state federation. An informal federation came into being and before long Cameroun Republic had forcibly assumed a colonial sovereignty over the Southern Cameroons. The status of the Southern Cameroons became indistinguishable from that of a colonial dependency of Cameroun Republic.

Again in the *Basic Facts about the United Nations* publication under the heading "Decolonisation", there is listed what the publication calls "Trust Territories that have achieved self-determination". There are 11 such territories in all, including "Cameroons under British administration." Out of these, 7 became independent sovereign states. Three united with another country to form a new state: British Togoland 'united' with the Gold Coast to form Ghana in 1957, Italian Somaliland 'united' with British Somaliland to form Somalia in 1960, and New Guinea 'united' with Papua to form Papua New Guinea in 1975.

Once more the entry regarding the Southern British Cameroons is characteristically Delphic and uninformative. All it says is that the territory 'joined the Republic of Cameroon'. Again there is no elaboration. Why? Why does the entry not say 'joined Cameroon Republic to form the Federal Republic of Cameroon'? Again it is very tempting to interpret the evasive entry to mean the UN did not recognise the so-called "joinder" since the agreed and declared policies of the two countries were never finalised and Cameroun Republic simply took over the Southern Cameroons.

Be that as it may, it can be stated without fear of contradiction that the colonial takeover of the Southern Cameroons by Cameroun Republic began in October 1961 in the form of a disguised and creeping annexation. In 1972 there was open theft of the people's land and freedom: the Southern Cameroons was formally annexed following the overthrow of the informal federation. Factually a federation was in existence from 1961 to 1972. There was a document, controversial to say the least, known as the "Constitution of the Federal Republic of Cameroon." There was also a large literature on the Federation,[22] all of which assumed the legal existence of the said Federation.

Factual situations, especially when they endure, do produce legal effects. The Federal Republic of Cameroon, albeit an informal federation, was therefore a subject of international law and a legal person in both the municipal and international legal orders. Like Judge Wellington Koo remarked, *obiter,* and, it is submitted, correctly, in a separate opinion in the *Northern Cameroons Case,* 'the Southern Cameroons [...] constitutes a part of the sovereign and independent *Federal Republic of Cameroon.*[23] Today, however, the Southern Cameroons is a territory under Cameroun Republic's colonial domination and oppression.

The people of the Southern Cameroons have since been struggling against a latter-day colonialism with a black face, colonialism by Cameroun Republic. They point to repeated demands they have made peacefully and in the most civilised manner: demand for an end to annexation and terrorisation, demand for the restoration of the Southern Cameroons' suppressed self-determination, even demand for the restoration of the federal system agreed to and declared by the two parties before the plebiscite, and also even a demand for the holding of a genuine internationally-supervised referendum with the following two straightforward questions to the people of the Southern Cameroons: "Do you wish to establish a sovereign independent state?" and, "Do you wish to be part of Cameroun Republic?"

Cameroun Republic has spurned these reasonable demands and every single call for a peaceful and democratic solution to the Southern Cameroons' colonial question. Over the years, peaceful demonstrations have been staged in the Southern Cameroons and abroad. Humble petitions and deputations have been sent to the colonial government of Cameroun Republic, to the Organisation of African Unity (OAU) and its successor the African Union (AU), to the Commonwealth and to the UN. While the Southern Cameroons waits for a peaceful and satisfactory resolution of this question, it is taunted by Cameroun Republic to take up arms as evidence of its seriousness to liberate itself. The Southern Cameroons is the object of negative lectures on the 'need' to accept annexation and subjugation. The admonition that the Southern Cameroons should win its liberties by peaceable means if it can has an ulterior motive because Cameroun Republic is always contemplating its continuing brutal and bloody repression in the territory.

In spite of the challenge to pick up the gun, the Southern Cameroons National Council (SCNC)[24] advisedly adopted "the force of argument not the argument of force" as its political credo. The "force of argument" is a form of political struggle based on passive resistance. The SCNC believes the "force of argument" is a viable non-violent liberation strategy. The credo encapsulates the doctrine of peaceful or consensual decolonisation. It embodies an appeal to law, morality, compelling argument, political wisdom, and to the strength of passive resistance, all aimed at getting Cameroun Republic to end its annexation of the Southern Cameroons and pull out its colonial administration from the territory. But the controlling state of Cameroun Republic continues to drown these pacific forms of struggle in blood.

So, many citizens of the Southern Cameroons now doubt the wisdom of continuing to preach the 'force of argument' doctrine. They argue that it is not possible to overcome the coloniser without fighting and that at the risk of going down in history as a cowardly people, sometimes a colonised people has got to fight to be free. They argue further that passive resistance can never work in a system that has no regard for law, is congenitally repressive and is impervious to reason and rational argument.

When, on 30 December 1999, the SCNC peacefully took over Radio Buea, in the capital of the Southern Cameroons, it proclaimed the revival of the Southern Cameroons as a polity and the restoration of its independence and statehood. It called on Cameroun Republic 'to withdraw forthwith its colonial administration, both civil and military, from the Southern Cameroons and to come to the negotiation table for discussions on consequential matters.'

Cameroun Republic has stubbornly refused to do so. It has refused to change its expansionist mindset. It continues to pursue its national policy of terrorisation and bloody repression of the people of the Southern Cameroons. It continues to pursue its policy of institutionalised torture, warmongering and unchecked violence in the territory. It continues to hold the people of the Southern Cameroons in colonial bondage. It continues to claim a phony sovereignty right over the Southern Cameroons, a claim the people of the territory have decisively rejected and have consistently refused to recognise.

Notes

1. Victoria Centenary Committee, *Victoria: Southern Cameroons 1858 – 1958*, Spottiswoode, Ballantyne & Co., London, 1958.

2. On 13 March 1959, the Assembly adopted resolution 1350 (XIII) recommending a plebiscite in the Southern Cameroons to ascertain the wishes of the people concerning their future. This was followed by another Assembly Resolution,

1352 (XIV) of 16 October 1959, imposing both the time of the plebiscite and the questions to be put to the people. The UN ordered a plebiscite to be held 'between 30 September 1960 and March 1961.' This was in total disregard of the request by Foncha and Endeley, political leaders of the territory, that the plebiscite be deferment to 1962. The UN further imposed the following questions: 'Do you wish to achieve independence by joining the independent Federation of Nigeria?' 'Do you wish to achieve independence by joining the independent Republic of Cameroons?' This imposition was also surprising as it was clear from the very representative Mamfe "Plebiscite Conference", held from 10-11th August 1959, that the territory's political leaders wanted the plebiscite questions to be either integration into, or secession from, Nigeria. On 31 May 1960 the Trusteeship Council adopted Resolution 2013 (XXVI) by which Britain was requested, inter alia, 'to take appropriate steps, in consultation with the authorities concerned, to ensure that the people of the Territory are fully informed, before the plebiscite, of the constitutional arrangements that would have to be made, at the appropriate time, for the implementation of the decisions taken at the plebiscite.' It was Britain's duty then to ascertain from both Nigeria and Cameroun Republic the terms and conditions under which the Southern Cameroons might be expected to join either of them. It was also the responsibility of Britain to fully inform the people of the Southern Cameroons, well before the plebiscite, of the conditions it had been able to ascertain from both Nigeria and Cameroun Republic. Given Britain's artful dilatoriness in this matter, and in line with Resolution 2013, Mr. Foncha, the Premier of the Southern Cameroons, and Mr. Ahidjo, President of Cameroun Republic, held several rounds of talks between August and December 1960. Those talks resulted in a signed and published agreement (expressed in the form of Joint Declarations and Joint Communiqués) which stipulated that should the plebiscite vote go in favour of achieving independence by 'joining' Cameroun Republic, the two countries would form a federal union of two states, legally equal in status. The agreement also spelt out the broad outlines of the prospective federation. In its *Note Verbale* of 24 December 1960 to the British Government, Cameroun Republic reiterated its commitment to the agreement and reconfirmed 'its desire for unification... on the basis of a Federation.' The agreement was made available to the UN and the British Government, and was widely used during the brief period of the plebiscite enlightenment campaigns. The electorate was informed that the implication for the Southern Cameroons 'joining' Cameroun Republic was that the two countries would form a federal union of two states, equal in status.

3. A Mazrui, & M Tidy, *Nationalism and New States in Africa*, East African Educational Publishers, Nairobi, 1984, p. 77: 'In reality the union was less a positive joining together of two parts of the former German Kamerun... than a rather negative

flight of the Southern Cameroons from Nigeria on ethnic grounds. The Southern Cameroonians were concerned above all to avoid Ibo and Yoruba domination in a federal Nigeria.'

4. There was thus an interval of several months between the popular decision to achieve independence (11 February 1961), and the effective date of independence (1 October 1961) arbitrarily set by the UN itself. It was the UN that also set the date of the 'joining'. Again, arbitrarily and untidily, it made the date of 'joining' to coincide with the effective date of independence. The Southern Cameroons had been the victim of a like unfair treatment before. In January 1959 the people of the Southern Cameroons had pronounced themselves at the polls in favour of secession from Nigeria. But it was not until 1960 that the Administering Authority put that decision into effect. In doing so Britain made the date of separation from Nigeria to coincide with the date of Nigeria's independence, 1st October 1960.

5. NN Mbile, *Cameroon Political Story - Memories of an Authentic Eye Witness*, Presbyterian Printing Press, Victoria, 2000.

6. *Official Verbatim Record of Debates in the Southern Cameroons House of Assembly* (Southern Cameroons Hansard), Government Printing Press, Buea, September 1961, pp. 88 et seq.

7. In reality, however, the two expressions "constitution" and "constitutional amendment law" were obfuscatory legal gymnastics, for the legislature of Cameroun Republic did in fact adopt a constitutional document.

8. It is submitted that Dr AM Maimo is grossly mistaken when he characterises as "a procedural event" the drafting and adoption by Cameroun Republic alone of the "federal constitution". Furthermore, his submission that that document 'should ... be treated as a valid legal document' lacks substance in law. See AM Maimo, *The Delicate Bridge between Historical Facts and Constitutional Reform: The Cameroon Anglophone Case*, a 14-page pamphlet, June 1993.

9. The UN "endorsed" the results of the plebiscite that the people of the Southern Cameroons 'decided to achieve independence *by* joining' Cameroun Republic. By contrast, the termination of trusteeship was to take place *upon* and not *by* joining. In other words, only if the Southern Cameroons did in fact "join" Cameroun Republic were the Trusteeship Agreement to be terminated and the independence date to become operative.

10. One such implication is the fact that the federation entailed the extinction of the legal personality of Cameroun Republic both in domestic and international law. Another one is that a federal state is a composite state, a superposition of states, not an absorption or fusion. Furthermore, in international law the outcome of

state succession (the succession of the Federal Republic to both the Southern Cameroons and Cameroon Republic) must be equitable, the states concerned being free to settle terms and conditions of agreement. Moreover, the peremptory norms of general international law and, in particular, respect for human rights and the rights of peoples and minorities, are binding on all parties to the succession.

11. L Sindjoun, *L'Etat Ailleurs - Entre Noyau Dur et Case Vide*, Economica, Paris, 2002.

12. This episode is discussed at length in chapter 8.

13. For example, human rights abuse reports by Amnesty International, US State Department, UN Special Rapporteur on Torture, and the Bamenda-based Human Rights Defence Group.

14. N Jayawickrama, *The Judicial Application of Human Rights*, Cambridge University Press, 2002, p. 231. See also M Pomerance, *Self-Determination in Law and Practice*, Matinus Nijhoff Publishers, The Hague, 1982; SKN Blay, 'Self-Determination versus Territorial Integrity in Decolonization' [1986] 18 *International Law and Politics* 441; R McCorquodale, 'Self-Determination: a Human Rights Approach' [1994] *International and Comparative Law Quarterly* 857; RC Ryser, 'Killing for Self-Determination', June 1999, www.cwis.org/fweye; R Higgins, 'Postmodern Tribalism and the Right to Secession – Comments', in Brolmann et al. (eds), *Peoples and Minorities in International Law*, Kluwer, 1993, p. 34.

15. ICJ Reports, 1963, at p. 22. Emphasis added.

16. P Gaillard, *Ahmadou Ahidjo: Patriote et Despote, Bâtisseur de l'Etat Camerounais*, Jeune Afrique Livres, Paris, 1994, p. 123.

17. FM Stark, 'Federalism in Cameroon: The Shadow and the Reality' *Canadian Journal of African Studies*, vol. x, no. 3, 1976, p. 441

18. J Vanderlinden, 'L'Etat Fédéral, Etat Africain de l'An 2000?' in *L'Etat Moderne Horizon 2000*, Librairie General de Droit et de la Jurisprudence, Paris, 1985, p. 307.

19. J Crawford, 'State Practice and International Law in Relation to Unilateral Secession' Report 1997, paragraph 21, http://canada.justice.gc.ca/en/news/nr/1997/factum/craw.html.

20. J Benjamin, *Les Camerounais Occidentaux – La Minorité dans un Etat Bi-communautaire*, Presse de l'Université de Montréal, Montréal, 1972; P Messmer, *Le Périlleux Chemin du Cameroun vers l'Indépendance*, Paris, 1998; P Messmer, *Les Blancs s'en Vont – Récit de décolonisation*, Ed. Albin Michel, Paris, 1998, pp. 134-135.

21. L Sindjoun, *L'Etat Ailleurs. Entre Noyau Dur et Case Vide*, Economica, Paris, 2002, pp. 127-129. The author's use of the term 'phagocytosis' speaks volumes

because the word suggests the engulfing and absorbing of the Southern Cameroons by Cameroun Republic, like a cell ingesting bacteria in the body.

22. See for example, VT Le Vine, *The Cameroons from Mandate to Independence*, Berkeley, 1964; HNA Enonchong, *Cameroon Constitutional Law*, Cepma, Yaounde, 1967; JM Nzouankeu, 'Remarques sur la Constitution Camerounaise' *Civilisation*, vol. 19, No. 2, 1969, p. 216; PF Gonidec, *La République Fédérale du Cameroun*, Berger-Levrault, Paris, 1969; WR Johnson, *The Cameroon Federation: Political Integration in a Fragmentary Society*, Princeton University Press, Princeton, 1970; N Rubin, *Cameroon - An African Federation*, Pall Mall, London, 1971; J Benjamin, *Les Camerounais Occidentaux*, Montreal, 1972; M Prouzet, *Le Cameroun*, LGDJ, Paris, 1974; FM Stark, 'Federalism in Cameroon: the Shadow and the Reality' *Canadian Journal of African Studies*, vol. X, No. 3, 1976, p. 423.

23. ICJ Report, 1963, at p.51. Emphasis added.

24. That is one of the principal organisations in the Southern Cameroons championing the independence of the Southern Cameroons. Other organizations are the Southern Cameroons Restoration Movement (SCARM), the Southern Cameroons Youth League (SCYL), the Ambazonia Movement, and the Southern Cameroons People's Organization (SCAPO). These organizations have saved the Southern Cameroons national reality from annihilation by Cameroun Republic.

Chapter Three
A Trust Betrayed by the United Nations

The case of the British Cameroons exemplifies how the UN sometimes acts in disregard of acknowledged rules or principles for reasons of politics, justifying such course of action on grounds of mere "adjustment", or on grounds of "special" or "exceptional" circumstances. First, the UN acquiesced in the dismemberment of the British Cameroons by the British Government, in spite of the UN's stated principle on the desirability of always maintaining the unity of colonial territories. The fact that the continuity of the British Cameroons Trust Territory was broken by the piece of Nigerian territory known as the 'Yola Arc', did not suffice to make it a special case in this regard since a country's territory need not be continuous.

The Administering Authority carried out the partitioning without even seeking the express views of the people of the Territory. Amazingly, at the plebiscite, the possibility of reuniting the two parts of the British Cameroons Territory to form a sovereign independent state was not presented or even considered as another alternative. In East Africa, the Belgians acted more honourably, for they partitioned Ruanda-Urundi after the people of that territory had been democratically consulted on the matter and they decided to achieve independence as two distinct states, Rwanda and Burundi.

The Ruanda-Urundi case is also instructive in another significant respect. Following the 1885 Berlin Treaty, that territory became part of German East Africa and remained so until the end of World War I. With Germany's defeat, German East Africa, like German Kamerun, was partitioned into two: Ruanda-Urundi ($1/17^{th}$ the size of the Territory) and Tanganyika (16/17th). The League of Nations mandated Belgium to administer Ruanda-Urundi, and Britain to administer Tanganyika. Belgium formed an economic and administrative union between Ruanda-Urundi and the contiguous colony of the Belgian Congo.

Ruanda-Urundi was thus administered as part of the Belgian Congo until Congo's independence on 1 July 1960. Two years later Ruanda-Urundi split into two and achieved independence on 1 July 1962, as the Republic of Rwanda (10,169 square miles) and the Republic of Burundi (10,740 square miles). Significantly, the UN did not impose a plebiscite on either Rwanda or Burundi to achieve independence by joining either the Congo or Tanganyika. Yet neither Rwanda nor Burundi is bigger in size or population, or more economically endowed, than the Southern Cameroons.

In the history of UN decolonisation of trust territories the British Cameroons Territory is the only case where a country's national unity and territorial integrity were totally disrupted. The two parts into which the Territory was divided were denied the right to remain as one country and to achieve sovereign statehood as such. Worse, neither of the two parts was even allowed to achieve sovereign statehood. Without any legal authority for so acting, the UN enjoined, separately, the Southern British Cameroons and the Northern British Cameroons to "join", willy-nilly, either of its two neighbours, Nigeria or Cameroun Republic. The imposition of these conditionalities meant that there was arguably no self-determination. There was instead a determination by the United Nations, not by the *self*.

This was odd indeed, especially when one considers how fairly other trust territories were treated as can be seen from the following examples that provide an edifying contrast to the scandalous way the British Cameroons was treated. British Togoland was not partitioned. It joined the Gold Coast and the conjoined territories achieved independence as Ghana. French Togo was not partitioned, nor was French Cameroun; each achieved independence from France intact. Neither British Somaliland nor Italian Somaliland was partitioned; each acceded to independence and then united to form the Republic of Somalia. Ruanda-Urundi separated through an informed decision by the people of the territory and became independent as two separate states. The Gilbert and Ellice Islands separated but emerged into independence as the separate states of Kiribati and Tuvalu.[1]

Second, quite early on the UN acquiesced in the Administering Authority's incorporation of each part of the partitioned British Cameroons into the adjoining British territory of Nigeria. It is of course the case that both the League of Nations Mandates Agreements and the United Nations Trusteeship Agreements made provision for 'administrative union'. But it is also the case that such union was not mandatory and both the Trusteeship Council and the General Assembly were very critical of it. At its 160th plenary meeting held on 18 November 1948, the General Assembly adopted Resolution 224 (III) on the question of administrative unions. The resolution states in part:

> *Noting* that the Trusteeship Agreements for some of [the Trust] Territories authorize the Administering Authority concerned to constitute the Territory into a customs, fiscal or administrative union or federation with adjacent territories under its sovereignty or control and to establish common services between the Trust Territory and such adjacent territories, *where such measures are not inconsistent with the basis objectives of the Trusteeship System* and with the terms of the Trusteeship Agreement [...]
>
> *Recalling* that the *General Assembly approved these Agreements upon the assurance of the Administering Powers that they do not consider the terms of the relevant articles in the Trusteeship Agreements as giving powers to the Administering Authority to establish any form of political association between the Trust Territories respectively administered by them and adjacent territories which would involve annexation of the Trust Territories in any sense or would have the effect of extinguishing their status as Trust Territories* [...]
>
> *Recommends* accordingly that the Trusteeship Council should: [...] (c) Request whenever appropriate, an advisory opinion of the International Court of Justice as to whether such unions are within the scope of and compatible with, the stipulations of the Charter and terms of the Trusteeship Agreements as approved by the General Assembly [...] [2]

The General Assembly was emphatic that any administrative union "must remain strictly administrative in its nature and its scope, and its operation must not have the effect of creating any conditions which will obstruct the separate development of the Trust Territory, in the fields of political, economic, social and educational advancement, as a distinct entity."

Third, and this point is canvassed at length in chapter 11, the people of the Southern Cameroons were not given all the internationally recognised self-determination status options to choose from. The so-called plebiscite 'alternatives' were false and incomplete. They were *false* because the UN misrepresented the process as one that was to lead to *independence* and not, as it turned out to be, a mere transition from colonial rule by one colonial authority to colonial rule by a successor colonial authority.

In 1953 the UN itself enumerated the following factors as "indicative of the attainment of independence": (i) full international responsibility of the territory for the acts inherent in the exercise of its external sovereignty and for the corresponding acts in the administration of its internal affairs; (ii) eligibility for membership of the United Nations; (iii) power to enter into direct relations of any kind with other governments and with international institutions and to negotiate, sign and ratify international instruments; (iv) sovereign right to provide for its national defence; (v) complete freedom of the people of the territory to choose the form of government which they desire; (vi) freedom from control or interference by the government of another state in respect of the internal government (legislature, executive, judiciary and administration of the territory); (vii) complete autonomy in respect of economic, social and cultural affairs.[3]

The UN knew for certain that none of these factors would be applicable to the Southern Cameroons after the plebiscite and following the "joining" it had prescribed for the territory. Therefore, the formula of the plebiscite question, 'do you wish to achieve independence...?' was a huge deception practised on the unsuspecting people of the Southern Cameroons.

The plebiscite "alternatives" were also incomplete because the internationally recognised political status option of separate independence was unjustifiably not made available. The 1960 UN declaration on decolonisation speaks of 'political status', that is to say, the status of a people within the international community. The political status options[4] are: sovereign independent state, free association with an independent state, integration with an independent state, or, indeed, emergence into any other political status.[5] None of these options, or any other, was in fact given.

The Southern Cameroons was instead ordered by the UN to "join" either Nigeria (from where it had just seceded a year earlier) or Cameroun Republic (a land literally soaked in blood) and steep in a culture of despotism. One of the British Plebiscite Supervisory Officers in the Southern Cameroons at the time would later observe:

> [T]he plebiscite, trumpeted by the United Nations as an exercise in democracy, only offered the people the choice [...] between frying pan and fire. I learned that over the previous two years efforts had been made, by some local politicians, to persuade the UN that the people of the Southern Cameroons would be happier if they could have their own country, however small and impoverished it might be, rather than being forced into a shotgun marriage with either of their larger neighbours, but the UN in its collective wisdom had decided that this was not an option. At the time, Nkrumah's wildly unrealistic vision of a united Africa was fashionable and UN delegates, especially those of the so-called 'Casablanca' group of African nations, were fiercely opposed to what they called 'Balkanisation'. That might have been fine for them, rubbing out lines on the map in New York, but here was I in a territory threatened with extinction. What on earth could I say to people who wanted their own country, however insignificant it might be? [...] They did not want independence if it meant merging with either of their more powerful neighbours.[6]

The UN did not even bother to indicate the political status option that "joining" entailed. It never indicated what political status the Southern Cameroons was to emerge into upon "joining" either Nigeria or Cameroun Republic as it had ordered. It said nothing about the political consequences for the Southern Cameroons of "joining" one or other of its two neighbours.

The excuse for the truncated decolonisation process was the self-serving reason given by the Administering Authority that the Southern Cameroons would not be economically viable to stand on its own as a sovereign independent state. This claim clearly had no merit and was a mere red herring since politics was the real reason. Yet, the UN acted on the economic non-viability claim in spite of the very clear principle that economic self-sufficiency is irrelevant to the issue of decolonisation. It is trite that Economic viability can be used to support a claim to independence, but it can never be used to deny entitlement to independence. The UN Declaration on the Granting of Independence to Colonial Countries and Peoples[7] provides:

> 3. Inadequacy of political, economic, social or educational preparedness should never serve as a pretext for delaying independence.
> 5. Immediate steps shall be taken, in Trust and Non-Self-Governing Territories or all other territories which have not yet attained independence, to transfer all powers to the peoples of those territories, without any conditions or reservations, in accordance with their freely expressed will and desire, without any distinction as to race, creed or colour in order to enable them to enjoy complete independence and freedom.

Fourth, the UN failed to provide the Southern Cameroons with much needed constitutional expertise. In October 1960 there was an Anglo-Southern Cameroons Conference in London. At the conclusion of the conference, the British Secretary of State for the Colonies, Mr. Iain Macleod, gave the assurance that "The UN and the United Kingdom would also be associated with [the post-plebiscite constitutional] conference" between the Southern Cameroons and French-backed Cameroun Republic.

But the UN and Britain failed to ensure the organisation of such a conference and failed to show up at the Foumban constitutional meeting. The UN pleaded financial constraints. Britain shamefully declared that *'the Southern Cameroons and its inhabitants are undoubtedly expendable.'*[8] Britain also made it known that it was not their objective to obtain the best terms possible from Mr. Ahidjo, and that 'UN participation should be avoided [as] there was no point in the UN taking part.'[9]

Fifth, the UN seemingly adopted the attitude that the Federal Republic of Cameroon was identical with Cameroun Republic. The Federal Republic, albeit a *de facto* federation, entailed the non-assertion of the international personality of the Southern Cameroons as a qualified subject of international law. It also entailed the extinction of Cameroun Republic as a subject of international law. The Federal Republic of Cameroon became the state successor to both the Southern Cameroons and Cameroun Republic. The legal identity of the Federation was different from that of either of the two countries that it succeeded to.

Yet the UN appears to have maintained the untenable attitude that the Federal Republic of Cameroon was identical with Cameroun Republic. The latter country achieved independence on 1 January 1960 and was admitted to membership of the UN on 20 September 1960. Its legal identity changed on 1 October 1961 when it became one of the two component states of the Cameroon Federation.[10]

At the UN, Cameroun Republic is listed simply as 'Cameroon'. The obfuscation caused by this polysemous entry in the UN records continues to give the distinct impression that the plebiscite in the Southern Cameroons had been mandated by the UN and organised by Britain simply to facilitate the territory's annexation by either of its two neighbours. Presumably that expedient may have been resorted to on the fallacious assumption that 'annexation', especially a disguised one, would not have the taint of colonialism or imperialism. If the Federal Republic of Cameroon was merely the continuation of Cameroun Republic, the inescapable conclusion must be that the Southern Cameroons is merely additional territory, which Cameroun Republic acquired with the conspiratorial assistance of the UN. That this territory has since been in revolt should therefore occasion no surprise.

Juridically, in the Cameroon Federation, there was no 'principal state' and no 'minor state' because both were on the same footing of legal equality. The Federal Republic was a new sovereign state under international law. It did not purport to be a continuation of the previous Cameroun Republic, but the state successor to both the Southern Cameroons and Cameroun Republic.

When in 1972 Cameroun Republic, through President Ahidjo, unilaterally scrapped the Federation and forcibly imposed on the Southern Cameroons direct rule from Cameroun Republic, the UN seems to have wrongly considered this veiled act of annexation as an internal affair of Cameroun Republic. Again, when in 1984 Cameroun Republic, through President Biya, revived Cameroun Republic both as a legal and a political expression, the UN again appears to have considered the matter an internal affair of Cameroun Republic. Quite early then, the UN would seem to have adopted the suspect attitude that Cameroun Republic continues and that the Southern Cameroons is merely additional territory for that State. Historically, whenever a territory has been acquired in a suspect manner it eventually revolts.

If the Southern Cameroons + Cameroun Republic = Federal Republic of Cameroon = United Republic of Cameroun = Cameroun Republic, then the Southern Cameroons + Cameroun Republic = Cameroun Republic. That equation is a fallacy. However, the claim is politically susceptible to two possible interpretations: (i) the Southern Cameroons was completely fused into Cameroun Republic which simply continues; or (ii) despite appearances to the contrary, no legal and recognised 'joining' ever took place between the Southern Cameroons and Cameroun Republic so that only the latter continues to appear on UN records.

It would be incredible to imagine that the UN sponsored the plebiscite not so much to decolonise the Southern Cameroons but to facilitate its transfer to a successor colonialist. For one thing, neither the international tutelage agreement nor the UN Charter conferred on the tutelary power any authority to cede the territory. Therefore, no valid cession could possibly be made and any purported transfer would necessarily be void and ineffectual.

Six, concerning the Southern Cameroons' question, the UN allowed itself to be unduly influenced by the Administering Authority. From 10 to 11 August 1959 there was a conference held at Mamfe in the Southern Cameroons on the impending plebiscite in the territory. All the delegates to that very representative conference agreed that there should be two questions at the plebiscite. There was unanimity that integration with Nigeria should be one question, and a substantial majority (70% of the delegates) indicated that secession from Nigeria should be the other question.

If the UN had been mindful of the outcome of the Mamfe Conference, the plebiscite questions would have been framed in such a way as to present a clear and sensible choice between integration into and secession from Nigeria. It was clear that secession from Nigeria necessarily meant becoming a sovereign independent state. For, at the Mamfe Conference, the Fon of Bafut, speaking for all the Chiefs of the Southern Cameroons and expressing the sentiments of the people of the territory, made this oft-quoted statement:

> We rejected Dr Endeley because he wanted to take us to Nigeria. If Mr Foncha tries to take us to French Cameroun we shall also run away from him. [...] French Cameroun is 'fire' and Nigeria is 'water'. I support secession [from Nigeria] without unification [with French Cameroun].

The Southern Cameroons was between the devil, Cameroun Republic, and the deep blue sea, Nigeria. The UN must have been aware of the unacceptability to the people of the Southern Cameroons of either of the two alternatives presented to them. Yet, surprisingly it chose to ignore the result of that conference. It later transpired that the disregard of the outcome of the conference was because of some arm-twisting at the UN, a manoeuvre that gives further credence to the theory of a conspiracy at the UN to deal with the Southern Cameroons' independence question in a manner that satisfied British interests rather than the interests of the people of the territory as ought to have been the case.

> Considering [that the various delegates to the Mamfe Conference did indicate where they stood on the plebiscite issue] and the representative nature of the Conference, one would have expected the United Nations to make Integration versus Secession the issue of the plebiscite. But that is not what happened. When the leaders returned to the United Nations in September 1959, Foncha placed the results of the Mamfe Plebiscite Conference before the United Nations, carefully described the organization and the representative character of the Conference and then invited the United

Nations to use those results as a guide for its decisions. None of the leaders contested those results [...] A fundamental problem was that the United Nations itself was already divided in partisan groups on the [Southern Cameroons] issue. The Integrationists had been identified as the friends of the British and non-conformists and, for that reason they received the support of British friends and anti-communists. Likewise, the Reunificationists had been identified as communists and, for that reason they were strongly backed by the Soviet bloc. The Foncharians had no ideological friends or enemies. While the agreement of the Integrationists and Reunificationists on the plebiscite issue made the work of the United Nations easier, the fact that the Foncharians were in power in the Southern Cameroons complicated it. If the United Nations used the principle of democracy to accept Foncha's position, its members would have abandoned their friends when they most needed help. Yet it could not impose a decision on a democratically elected Government in favour of the opposition parties. Faced with this problem, the United Nations decided to ignore the results of the Mamfe Plebiscite Conference and to talk Foncha out of his programme. After some struggle and logrolling, Foncha, without consulting those who voted him into power and receiving their permission first, agreed to make Reunification the second question of the plebiscite in exchange for a short period of continued trusteeship administration. Consequently, the United Nations made Integration versus Reunification the issue at the plebiscite.[11]

Seven, the UN stampeded the Southern Cameroons into a plebiscite. Foncha and Endeley, the political leaders of the Southern Cameroons, had requested deferment of the plebiscite to 1962. The Commissioner of the Southern Cameroons, Mr. J. O. Field even sent a cablegram to the UN, addressed to UK's Ambassador, Sir Andrew Cohen, correctly stating that the majority of the people of the Southern Cameroons found the 'alternative' of "joining" Cameroun Republic unacceptable. The cablegram read:

Foncha United Nations Delegation, United Nations, New York. Proposed plebiscite question announced today on radio most unacceptable to elected Ministers and majority people, Southern Cameroons Stop Urge that delegates return here for brief consultations and alternative that I join them in New York Stop Convey strength of local feelings and that debates should be adjourned […] Stop *We cannot be responsible for political and security consequences if second question that is unification is imposed in territory* Stop [emphasis added]

Honourable A. N. Jua, minister and an elected representative of the people of the Southern Cameroons, also sent a cablegram to the UN calling for postponement of the plebiscite:

Entire Cameroonians strongly oppose Decision on Plebiscite Questions. Request you suspend the Decision till 16th Plenary Session, i.e., 1962 following postponement of plebiscite dates. Urge you honour majority wishes of the people.

The UN ignored this simple and sensible request and went ahead to impose a plebiscite to be concluded 'not later than March 1961,'[12] as if the Southern Cameroons was in flames. This UN *diktat* deprived the Southern Cameroons of much-needed breathing space and time for cogitation. Why was the UN in such a hurry? If Britain was being tight-fisted with its money, the UN could have taken direct administration of the territory for a year or two pending a fully informed decision by the people on their political future. Speaking for the United States at the 896th General Assembly meeting on 6 October 1959, the American Permanent Representative to the UN, Ambassador Clement Zabloiski, prophetically cautioned the UN in these terms:

The results of a hurried choice imposed on the population of the Trust Territory would be catastrophic for their political future.

Earlier, on 1 October 1959, at the 892nd General Assembly meeting, Ambassador Chrishna Menon, speaking for India, recalled Memorandum T.1393 of 27 June 1958 submitted to the UN by Britain. In that memo, the UK Government stated that the Southern Cameroons had not been delayed in its political evolution towards full autonomy, then independence, as with the Federation of Nigeria. The Ambassador then drew the following inescapable logical conclusion:

> In this regard, my delegation sees no reason why the Southern Cameroons shall not achieve independence on the same date like Nigeria [...] Any other decision would not fully satisfy the population.

Eight, bad faith again underpinned the handling of the Southern Cameroons' issue at the UN in its April 1961 session. On 18 April 1961, the Fourth Committee adopted draft resolution A/C.4/L.685 and recommended it for adoption by the General Assembly. In the draft resolution Britain, the Southern Cameroons and Cameroun Republic were invited to initiate urgent discussions with a view to finalising, before 1 October 1961, "the arrangements by which the agreed and declared policies of the concerned parties for a union of the Southern Cameroons with the Republic of Cameroun into a Federal United Cameroon Republic will be implemented."

The same recommended draft resolution also provided for the appointment, by the General Assembly, of "a commission of three constitutional and administrative experts," to be nominated one each by three Member States designated by the General Assembly, to assist, at the request of the parties concerned, in the discussions "on a union of the Southern Cameroons with the Republic of Cameroun into a Federal United Cameroon Republic." The adoption and implementation of the recommended resolution was to entail a petty financial expenditure (mainly for hiring of the three constitutional experts) estimated at a mere $46,000.

Resolution 1608 (XV), eventually adopted by the General Assembly on 21 April 1961, turned out to be a dangerously watered-down version of the resolution recommended by the Fourth Committee. No mention was made of the appointment of constitutional experts. No mention was made of 'a union of the Southern Cameroons with the Republic of Cameroun into a Federal United Cameroon Republic.'

The UN pleaded financial constraints for leaving out these matters which it knew, or must be taken to have known, were very critical for safeguarding the status, dignity and self-determination of the people of the Southern Cameroons within the "joining" into which the UN had forced the Southern Cameroons. The UN refused, for claimed financial reasons, to provide the territory with much-needed constitutional experts to assist in constitutional talks with Cameroun Republic. The provision of such expertise by the UN would have been nothing new. Only ten years earlier it had done so in constitutional talks leading to the Ethiopia-Eritrea Federation.[13]

Once more the money factor plagued the Southern Cameroons "decolonisation" saga. Claimed economic non-viability of the territory was the excuse conveniently invoked in 1959 by the UN for ruling out separate independence for the Southern Cameroons. In April 1961, when it came to the effective implementation of the result of the very plebiscite it had imposed on the people of the territory, economic considerations again entered the calculus in working out the future of the territory and its people. The UN considered the paltry sum of $46,000 too large an amount to spend in order to secure and safeguard the Southern Cameroons and the dignity and worth of its people. In the eyes of the UN, the Southern Cameroons and its people were not worth spending $46,000 on!

Notes

1. See Nihal Jayawickrama, *The Judicial Application of Human Rights Law*, Cambridge University Press, 2002, p. 222.

2. UN General Assembly Resolution 224 (III) of 18 November 1948. Emphasis added.

3. UNGA Resolution 742 (VIII), 27 November 1953.

4. UNGA Resolution 2625 (XXV), 24 October 1970. See also the earlier UNGA Resolution 1541 (XV) of 15 December 1960 which provides the following three ways as those in which a non-self-governing territory could be said to have reached a full measure of self-government: by emergence as a sovereign independent state; by free association with an independent state; or by integration with an independent state. Since the Southern Cameroons was to

achieve independence by joining an independent country and had to make that decision through informed and democratic process, it is clear that the political relationship between the Southern Cameroons and Cameroun Republic was conceived as that of *free association*. Principle VII of that Resolution provides that free association "should be one which respects the individuality and cultural characteristics of the territory and its peoples, and retains for the peoples of the territory which is associated with an independent state the freedom to modify the status of that territory through the expression of their will by democratic means and through constitutional processes. The associated territory shall have the right to determine its internal constitution without outside interference, in accordance with due constitutional processes and the freely expressed wishes of the people. This does not preclude consultations as appropriate or necessary under the terms of the free association agreed upon."

5. This 'any other political status' option is available to a smaller collectivity living within a territory such as an indigenous people or an ethnic, religious or linguistic minority, the viable alternatives being regional autonomy, self-government or assimilation: Nihal Jayawickrama, *The Judicial Application of Human Rights Law*, Cambridge University Press, 2002, p. 234

6. J Percival, *The 1961 Cameroon Plebiscite: Choice or Betrayal*, Langaa Research & Publishing, Bamenda, 2008, pp. 32-33.

7. General Assembly Resolution 1514 (XV) of 14 December 1960.

8. Statement of Lord Perth, Minister of State at the Colonial Office, in a secret memorandum dated 12 October 1960. *Declassified Secret Southern Cameroons Files*, (Public Records Office), London.

9. Statement of Mr. Christopher Eastwood, Colonial Office, at a meeting held in the Colonial Office on 25 January 1960. *Declassified Secret Southern Cameroons Files*, (Public Records Office), London.

10. The list of UN Members includes the state denoted simply as 'Camer*oon*', the independence date of which is given as 1 January 1960 and the UN Membership date of which is given as 20 September 1960. The official name of the country in question is *République du Cameroun*, in shorthand, *Camer**oun***. In the contemplation of the UN was 'Camer**oon**' simply an English translation of Camer**oun**?

11. B Chem-Langhee, & MZ Njeuma, 'The Pan-Kamerun Movement 1949-1961' in Ndiva Kofele-Kale (ed), *An African Experiment in Nation-Building: The Bilingual Cameroon Republic since Reunification*, Oxford Westview Press, 1980, p. 52.

12. United Nations General Assembly Resolution 1352(XIV) of 16 October 1959.

13. See, UNGA Resolutions 390A (V) of 2 December 1950 and 617 (VII) of 12 December 1952. See also, 'The Question of Eritrea' *Yearbook of the United Nations*, 1952, pp. 262-266.

Chapter Four
A Trust Betrayed by the British Government

From the very beginning of the Southern Cameroons' 'decolonisation' saga, the attitude of the British Government was anything but fair and honest. It was clear the Administering Authority was more interested in yoking the Southern Cameroons to Nigeria. It considered the Southern Cameroons as merely material for "in-filling on the Nigerian border"[1] just as it considered British Togoland as material for in-filling on the Gold Coast border. The first act of betrayal by the British Government was the dismemberment of the British Cameroons Trust Territory. The British Government divided the Territory into two, each part being administered separately as a dependency of the region of Nigeria contiguous to it. This was a disguised annexation of the Trust Territory to Nigeria.

The British purposefully failed to develop political, economic and social institutions common to both parts of the Trust Territory. This failure had the untoward consequence of keeping both parts of the Trust Territory completely separate and divorced from each other. Each part pursued its own path of political, economic and social development. This impairment of the territorial integrity of the British Cameroons Trust Territory flew in the face of the UN's prohibition regarding administering powers partitioning non-self-governing territories. Indeed, the 1960 Declaration on decolonisation states that '[a]ny attempt aimed at the partial or total disruption of the national unity and the territorial integrity'[2] of a non-self-governing territory 'is incompatible with the purposes and principles of the Charter of the United Nations'.

Having partitioned the British Cameroons Trust Territory, the British Government proceeded to administer each part as an integral part of the contiguous region of Nigeria. This was denoted as "administrative union". The Administering Authority brushed aside the Trusteeship Council's criticisms of administrative unions and insisted on continuing to administer the Southern Cameroons as an integral part of the Eastern Region of Nigeria. One disastrous consequence of this controversial administrative union was that the identity and legal personality of the Southern Cameroons became blurred. The territory became a mere appendage of Nigeria and consequently a backwater to developments in that country. This had the effect of practically extinguishing the status of the territory as a Trust Territory, a violation of UN General Assembly Resolution 244 (III) of 18 November 1948. The territory was often referred to as a colony within a colony.

The Administering Authority failed to develop the territory and then perversely turned round and pleaded its own failing in this regard as a reason for standing in the way of the Southern Cameroons' independence as a sovereign state. Indeed, having failed to develop the territory the Administering Authority later railed about the territory's alleged economic non-viability and advanced this as a 'reason' for opposing the territory's emergence into statehood.

Furthermore, by administering the Southern Cameroons from Nigeria as an integral part thereof rather than directly from Britain, the Administering Authority created an environment that virtually eclipsed the issue of separate independence for the territory. As a result, much of the political struggle in the territory was about asserting its identity and legal personality as well as securing its separation from Nigeria. Had there been no forced administrative union with Nigeria, the issue of outright independence would have been the primary focus of Southern Cameroons' politicians, and the disastrous diversion of "joining" Nigeria or "joining" Cameroun Republic would hardly have arisen. The false issue of "economic non-viability" introduced into the independence equation by the British Government would also never have arisen.

Further still, a strong majority of the people of the Southern Cameroons clearly did not want to "join" Nigeria or Cameroun Republic. The majority wanted to establish a sovereign independent state[3] and it was clear that had the option of separate independence been offered at the plebiscite, that option would have carried the day. The Southern Cameroons' Government stated that it wanted a continued period of trusteeship administration to be followed by outright independence before any discussion could be initiated, if at all, on whether to "join" either Nigeria or Cameroun Republic.[4]

Notwithstanding its awareness of the open sentiments of the majority of the people in favour of outright independence and the publicly stated and politically sound position of the Southern Cameroons' Government, the British Government, eager to keep its "golden key to the Bank of England", presumptuously claimed that 'many of the best friends of the Cameroons do not foresee a destiny more likely to promote her happiness and prosperity than in continued association with Nigeria.'[5] The British Government was determined to sink the Southern Cameroons into Nigeria!

> The British view is that in the particular circumstances of the British Cameroons the progressive development of the inhabitants towards self-government or independence must appropriately be promoted in association with the socially advanced protectorate of Nigeria. The British delegation has impressed this view with consistent firmness and frankness upon the Trusteeship Council and the Council has been obliged to accept it grudgingly, but with an increasing appreciation of its logic, albeit qualified by a natural and legitimate anxiety that our policy should be accompanied by adequate measures to preserve the identity of the Trust Territory.[6]

So saying the British Government unfairly and unwarrantedly introduced into the independence debate at the UN the spurious question of economic viability and applied concerted and sustained pressure on the Government of the Southern Cameroons to hush up its stated view and to prevent the emergence of any association or organisation in the territory in favour of separate independence.

'Economic non-viability' is a notoriously vague concept. There is no appropriate typology for the description and the analysis of "an economically non-viable state." Furthermore, in the law of self-determination it is for the people to determine the destiny of the territory and not for the territory to determine the destiny of the people.[7] That is why the 1960 Declaration on decolonisation declares economic self-sufficiency to be irrelevant to the question of independence for a dependent people. By bringing into play the claimed economic non-viability of the Southern Cameroons, the British Government was incorrectly saying the territory of the Southern Cameroons had to determine the destiny of its people.

That was not all. In June 1959, the British Government commissioned Sir Phillipson to prepare a report on the economic consequences of separation of the Southern Cameroons from Nigeria. This one-man economic report on the Southern Cameroons was clearly uncalled for since the Southern Cameroons was legally not a part of Nigeria and it was mandatory for the Administering Authority to ensure the separation of the Southern Cameroons from Nigeria before 30th September 1960 regardless of the economic consequences. But the British Government needed a report to serve a specific purpose at the United Nations, namely to form the basis of its preposterous claim that the Southern Cameroons is not economically viable to accede to sovereign statehood.

Sir Phillipson arrived in Buea, the Southern Cameroons, in mid-July 1959 and on 3rd September, after only a two-day visit to the Cameroons Development Corporation (CDC) plantations in Victoria and Tiko, he submitted an "interim report" in which he expressed the opinion that the Southern Cameroons would not be viable as a separate independent state. The consultant appeared to have misunderstood his mandate. He took it that he was required to ascertain whether on separation from Nigeria the Southern Cameroons would be economically self-sufficient to stand on its own. If that was the purpose of the whole exercise then it was, on principle, a meaningless exertion because whether economically self-sufficient or not the Southern Cameroons had to be separated from Nigeria and Britain was treaty-bound to lead it to 'self-government or independence.'[8]

One would have thought that Sir Phillipson's charge simply required him to ascertain the consequences that separation would entail (so that the Southern Cameroons' Government could start working on how to face any such difficulties), rather than to pronounce himself on the ultimate issue of sovereign statehood (a matter that was outside his mandate). His report was based mainly on a two-day visit to CDC plantations in Victoria and Tiko and interviews with some civil servants and economic operators in the Buea-Victoria-Tiko conurbation.

It was only a week after he had submitted his interim report, that Sir Phillipson made a fieldtrip inland. Even then, it was a whirlwind three-day trip that took him to Bamenda, Wum and

Nkambe. His visit to the Santa Coffee Estate and the Ndu Tea Estate were perfunctory, suggesting he had already made up his mind (or perhaps already written his report) and was merely seeking some data to validate his bias.[9]

Why was Sir Phillipson in such a hurry? There had to be an interim report, a rushed one, because the British Government wanted it for use at the 14th session of the General Assembly as "evidence" in support of the claimed "economic non-viability" of the Southern Cameroons. Moreover, Sir Phillipson also calculatedly made available his interim report to politicians from the Southern Cameroons attending that UN session. The reason for this ploy was that these politicians would acquaint themselves with Sir Phillipson's "economic non-viability" provisional conclusion, the labours of an "expert", and would be deflected from pushing the separate independence issue.

The report thus served its intended purpose by "informing" the UN decision to exclude from the plebiscite the political status option of outright independence for the Southern Cameroons. Miss A. Brooks, the Liberian Chairlady of that session of the Fourth Committee concluded the debates by saying that the plebiscite questions in the draft resolution of the Committee were to be framed in such a way that it 'would serve to allay any apprehension that the Southern Cameroons might become independent as a separate entity, an eventuality which all were agreed should be ruled out in view of the territory's limited economic potential.'[10]

After submitting his interim report, Sir Phillipson resumed work on his consultancy assignment and this time submitted a final report on 9th October 1959 that was finely nuanced. In that report he in effect stated that the interim report of five weeks earlier was meant to influence decision at the UN. The interim report, he said, was 'of restricted circulation as it seemed advisable that those attending the 14th session of the General Assembly of the United Nations from the Southern Cameroons should be acquainted with my provisional conclusion.' He then confessed that, 'this report replaces that interim report, which should now be regarded as obsolete.'[11]

The same Sir Phillipson would later be appointed 'constitutional and economic adviser' by the British to assist the Southern Cameroons' Government in an examination of the constitutional, fiscal and economic problems likely to arise out of "joining" Cameroun Republic. Since he had taken the view that the Southern Cameroons could not economically stand on its own, he was not a person likely to counsel the taking of a robust attitude in discussions with Cameroun Republic.

But he served the British Government very well as its hatchet man on mission in the Southern Cameroons. Sir Phillipson's consultancy mandated him to write a report on the consequences of the separation of the Southern Cameroons from Nigeria. But the consultant "sidetracked" his terms of reference and laboured to show that the Southern Cameroons would not be economically viable as a sovereign independent state. Sir Phillipson was still on his consultancy work when the British Government decided to appoint him so-called neutral chairman of the Mamfe Plebiscite Conference and he demonstrated his 'neutrality' by hurriedly closing the conference declaring, in spite of clear evidence to the contrary, that the delegates had failed to reach agreement on the alternatives that should be presented at the plebiscite. No sooner had Sir Phillipson finished his consultancy report than the British Government appointed him yet again, this time as a double expert, on constitutional law and on economics, to assist the Southern Cameroons in its negotiations with Cameroun Republic. The assistance he provided was, in fact, his success in putting the Southern Cameroons in a weaker bargaining position vis-à-vis Cameroun Republic on account of his economic non-viability claim.

During Anglo-Southern Cameroons' talks in London in October 1960, the British Government informed the Southern Cameroons' delegation that by framing the plebiscite questions the way it did, the UN ruled out a period of continuing Trusteeship and also ruled out the question of separate independence for the Southern Cameroons. But the British were unable, and still are unable, to say the political status the UN proposed for the territory within the "joining" forced on it..

The Secretary of State for the Colonies, Mr. Iain Macleod, stated that if the plebiscite went in favour of "joining" Cameroun Republic, arrangements would have to be made 'for the early termination of Trusteeship and *the transfer of sovereignty to the Republic*.[12] In a March 1961 brief, prepared for an upcoming meeting of Commonwealth Prime Ministers, the Colonial Office stated that Nigeria was kept fully informed of 'every move in the discussion of *the hand-over of the Southern Cameroons to the Cameroun Republic*.' [13]

It is very strange indeed that the British Government should have been talking about 'transfer of sovereignty' and 'hand-over' of the Southern Cameroons to Cameroun Republic. The Administering Authority had no mandate to do any such thing. The 1960 Declaration on decolonisation requires the transfer of all powers to the people of the territory in order to enable them to enjoy complete independence and freedom. No law, whether international law or its own domestic law, required the British Government to transfer or to handover the Southern Cameroons to a foreign state. The very idea of a trust (tutelage or *fideicommissum*) implies a transitional arrangement where the administering authority should enjoy only delegated and a fundamentally limited authority in respect of the trust territory. The administering authority thus would not enjoy an unrestricted plenitude of powers in the trust territory. In fact, the British Government, as trustee, was prevented by the terms of the trusteeship agreement from doing a number of things, which an owner of territory can lawfully do. For example, Britain did not acquire the right of ownership in the Southern Cameroons; Britain exercised its trusteeship on behalf of the UN, for the trusteeship agreement contained no cession or transfer of the territory to Britain; Britain had no power, without the consent of the UN, to annex, cede or otherwise dispose of the territory.

The Administering Authority's unfortunate pronouncements, together with its entire attitude and conduct regarding the Southern Cameroons' decolonisation question, have rightly formed the basis of the view that the Southern Cameroons was never decolonised but simply transferred as a colonial territory to Cameroun Republic. Colonial rule by Britain ended and colonial rule by Cameroun Republic began. However, it is doubtful that the British Government actually executed a deed of transfer to that effect, as opposed to a mere notification to Cameroun Republic that its responsibilities over the Southern Cameroons would cease at mid-night of 30 September 1961. But this "transfer thesis" finds further support in the following scandalous statement of Mr. Hugh Fraser, then the British Under-Secretary of State for the Colonies.

On 1 October 1961, Mr. Fraser stated in the House of Commons that, as he was speaking, the Southern Cameroons had already been 'transferred' to Mr. Ahidjo and that it was only the said Ahidjo who could call for the postponement of the termination of the Trusteeship Agreement, because Cameroun Republic 'compared with the size of the Southern Cameroons is a three to one.' Here was a British Minister making a statement that had little meaning factually, legally and politically. Hugh Fraser was evasively responding to the well-founded criticism by the venerable Lord Thompson (then Honourable G.M. Thompson, Member of Parliament (MP) for Dundee East) of Britain's rather inglorious handling of the Southern Cameroons' "decolonisation" question. The Honourable MP pointed out that Britain had 'a very strong moral responsibility' in the Southern Cameroons 'quite apart from our legal responsibilities' and submitted that the British Government had failed to discharge itself creditably.[14]

There is yet further evidence of the betrayal of the Trust conferred on Britain. Consider this passage in a June 1960 top-secret dispatch from C.B. Boothby, Head of the African Department at the British Foreign Office, to Mr. P. M. Johnston, British Ambassador to Cameroun Republic, stating Britain's opposition to an independent Southern Cameroons:

> [W]e are not attracted to the idea of an independent Southern Cameroons because it would certainly not be able to pay its way and, as you suggest, we are not at all anxious to have to do so on its behalf. We cannot expect to get any advantage from being foster mother to an independent Southern Cameroons and it is clear that it would have to be fostered by somebody. The responsibility would only be likely to embarrass us with the Nigerian and Cameroun Governments in turn. In fact, the sooner we can provide decently for the future of the Southern Cameroons and wash our hands off it, the more pleased we shall be.[15]

These same views were strongly echoed by Sir Andrew Cohen, British Representative at the UN, in a number of confidential dispatches to the Colonial Office as well as to the Foreign Office.

Sir Andrew, a man of ability and a former colonial district commissioner in Uganda, was something of a vain man and his antipathy toward the Southern Cameroons was transparent. In his confidential dispatches, the distinguished British Representative stressed the need for the British Government to be firm with Premier Foncha so as to scotch the ever-growing sentiment among the entire political leadership and people of the Southern Cameroons that the territory should be granted outright independence.

> I believe a firm attitude on this now may save us a great deal of trouble later and I think that H.M.G.'s position should be made abundantly clear to Foncha in an effort to scotch tendencies towards the third question. [...] I think it may be necessary to tell Field [Commissioner of the Southern Cameroons] firmly that the policy of H.M.G. is to discourage any tendency towards a 'third question' very strongly.[16]

This was a case of concerted and sustained efforts by the British Government to deliberately suppress the legitimate aspirations and inalienable right of the people of the Southern Cameroons to establish freely, without external interference, a sovereign and independent state and to pursue their economic, social and cultural development. This line of conduct by the British Government was wholly inconsistent with its legal commitments under Articles 3 and 6 of the Trusteeship Agreement and with its treaty obligations under Articles 1(2) and 76b of the UN Charter.

The British wanted a successor colonialist to take over the Southern Cameroons as 'foster mother'. The trusteeship over the Southern Cameroons was never forced on Britain. It seems therefore odd to the extreme that the British Government should later have been complaining about having to meet financial commitments in the territory, so much so that she led a campaign to deprive the people of the Southern Cameroons of their inalienable right to govern themselves and control their own destiny.

Britain even refused to provide for the security of the Southern Cameroons. As the ominous date of 1 October 1961 approached, the Southern Cameroons Government had serious legitimate concerns about the territory's security on account of the bloody terrorism raging in Cameroun Republic, and the impending departure of British troops[17] from the Southern Cameroons. It informed the Administering Authority that it was committed to raising and maintaining its own army and police and requested British assistance in the realisation of that objective.

Oddly enough, the British reply was that Cameroun Republic troops would maintain security in the Southern Cameroons when British troops leave. This was hardly reassuring as it meant one foreign force would replace another foreign force in the territory. The Southern Cameroons' Government was alarmed at such a prospect. It argued that to allow Cameroun Republic forces into the Southern Cameroons even as a temporary measure would smack of countenancing an army of occupation in the state. Such a situation, it pointed out, would be all the more repugnant and unacceptable on account of the suspect level of education and training of those forces, and their continued practice of brutal repression and torture.

The Southern Cameroons pleaded with the Government of the United Kingdom to accede to its long-standing request to assist in the provision for, and secondment of, trained personnel to a future Southern Cameroons' army and police. The British were unmoved. They repeated their familiar line: lack of money.[18] A direct consequence of this latest British betrayal was that two weeks before the Union Jack was lowered at Buea, capital of the Southern Cameroons, French-led Cameroun Republic soldiers, indistinguishable from colonial regiments, moved in and were permanently stationed in the Southern Cameroons occupying to this day the very housing facilities built by the Royal Engineers of the departed British troops.

On 1 October 1961, Her Majesty, Queen Elizabeth II, addressed a message of 'sincere good wishes [...] on the occasion of the ending of United Kingdom trusteeship in the Southern Cameroons.' Oddly enough, the message was not addressed to Mr. Foncha, Prime Minister and political head of the "decolonised" British Southern Cameroons, as traditionally ought to have been the case. The Queen instead addressed her message to Mr. Ahidjo, President of Cameroun Republic, on the ground that he was the one 'now [to] preside' over the 'united territories'.[19] He was in effect the new colonial overlord in the Southern Cameroons.

In her message, the British Head of State expressed her gladness that 'friendly cooperation' between Britain and Cameroun Republic 'made it possible for the Southern Cameroons to attain independence in accordance with the results of the February plebiscite.'[20] If the Southern Cameroons did attain independence why did the Queen not address her message to the political leader of the new state that had just achieved independence from Britain? The Queen's act of addressing her message to Ahidjo rather than to Foncha only went to reinforce the view that the Southern Cameroons was, as indeed Hugh Fraser himself told the House of Commons, transferred to Cameroun Republic. Cameroun Republic has thus been able to argue, lamely of course, that in recognition of the validity of its territorial claim to the territory of the Southern Cameroons the British Government invited President Ahidjo to Buea, capital of the Southern Cameroons, and formerly transferred to him sovereignty over the territory.[21]

By a vote taken on the matter in April 1961, the UN endorsed the decision of the outhern Cameroons to achieve "independence." Yet, the Administering Authority did not bother to sponsor, as is the practice or tradition in such circumstances, the admission of independent Southern Cameroons to membership of the UN. That membership would not have been inconsistent with the Cameroon federal union, especially the informal federation that it was. Ahidjo was President of the Federation. He did not apply for Federal Republic of Cameroon membership of the United Nations. But that was a calculated omission designed to foster his annexation agenda by giving the impression that the Federal Republic of Cameroon was a mere continuation of Cameroun Republic in a different name.

On the question of UN membership, it may be noted that Article 4 of the 1978 Vienna Convention on the Succession of States in Respect of Treaties, embodies a principle of customary international law according to which membership in international organisations is not subject to the general continuity rule. Membership has to be asked for by the state successor and accepted by the members of the organisation according to the rules governing the organisation. Since the Cameroon Federation, as state successor to both Cameroun Republic and the Southern Cameroons, did not ask for UN membership it did not continue the membership of Cameroun Republic, obtained on 30 September 1960.

Under Article 73 of the UN Charter, Members of the UN are obliged to develop self-government in dependent territories and, by virtue of Article 103 this obligation prevails over those under other international agreements. When this obligation is fulfilled a dependent territory attains its independence and there must be a constitutional transfer of sovereign powers to an independent government of the emergent state.

One would therefore have expected that termination of the Southern Cameroons' tutelage status would have entailed the concomitant transfer of sovereign powers to an independent Southern Cameroons' government as indeed is required by the 1960 Declaration on decolonisation and as is necessarily implied in Article 76b of the UN Charter. Consistent with its pre-plebiscite agreement with Cameroun Republic for a federal political association of the two countries, the independent Government of the Southern Cameroons would then have advised itself on the surrender of residuary powers of sovereignty to the Federal Government.

Instead, on 1 October 1961, the Administering Authority purported to have transferred their sovereign powers over the Southern Cameroons to a foreign prince called Mr. Ahidjo, President of Cameroun Republic. The argument sometimes advanced is that this was done because Mr. Ahidjo was President of the Federal Republic of Cameroon; this does not hold water at all. There was no federal government yet on 1 October[22] and nowhere was it agreed between the Southern Cameroons and Cameroun Republic that Mr. Ahidjo, as an individual, would constitute a body representing the federation and the federal government on 1 October 1961. Moreover, Mr. Ahidjo had no standing regarding the British Cameroons Trusteeship Agreement and was thus an interfering body. The transfer of sovereign powers to him (assuming there ever was such a thing) was therefore invalid. Assuming, but without conceding the point, that the transfer was valid, what was transferred could only have been the exercise of colonial sovereignty, which is the only type of sovereignty that was vested in the trustee power. The trustee power could therefore not transfer what it did not have. The maxim of the law is, *nemo dat quod non habet* (nobody gives what he does not have). The residuary sovereignty in the trust territory remained vested in the UN and the national sovereignty in the people of the territory. Neither of these was ever conceded to Cameroun Republic.

There appears therefore to be overwhelming evidence that neither the British Government nor the United Nations acted in the best interest of the people of the Southern Cameroons. They betrayed the "sacred trust of civilization" assumed by them in respect of those hapless people.

Notes

1. E Ardener, 'The Political History of Cameroon' *The World Today*, vol. 18, No. 8, August 1962, p. 343.

2. Declaration on the Granting of Independence to Colonial Countries and Peoples (General Assembly Resolution 1514 (XV) of 14 December 1960), numbered paragraph 6.

3. N Jua & P Konings, 'Occupation of Public Space: Anglophone Nationalism in Cameroon,' (2002): http://etudesafrica ines.revue.org/document4756.html (Visited: 6 December 2007); N Omoigui, 'The Bakassi Story', published on the Internet in 2007; J Percival, *The 1961 Cameroon Plebiscite: Choice or Betrayal*, Langaa Research & Publishing, Bamenda, 2008, pp. 31-34.

4. The Communiqué issued after the Anglo-Southern Cameroons Conference of 10-13 October 1960, stated this to be the position of the Southern Cameroons. 'Mr. Foncha, the Premier of the Southern Cameroons expressed the hope that the United Nations would be prepared, if the vote went in favour of the Cameroun Republic, to agree to a period of independence for the Southern Cameroons during which preparations would be made for the unification of the Southern Cameroons with the Cameroun Republic on a federal basis.' See *Report of the United Nations Plebiscite Commissioner for the Cameroons under United Kingdom Administration*, UNGA Document A/4727 of 11 April 1961, paragraph 68.

5. This was the statement of the British Secretary of State for the Colonies, Mr. Alan Lennox-Boyd at the conclusion of discussion during the May/June 1957 London Conference on the Nigerian Constitution. He, it is, who also made the 'golden key to the Bank of England' statement.

6. Confidential Memo of the British Consul General at Brazzaville dated 24 January 1952: Foreign Office File No. F.O.371/10/390.

7. Per Judge Dillard in his separate opinion in the *Western Sahara Case* 1975 ICJ 12, 114.

8. Charter of the United Nations, Article 76 b.

9. Sir Phillipson's itinerary was as follows: July 11/12: London-Lagos; July 13: Lagos-Tiko-Buea; July 28: Buea-Victoria-Buea; July 29: to CDC for visits to

Limbe Nurseries, Bota Oil Mill, Bota Wharf, Industrial Area, Middle Farm, Bota Hospital and School, Workers' Shop and Community Hall, Motor Transport Garage (Moliwe); July 30: to CDC for visits to Tole Tea Factory (Buea), Rubber Factory (Tiko), Rubber Plantation (Missellele), and further tour of industrial area; August 7/8: Buea-Kumba-Mamfe; August 10/11: Conference on plebiscite questions and register; August 12: Mamfe-Buea; September 11: Buea-Mamfe-Bamenda (air between Tiko and Mamfe); September 12: Bamenda-Bafut-Wum-Bamenda: September 13: Bamenda-Bali-Bamenda (a.m.), Bamenda-Santa Coffee Estate-Bamenda (p.m.); September 15: Bamenda-Ndu Tea Estate-Bamenda; September 17: Bamenda-Mamfe; September 18: Mamfe-Tiko (by air)-Buea. See page 54 of his final report.

10. 898th Meeting of the Fourth Committee in October 1959. According to this view then the Southern Cameroons was to become 'independent as a dependent entity', like Leopold II's *'Etat Indépendant du Congo'* or France's *'République Indépendante du Togo au sein de l'Union Française'*. This was new and strange learning.

11. Sir Sydney Phillipson, *Report on Financial, Economic and Administrative Consequences to the Southern Cameroons of Separation from the Federation of Nigeria*, Lagos, Federal Government Printer, 1959, p. 45.

12. See *Report of the Plebiscite Commissioner*, op. cit., paragraph 68. Emphasis added.

13. Colonial Office brief of 7 March 1961 on preparations for the 1961 Commonwealth Prime Ministers Meeting. Cited by Professor M Shaw during the oral pleadings in the 'Bakassi case.' Emphasis added.

14. See *House of Commons Debates*, August 1, 1961, pp. 1335-1351.

15. *Declassified Secret Southern Cameroons Files*, (Public Records Office), London, 13 June 1960

16. Ibid. Directive by Sir Andrew in a despatch from New York to Eastwood dated 7 June 1960,

17. The troops consisted of the First Battalion, King's Own Royal Border Regiment, supported by elements of the Royal Engineers, the Royal Army Medical Corps, and a detachment of the 230th Squadron, Royal Air Force.

18. 'Record of the Tripartite Conference between Representatives of the Republic of Cameroun, the Southern Cameroons, and the United Kingdom, held in the House of Assembly at Buea from 15-17 June 1961, under the Chairmanship of His Honour the Commissioner of the Southern Cameroons, Mr. J.O. Field, CMG.' *Declassified Secret Southern Cameroons Files*, (Public Records Office), London.

19. Her Britannic Majesty's message is reproduced in *Press Release* No. 1562, Bulletin No. 1, West Cameroon Information Service, Buea, 9 October 1961, p. 3.

20. Ibid., p. 3.

21. L Sindjoun, *L'Etat Ailleurs*, op. cit. According to the author at p. 171, the Government of the United Kingdom effected 'le transfert solennel de la souveraineté du Cameroun méridional au président Ahidjo, le 30 septembre, 1961 à Buea.' This would seem more of a myth or wishful thinking than the true state of affairs. No evidence is provided of any such alleged transfer of sovereignty, e.g. the instrument of transfer. The British Government itself exercised sovereignty by virtue of an instrument, the Trusteeship Agreement, and could not therefore transfer that sovereignty verbally or informally. And, even if, as a mere theoretical proposition, such an event took place, only a colonial sovereignty could have been transferred to Ahidjo since the British Government itself exercised only a colonial sovereignty over the Southern Cameroons. The British Government could not even have transferred sovereignty over the Southern Cameroons because it did not own the territory.

22. It was only on the 10th of October 1961 that a federal government was formed. Ahidjo chose the members of that government. The legal capacity in which he did so remained doubtful to the extreme.

Chapter Five
A Black Colonialist Makes an Expansionist Claim

Cameroun Republic asserts sovereignty over the Southern Cameroons. The claimed bases of that assertion are two arguments, one founded on "history" and the other on so-called "popular consent to incorporation."

According to Cameroun Republic, the 20-odd years of German colonisation of a swathe of territory at the hinge of Africa created a "Kamerun nation" Cameroun Republic succeeded to that "nation" on 1 January 1960 when it attained independence from France and became an international person.

Further, Cameroun Republic also acquired, on account of its larger spatial and demographic configuration compared to that of the Southern Cameroons, the status of "mother country" with a historic mission to reassemble all the territories that made up the extinct German *Kamerun* protectorate and so create "Greater Cameroun Republic." A former Cameroun Republic academic and later a government minister starkly expressed the territorial ambition of Cameroun Republic in these terms:

> L'un des objectifs fondamentaux de la République du Cameroun est d'arriver à réaliser l'unité du territoire.[1]

> Lorsque la République du Cameroun proclame [...] le respect des frontières nées de la décolonisation, elle vise les frontières du Cameroun telles qu'elles se présentent en 1910 [...] elle revendique le retour aux frontières coloniales.[2]

In 1961, Ahidjo canvassed for the first time Cameroun Republic's expansionist argument. Making his closing speech at the aborted Foumban constitutional meeting in August 1961, Ahidjo told the unsuspecting Southern Cameroons' delegation:

> Consequently, it fell upon Cameroun Republic which already enjoyed its international sovereignty and which already

had its institutions, to adjust its very constitution in order to form a union with the brother territory of the Southern Cameroons.³

That was an elliptical statement. In effect this is what Ahidjo was saying: there was no new constitution to be worked out by common bargain between the two parties; Cameroun Republic would simply tinker with its existing constitution to facilitate the constitutional accession of the Southern Cameroons to Cameroun Republic. A few weeks later, Ahidjo expressed his expansionist pretensions in plain language.

Addressing his country's National Assembly later in the month, Ahidjo claimed that the United Nations, by its Resolution 1608 (XV), 'imposed on us the obligation to adjust the institutional structures of Cameroun Republic so as *to receive back a dismembered part of our country.*' ⁴

Ahidjo's "Federal Constitution" was thus an entirely Cameroun Republic affair, drafted by Cameroun Republic and adopted by the legislature of that country. The long title of the document rehearsed the expansionist argument by declaring that Cameroun Republic amended its constitution 'so as to allow for *the return of part of its territory.*' In a speech to the congress of his *Union Camerounaise* political party in Ebolowa in July 1962, Ahidjo put his expansionist claim much more bluntly:

> The reunification of the Southern Cameroons and Cameroun Republic did not necessitate a fundamental change of the constitution of Cameroun Republic, but only a minor amendment *to allow for part of the territory to rejoin the mother land* [...] It was Cameroun Republic which had to transform itself into a Federation, taking into account *the return to it of a part of its territory*, a part possessing certain special characteristics.⁵

Ahidjo was no lawyer and was of course not talking law. His French advisers 'forget' to tell him he could not credibly talk of 'recovering lost territory' because the very fact of the UN-ordained plebiscite in the Southern Cameroons was in itself the complete legal and political rebuttal, by the international community, of his nonsensical talk about 'recovery of lost territory'. If indeed, the Southern Cameroons were a lost-and-found part of Cameroun Republic, there would have been no need for the plebiscite; the UN and Britain would simply have returned the Southern Cameroons (and the Northern Cameroons as well) to Cameroun Republic in the same way Spain returned Ifni to Morocco and Britain returned Hong Kong to China.

The legal implications of the plebiscite were that the UN recognised the fact that the native inhabitants of the Southern Cameroons constitute a people within the meaning of the right of self determination; that the people of the Southern Cameroons have the unquestionable and inalienable right to self-determination; that the people of the Southern Cameroons have sovereign title to the territory of the Southern Cameroons; that the Southern Cameroons constitutes a unit of self determination; and that the Southern Cameroons, the frontiers of which are well delimited by territorially-grounded treaties, constitutes a distinct, separate, legal and political entity entitled to achieve independence.

Ahidjo was thus merely engaged in blowing political hot air. Even so, he sounded defensive. He appeared to be anxious to gain political mileage as the so-called architect of so-called 'reunification' by demonstrating to a 'radical' political persuasion in Cameroun Republic[6] that the Southern Cameroons was indeed grabbed by Cameroun Republic on 1 October 1961, the 'federation' window-dressing notwithstanding. The hackneyed line of that hawkish political persuasion was that on 1 October 1961 Cameroun Republic should simply have annexed the Southern Cameroons outright. In their hankering for the outright annexation of the Southern Cameroons, politicians of that shade of view argued that the federal association fell far short of the so-called "unity" they had supposedly "struggled" for.

But Ahidjo had in fact achieved the same goal by resorting to a ruse and by making and emphasising allegations he knew were false but, nevertheless, important in serving the expansionist interests of Cameroun Republic. First, Ahidjo averred that no political association, less still a political association of two countries took place on 1 October 1961. Second, he said that Cameroun Republic simply continued, but had to rework itself to accommodate the return of its lost people and territory, with consequential border adjustments. Third, he claimed that Cameroun Republic by an act of state transformed itself into a federation precisely so as to accommodate a 'returned part of its territory having special characteristics'. Fourth, in Ahidjo's view the "return" of that claimed part of the territory of Cameroun Republic was no more than a rectification of its south western borders, enabling it to return to the German colonial frontier at that point. Fifth, for Ahidjo what took place on 1 October 1961 was simply a case of the constitutional accession of the Southern Cameroons to Cameroun Republic, in other words, the incorporation of the Southern Cameroons into Cameroun Republic.[7]

These allegations are not borne out by facts or by law. But from them Cameroun Republic feels able to characterise Southern Cameroons' independence struggle as a secessionist bid.

The merit of Cameroun Republic's assertions is worth examining in some detail.

Notes

1. AN Njoya, *Le Cameroun dans les Relations Internationales*, Librairie General de Droit et de la Jurisprudence, Paris, 1976, p. 189. My translation: "One of the fundamental objectives pursued by Cameroun Republic is to be able to bring about the unity of the territory."

2. Ibid., p. 188. My translation: "When Cameroun Republic speaks of respect for frontiers as at the time of decolonisation, it has in mind Cameroun's boundaries as they stood in 1910... it claims the return to colonial boundaries." He does not explain his arbitrary choice of 1910. Nor does he indicate the boundary treaties executed in or before 1910 attesting to 'the 1910 frontiers' he talks of. By 'return to colonial boundaries' the writer is evidently referring to the colonial boundaries of German Kamerun, and, inexplicably, arbitrarily decides that these boundaries must be those as they stood in 1910.

3. Closing speech at the Foumban meeting. See *Recueils des Discours Presidentiels 1958-1968*, Paris, 1968. Emphasis added.

4. Ahidjo's public speeches, in French of course, are published in two collections, *Recueils des Discours Présidentiels 1958-1968*, Paris, 1968; and *Anthologie des Discours 1968-1978*, Paris, Les Nouvelles Editions, 1979. Passages cited in the text are from these documents and the translation is mine. Emphasis added.

5. 1962 address at the *Union Camerounaise* party congress in Ebolowa. See Recueil des Discours Presidentiels, op. cit. Emphasis added.

6. The communist-leaning UPC political party and a veiled political group operating as *'le Cercle Culturel Camerounais'* passed for radical political parties or were so considered.

7. *Anthologie des discours*, op. cit., p. 143.

Chapter Six

Refutation of the 'History' Thesis

As a trust territory, the Southern Cameroons possessed international status and a degree of international personality. These were underpinned by secure frontiers, well delimited by boundary treaties.¹ The status of the Southern Cameroons as a territory firmly on the path of sovereign statehood was further strengthened when it achieved self-government status in 1954 and became a state in *statu nascendi* in 1960 with its own separate constitution, *'The Southern Cameroons Constitution Order in Council'*. Its national sovereignty was in abeyance waiting to revive and rest on the new state at the moment of its independence.

The Southern Cameroons had, during that time, capacity to conclude various types of international agreements, since the period of self-government of a territory is often characterised by its capacity to conclude such agreements.² It is partly for this reason that in interpreting the second plebiscite question the British Colonial Secretary, Mr. Iain Macleod, stated in October 1960, that arrangements for a future Cameroon Federal Republic would be worked out after the plebiscite 'by a conference consisting of representative delegations of equal status from the Republic and the Southern Cameroons.'

Cameroun Republic did not contest this formula. It did not make any reservation to it. On the contrary, it fully endorsed the formula on 2 December 1960, thereby acknowledging the fact that both countries were, after the plebiscite, legally equal in terms of political status (i.e. independent countries). Indeed, in 1959 and throughout 1960, Ahidjo denied on several occasions any hidden intentions of annexing the Southern Cameroons, stressing that both sides would carry out negotiations for what he called and persisted in calling "reunification" on a footing of strict equality. In a foreword to an official publication by Yaounde in late 1961 Ahidjo wrote: 'When the solemn re-unification of *the two Cameroons* took place on 1ˢᵗ October 1961, it was necessary to endow this re-united country with a Constitution adapted to the Federal System agreed upon between *the two sister States*.'³

The July 1961 Foumban constitutional meeting was therefore a meeting of two independent states, the Southern Cameroons having in contemplation of law achieved independence by its vote to that effect five months earlier, on February 11, though the effective date of that independence was postponed by the UN to 1 October 1961. Ahidjo's implied claim that the Southern Cameroons delegation at Foumban was inferior in status was merely political hot air and had no legal basis.[4] For, in a stunning admission, as indicated in the preceding paragraph, Ahidjo later spoke of "the Federal System agreed upon between *the two sister States*."[5]

The pre-plebiscite agreement between the Southern Cameroons and Cameroun Republic concluded in 1960 was, arguably, predicated on the fact that the former was possessed of some degree of international personality, at least for the purpose of the matter at hand. Object and subject of international law cannot conclude a treaty; but they can validly conclude an agreement expressed as governed by an agreed municipal law. In the instant case, however, the pre-plebiscite agreement did not state any agreed municipal law that was to govern it, the inescapable implication being that the agreement was governed by and binding under international law as one concluded between a subject and at least a qualified subject of international law. It was the future federation that was to be governed by domestic law, that domestic law being the federal constitution that was itself still to be drafted and adopted.

If, therefore, Cameroun Republic concluded the pre-plebiscite agreement with the Southern Cameroons possessed of some degree of international personality, even if limited to the conclusion of said agreement, then the fact that the agreement was expressed in the form of a Joint Declaration or Communiqué can hardly be of any consequence, except to suggest that the agreement was concluded with less solemnity. In the eyes of international law, the nomenclature of an agreement between international persons binding in virtue of the maxim *pacta sunt servanda* is immaterial. For example, the Anglo-Chinese Agreement in 1984 regarding Hong Kong took the form of a Joint Declaration to which were adjoined three annexes.

Admittedly, not all agreements between subjects of international law are legally binding instruments. Some agreements though they may exercise an influence in international politics, may be merely statements of commonly held principles or objectives or policies;

or they may be no more than a policy manoeuvre or a statement of political commitments taking the form of gentlemen's agreements, joint statements or declarations.[6] Indeed, UN Resolution 1608 (XV) would seem to have considered the pre-plebiscite agreement as mere 'policies' agreed upon, implying that they were not legally binding.

But it is doubtful that the agreement was not legally binding. All the facts and circumstances of the situation clearly indicated that the parties intended to set up juridical relations between themselves. They intended to establish binding obligations. The agreement was negotiated over a long period of time and was signed by the political leaders of the two countries. It was made available to the United Nations and to the British Government as the agreed constitutional arrangement for political association between the Southern Cameroons and Cameroun Republic. Cameroun Republic subsequently confirmed the agreement by a *Note Verbale* from its Ministry of Foreign Affairs to the British Government. The agreement was framed not in facultative terms but in the phraseology of legal obligations. The rights and the status of the Southern Cameroons thereunder did not depend upon the permission and pleasure of the Government of Cameroun Republic.

Any suggestion that the agreement was non-binding and that therefore Cameroun Republic was not bound to implement federalism, would, by parity of reasoning be valid also with regard to the Southern Cameroons, meaning that it was also not bound to "join" Cameroun Republic. If the agreement was ineffectual, then it was so regarding both parties. A party cannot approbate and reprobate.

Successor-state fantasy

Cameroun Republic declares itself to be the successor state to a so-called "Kamerun nation", a mythical nation (mythical because no such *nation* exists or ever existed, as distinct from a once short-live colonial entity) supposedly created by fiat of an evanescent German colonialism. This claim is preposterous. By what magic did Cameroun Republic whose existence as a legal and political entity dates from 1922 succeed in 1960 to an entity extinct *de jure* in 1919? In law, an extinct entity is one that juridically no longer exists. By what miracle then could Cameroun Republic have succeeded to a non-existent entity?

Upon the defeat of Germany and the consequential extinction of the "Kamerun" German colonial possession, all treaties affecting that colonial territory also became extinguished, survived only by the territorially grounded treaties. Cameroun Republic did not succeed to extinct "Kamerun" for the simple reason also that in the law of state succession a successor state succeeds to an immediate, and not to some remote, predecessor state or entity. What Cameroun Republic succeeded to at its independence on 1 January 1960 were the subsisting rights and obligations of France over the colonial territory of French Cameroun. Cameroun Republic therefore acquired its territories not from Germany but from France. At its independence it inherited the territories of French Cameroun because its independence was achieved within the territorial framework of the French trusteeship. The territory of Cameroun Republic devolved upon it as the emergent successor state on the basis of the pre-existing boundaries as established by treaty.

The legal foundation of Cameroun Republic as a country goes back to the inception of French, not German, colonisation. This can even be seen from the following facts. Cameroun Republic's language of public administration is French not German. Its educational and economic systems, its value system, and its legal, judicial, administrative and political culture are all French-derived. Its currency is French-backed and its military and policing training and tradition are French-based. The German orthography *Kamerun* has never been in use in that country, whether by government or by associations, during or after French colonial rule. In short, the Francophone nature of Cameroun Republic and the visceral Francophile feeling of its political rulership expose the lie behind that country's claim to being the heir to extinct "German *Kamerun*." Ironically, the greatest number of words of European origin that have been assimilated into native languages in Cameroun Republic, like Duala, Bulu and Ewondo, are derived, not from German or even French, but from English!

The "*Kamerun* nation" idea and its progeny, the "reunification" idea, are mere figments of the imagination. They are political myths invented to serve expansionist political goals. The period of German colonial rule was so short that the German language was not in use beyond the narrow coastal strip where German presence was really felt. There was no local representative body whatsoever of a political nature or other political institution set up in the protectorate[7] and which could possibly have promoted a form of structured contact and interaction between the various communities of the protectorate.

Had the period of effective and peaceful German rule lasted much longer, had the German language been in general use, had some representative body existed, then, arguably, there could have been generated, at least a modicum of a feeling of common belonging among the disparate and far-flung peoples of the territory. As this never happened, the natives within the borders of erstwhile *Kamerun* never coalesced into anything like a country or nation that the borders of territorial entities usually imply. As a result, the period of German colonisation never elicited any sense whatsoever of a common national belonging, identity, or allegiance in the territory. Thus, when France excised from its French Cameroun territory two large chunks of it known as the *Duckbill* and the *Neue Kamerun* and incorporated them into French Equatorial Africa the inhabitants thereof did not claim and have never claimed, nor has Cameroun Republic itself ever claimed, that they have any ties or sense of belonging to a so-called "*Kamerun* nation."

What is more, the modern history, as distinct from the legal foundation, of Cameroun Republic practically dates from the inception of German colonisation in 1884. By contrast, the modern history of the Southern Cameroons dates from the 1840s with the anti-slavery activity of the British at Ambas Bay and more particularly from 1858 when the Ambas Bay district was claimed for England and the small European settlement there named Victoria after the then reigning British monarch.

Before the 20 or so years of its German connection, the Southern Cameroons had had 30 years of British connection (in fact 44 years, if one takes 1844, the date of the first Anglo-Bimbia treaty, as the cut off date) and, after the German interregnum, a further period of 46 years of British rule. How then can it credibly be argued that the Southern Cameroons and Cameroun Republic formed a so-called "nation" created by German colonialism and that the attempt of political association in 1961 between the two countries represented so-called "reunification" or even "unification"? According to

Cameroun Republic's demagogic logic the Southern Cameroons should consider the 20 years of its tenuous German connection more important than the combined, intense 90 years of its British connection!

Upon the outbreak of World War I in 1914, German resistance in *Kamerun* collapsed in the face of overwhelming British forces moving in from British West Africa and French forces from French Equatorial Africa. From 1914 to 1916 the protectorate was occupied as enemy territory consistent with the laws of war at the time. The utter defeat of Germany in the territory in 1916 saw its partition by Britain and France. On that date therefore Germany ceased to exercise any form of territorial authority in that territory or any part thereof. At the end of the War in 1918 and consequent upon her defeat, Germany signed the 1919 Treaties of Versailles under which she renounced and relinquished title and right to all her colonial possessions, including the Kamerun territory already partitioned in 1916 between Britain and France.

Kamerun thus became extinct both as a German colony and as a single entity. In its place there emerged two separate and distinct legal and political entities, British Cameroons and French Cameroun. In order to avoid the perception that European powers were indulging in wholesale annexations in the good old imperialist fashion, it was agreed at Versailles that the conquered enemy territories be placed under a mandate system, the goal being ultimate independence of the natives.[8] The 1916 Anglo-French partition and the 1919 Anglo-French boundary treaty (Milner-Simon Declaration) were thus confirmed in 1922 when the League of Nations granted a mandate to Britain over the British Cameroons and another mandate to France over French Cameroun. The frontier alignment between British Cameroons and French Cameroun, as defined by the 1919 boundary treaty was more particularly determined in the 1931 Anglo-French boundary treaty (Graeme-Marchand Declaration) and confirmed by the UN in the Trusteeship Agreements in 1946, relative to the British Cameroons and to French Cameroun.

This had legal implications. *Kamerun* as a unitary colonial territory had already ceased to exist in 1916, following the partition of the territory along the Simon-Milner Line. In 1919 it became extinct and inexistent in law and in fact. The inhabitants of British Cameroons as well as those of French Cameroun were divested of their nominal German nationality, though they did not automatically become invested with the nationality of their respective mandatory power.

In theory of law those two territories, the British Cameroons and French Cameroun, were separate, new legal and political entities created in 1922 by the political force represented by the mandate system. The juridical basis of their respective existence and the international basis of the frontiers between the two are the mandate system, transmuted into the trusteeship system after World War II. At the Anglo-French boundary delimitation in 1922, the boundaries of the British and French mandated territories were neither the pre-1911 nor the post-1911 ones of German *Kamerun*. The *Neue Kamerun*[9] gained by Germany in 1911 was questionably excised by France and incorporated into French Equatorial Africa. France, however, kept as part of the territory of its Cameroun mandate one small gain, the Duckbill that had been ceded to Germany in 1911. But even that is now part of Chad.

The view that a unitary *Kamerun* territory was cut into two in 1922 is misconceived because the boundary of the two mandates were formally defined in 1922 in a way that did not precisely match those of the German protectorate at any period. They were neither the boundaries of 1894 nor those of 1911, but a superimposition of the two, which had the effect of excluding all parts of *Kamerun* that had been occupied by France at either of those dates.[10] The boundary separating British Cameroons from French Cameroun was and remained an international boundary attested by boundary treaties.

At the end of World War II the Mandates System was transmuted to the Trusteeship System under Chapters XII and XIII of the UN Charter. The British Cameroons, like French Cameroun, was a Category B UN Trust Territory under a Trusteeship Agreement approved by the UN General Assembly on 13 December 1946. Though held as one Mandate/Trust Territory, the British Cameroons consisted in fact of two separate territories, Southern and Northern British Cameroons; the Northern Cameroons itself comprising of two unconnected stretches of land, the result of a wedge-like projection of a piece of Nigerian territory known as the 'Yola arc'.

"Father-state" delusion

Cameroun Republic arrogates to itself the dubious status of a "father-state" or "fatherland" (*la patrie*). That claimed status appears to rest on three things: its larger area and population compared to those of the Southern Cameroons; its delusive self-anointment, arising from delusions of grandeur, as the so-called successor state to extinct German *Kamerun*; and its practice of hiring citizens of the Southern Cameroons to serve in its institutions and organisations. But a country does not acquire the status of "mother- or father-state" in relation to another country by dint merely of larger space and demographics. The envisaged political association between the Southern Cameroons and Cameroun Republic was predicated on a federal system and, indeed, a federation, however informal and distorted, came into being and lasted for a good ten years.

A federation is based on the concept of legal equality among component states, irrespective of the size, population and economic endowment of each. It involves a dovetailing rather than a supersession of legal orders. It entails the division of sovereignty between the federation on the one hand and the component states on the other. There is no concept of "mother" or "father" or "principal" state in a federation, and there was none in the Cameroon Federation for the simple reason that at no time prior to 1 October 1961 were there political, legal, cultural or economic ties, or ties of territorial sovereignty between the Southern Cameroons and French Cameroun/Cameroun Republic. It is partly for this reason that UN Resolution 1514 (XV) was applied in the decolonisation of the Southern Cameroons, in particular, the principle of self-determination.

In 1961 Cameroun Republic could not therefore have been a "father' country in relation to the Southern Cameroons. At no time before its formal annexation by Cameroun Republic in May 1972 was the Southern Cameroons ever a dependency of Cameroun Republic. If mere size and population were critical in this matter Britain and France, for example, would not have, in the colonial period, qualified as the mother-state or parent state in relation to the vast colonial empire which each had.

Cameroun Republic's so-called "father-state" thesis is a typical political argument. Political arguments have always been rejected as a basis of claim to territory within another country. Even as a political argument, the "father-state" or "fatherland" thesis lacks substance and is of little legal relevance. Claims founded on such arguments have never been acceptable to the international community as a whole. The UN's political organs and its principal judicial organ, the International Court of Justice, have never accepted them. A similar fanciful "right" was invoked to no avail by Morocco as the basis of its extensive claim to both Mauritania[11] and the Western Sahara;[12] by Guatemala as the basis of its claim to Belize;[13] by Iraq as the basis of its claim to Kuwait; by Somalia as the basis of its claim to the Ogaden in Ethiopia, to Northern Kenya and to Djibouti; and by Indonesia as the basis of its claim to East Timor. No merit whatsoever was found in such claims.

If mere geographical propinquity and a controversial period of history going back to a dim and remote past justifies territorial acquisition, as Cameroun Republic anarchistically contends, almost every country in the world would become prey to a larger or some other limitrophic neighbour. For example, Italy would claim to be the successor of Ancient Rome and would then assert a claim to all of the old Roman Empire. Turkey would be able to do likewise regarding the old Ottoman Empire. Germany would assert a claim over Alsace-Lorraine. France would claim all the territories conquered by Napoleon Bonaparte; Italy would claim Corsica, Savoy and Nice from France; and Mongolia would claim China, Russia, Poland and Hungary, territories conquered by Genghis Khan and his successors. Guyana would be able to lay claim to French Guyana on account of their common name and geographical contiguity. India would be entitled to claim back Pakistan and Bangladesh.

The outlook would be similar in Africa if the claim of Cameroun Republic to the Southern Cameroons were ever to be sustained. A calamitous precedent of apocalyptic proportions would thus be set that would spell doom for Africa. South Africa would be entitled to claim Namibia, Botswana and Swaziland over which it exercised a colonial sovereignty even as recently as the early 20th century. Egypt would be entitled to claim Sudan over which it exercised sovereignty along with Britain. Tanzania would be entitled to claim Burundi and Rwanda since they all formed part of German East Africa. Togo, on the same basis of a shared colonial experience under German rule, would be entitled to claim the former British Togoland now part of Ghana.

Nigeria would be entitled to claim Cameroun Republic since Nigerian Muslim rulers exercised a pre-colonial sovereignty over half of Cameroun Republic. It would even be entitled to stake a claim to the Southern Cameroons that was administered by the British for 45 years as an integral part of Nigeria. Guinea Bissau would be entitled to claim the Cape Verdes since both were, up to the eve of independence, under Portuguese rule as one country. It would also be entitled to claim the Casamance region in Senegal. Cameroun Republic would be able to claim the huge chunks of territory known as *Duckbill* and *Neue Kamerun*, areas now parts of Chad, Central African Republic, Congo and Gabon, with the possibility of Gabon becoming extinct. It would even be entitled to claim Equatorial Guinea and Gabon on account of their common Pahouin ethnicity. Further, it would be entitled to claim erstwhile British Northern Cameroons on account of a brief common German connection more than a century ago.

Mauritius would be entitled to claim Seychelles which was administered by the British as a dependency of Mauritius. Rwanda and Burundi would each be able to stake a claim to parts of the Democratic Republic of Congo in the Goma region. Democratic Republic of Congo would be able to lay claim to Congo-Brazzaville on account of their common name and geographical propinquity. Guinea Conakry would be able to lay claim to Guinea Bissau on account of their contiguity, ethnicity and common name.

Somalia would be able to claim Djibouti, formerly French Somalia. Swaziland would be able to claim the KaNgwane and Ngwavuma areas from South Africa. Zimbabwe could claim Zambia and Malawi on the basis of a shared common British colonial administration as the Central African Federation. Morocco would renew its old claim to Mauritania and southern Algeria; Libya would renew its old claim to the Aouzou strip; and Somalia would renew its old claim to Djibouti, the Ogaden and Northern Kenya.

Clearly, the doctrine being propounded by Cameroun Republic, and under which it is laying a baseless claim to the Southern Cameroons as part of its territory, is thus a very dangerous doctrine with dire consequences for Africa, were it to be accepted. Consequently, it cannot be.

Interestingly, in its Application to the International Court of Justice in *Case Concerning the Northern Cameroons, 1963*, Cameroun Republic invoked as the basis of its suit a claimed 'special interest in the reunification of all the peoples of the Cameroons.' Already, following the announcement of the plebiscite results in the Northern Cameroons, Cameroun Republic circulated to members of the UN General Assembly, at the end of March 1961, a so-called White Book in which it alleged want of 'respect for the Camerounese personality' by the British Government. The claimed "special interest" and "Camerounese personality" were merely euphemisms for German *Kamerun*, the supposed progenitor of the fictional "Kamerun nation."

The *Northern Cameroons Case* turned around a dispute about the interpretation and application of the British Cameroons Trusteeship Agreement relative to the British Northern Cameroons. This treaty was no longer in force because, after the termination of the trust over the British Northern Cameroons on 1 June 1961, no Member of the UN could any longer claim any of the rights which might have been originally granted by the Trusteeship Agreement as regards the British Northern Cameroons.

In that case, Cameroun Republic surreptitiously laid claim to territorial title to the Northern British Cameroons by invoking what it called 'a special interest in the reunification of all the peoples of the Cameroons.' This was an expansionist claim, an annexationist claim dressed up as a challenge to alleged irregularities by Britain in the conduct of the plebiscite in the Northern British Cameroons. Cameroun Republic was unable to identify who these so-called 'peoples of the Cameroons' were and was also unable to exhibit any mandate from any such people requiring it to act as knight-errant in an elusive quest for a so-called "reunification" (whatever that meant).

Cameroun Republic contended that it was merely asking for a declaratory judgment. Importantly, it conceded that it was not asking for the detachment from Nigeria of the territory of the Northern Cameroons incorporated into that country as directed by the UN under paragraph 4(a) of Resolution 1608 (XV). It further conceded that it was not asking for the restoration to Cameroun Republic of the people or territory of the Northern Cameroons as it could not possibly claim to have had and lost them. Clearly, the scheme of Cameroun Republic in asking for a declaratory judgment legally devoid of purpose was to obtain some favourable ruling for use politically to shore up its pathetic claim to territories outside those it inherited from its colonisation on the date of its independence from France on 1 January 1960. The Court saw through this ploy and non-suited Cameroun Republic, ruling that its claim was without object. That country thus bitterly failed in its veiled attempt to grab the British Northern Cameroons on the basis of historical accident and geographical contiguity. Any claim by that country to the Southern Cameroons must similarly fail.

Contrary to the impression that the Camerounese Government gave to its uninformed populace, the *locus standi* of that country in the *Northern Cameroons Case* did not stem from its self-proclaimed so-called "fatherland" status. Nor was the interest relating to the application of the Trusteeship Agreement a special interest vested in Cameroun Republic. It was an interest possessed not only by the UN primarily or by Cameroun Republic alone, but a common interest possessed also by every other Member of the United Nations. Article 19 of the Trusteeship Agreement for the Cameroons under British Administration gave any United Nations Member State a procedural right exercisable in the event of a dispute relating to the interpretation or application of the provisions of the Agreement. It was precisely on the basis of such a right conferred by a similar provision, Article 7 of the Mandate Agreement for South West Africa (Namibia), that Ethiopia and Liberia instituted proceedings against apartheid South Africa in the *South West Africa Case*.[14]

Participation in a state's affairs by aliens

One line of argument sometimes canvassed by citizens of Cameroun Republic as a basis for their country's claim to the territory of the Southern Cameroons is that citizens of the Southern Cameroons participate in their country's institutions, including participation in their country's sports movement. But clearly participation in a state's affairs by aliens can never found a territorial claim to the country of provenance of those aliens. Such participation is often hardly meaningful.

But quite apart from the meaningfulness of such participation, history teaches that tutelary states have always recruited into their institutions, into their national football squad and into their athletic teams, deserving individuals from among their subjugated peoples.

It is a strategy meant to serve two ends, assimilation and pacification. The colonialist may thus co-opt into its rulership, select to join its sports teams, and hire to its administration and security forces meritorious persons from among the colonised people. It may even give the vote, give identification papers, and grant citizenship to the colonised. But all that changes nothing. The colonised territory does not thereby, and without more, become part of the territory of the colonising or annexing state.

A case in point is the French colonial practice of having representation from the colonies in parliament in Paris, of appointing deserving politicians from the colonies as Ministers in the French Government[15] or as colonial governors,[16] of giving French citizenship individually or collectively to some colonised peoples, and of recruiting into its military fit persons from the colonies. Thus, the French decrees of 1957 and 1958 *'portant statut du Cameroun'* made provision for the participation of French Cameroun, through its elected representatives, *"au fonctionnement des organes centraux de la République Française."* Under those decrees also, *"les ressortissants camerounais [...] jouissent des droits civils, civiques et sociaux des citoyens français; ils ont notamment accès à toutes les fonctions civiles et militaires et sont électeurs et éligibles dans l'ensemble de la République française."*[17] There were, therefore, in the employment of the French Government in Paris not only French nationals of European origin but also native Camerounese French.

Furthermore, during the fifty-odd years of Britain's administration of the Southern Cameroons as an integral part of Nigeria, Southern Cameroons' citizens served in Nigeria in various capacities: as ministers of government, members of parliament, soldiers, policemen, civil servants, journalists, businessmen, sportsmen and so on. The people of the Southern Cameroons did not by that fact alone become Nigerians; nor did the Southern Cameroons legally become a part of Nigeria.

Up to late 1961, the inner cabinet of President Ahidjo of Cameroun Republic consisted of a Malian, Cheick Sissoko, and eight Frenchmen, Godefroy, Marchand, Rousseau, Domissy, Audat, General Briand, and Colonels Richard and Blanc. That did not make them nationals of Cameroun Republic; nor did it mean that Mali and France had thereby become part of Cameroun Republic.

The fact of the matter is that any country is at liberty to hire heads and hands from anywhere it can. The practice goes back to ancient times: it was not uncommon in Europe to commission capable foreign nationals as soldiers, explorers, navigators, advisers, and diplomats, or to appoint them to political office. In Biblical times the King of Egypt appointed Joseph, a Jew, to the exalted position of Prime Minister of Egypt by putting him "in charge of the whole land of Egypt."[18] In Babylon King Nebuchadnezzar appointed and promoted Shadrach, Meshach, and Abednego, Jews also, to exalted positions[19]. King Darius similarly honoured Daniel[20]. In ancient Persia 'Mordecai the Jew was second in rank to King Xerxes.'[21] In 1875 France confided a mission of exploration in Africa to the Italian Pierre Savorgnan de Brazza. He became a naturalised French citizen. King Leopold of Belgium entrusted Henry Stanley Morton, a British citizen, with a similar mission of exploration. A few years back a native Japanese became President of Peru. Presidents Ahidjo and Biya are said to be paternally aliens in Cameroun Republic.

Southern Cameroons' citizens have the requisite expertise, the knack to work hard, the right mental attitude for work, and a high sense of commitment, honesty, loyalty, and fair play. Cameroun Republic is chronically deficient in such quality human resources and needs to supplement the small number it has. It is principally for these reasons that Cameroun Republic habitually contracts Southern Cameroons' citizens to serve in various offices in that country. But it does so in the hope also of making political capital out of that practice, by presenting it as evidence that the Southern Cameroons is part of its territory. But that proves nothing. At any rate, Cameroun Republic is an occupying State with self-assumed responsibilities for the administration of the territories of the Southern Cameroons as its dependencies. Part of those responsibilities is to provide jobs to citizens of the Southern Cameroons.

Further, Cameroun Republic, as an occupying State, is duty bound to ensure the political, economic, social and cultural advancement of the Southern Cameroons and the just treatment of its people, consistent with Article 73 of the UN Charter. It must allow the people of the Southern Cameroons access to essential resources and services needed for decent living. It must provide citizens of the Southern Cameroons necessary travel documents to enable them to enjoy the right to freedom of movement. These are continuing legal obligations that fall on Cameroun Republic until it relinquishes, as it must, its colonial hold of the Southern Cameroons.

As a matter of law, Cameroun Republic must immediately dismantle its colonial administration in the Southern Cameroons. It must immediately relinquish all powers to the people of the territory without any conditions or reservations to enable them to enjoy complete independence and freedom. This is not a matter of favour. It is a requirement of international law.

Notes

1. The frontier with Nigeria to the west and north: the 11 March 1913 Anglo-German boundary treaty; the British 1946 Order in Council (Second Schedule determining the boundary between Southern and Northern British Cameroons; and the British 1954 Order in Council (Definition of the boundary between the Southern Cameroons and eastern Nigeria). The frontier with Cameroun Republic to the east: the Anglo-French [Milner-Simon] Declaration of 10 July 1919 defining the frontier between British Cameroons and French Cameroun, this frontier being more exactly determined in the Anglo-French [Graeme-Marchand] Declaration of 9 January 1931. This territorial framework was confirmed by the League of Nations, reconfirmed by the United Nations, and became frozen on 1 October 1961 when the British Southern Cameroons achieved independence upon the termination of the trusteeship over the territory on that date.

2. For example, shortly before the achievement of their respective independence the Belgian Congo, French Cameroun and Uganda concluded various accords with their respective parent States. Australia, Canada, India, New Zealand, and South Africa were admitted to original membership of the League of Nations despite the fact that constitutionally they remained subordinate to the British Crown. When they were still mandated territories, Iraq in 1930 concluded a Treaty of Alliance with Britain, and Syria and Lebanon in 1936 signed, separately with France, a Treaty of Alliance and Friendship.

3. Commissariat Général à l'Information, *Institutions et Constitution de la République Fédérale du Cameroun*, Imprimerie Meyerbeer, Nice, 1962, p. 2. Emphasis added.

4. The point must, however, be made that the Southern Cameroons delegation failed to carry itself and to conduct business at Foumban consistently with the fact that it was legally equal in status with the delegation of Cameroun Republic. The delegation should have seen through Cameroun Republic's chicanery, walked out of the meeting and refused to go ahead with the proposed political association.

5. Commissariat Général à l'Information, *Institutions et Constitution de la République Fédérale du Cameroun*, Imprimerie Meyerbeer, Nice, 1962, p. 2. Emphasis added.

6. NM Shaw, *International Law*, Cambridge University Press, Cambridge, 1997, pp. 93, 634.

7. See Rudin, op. cit.; S Ardener, *Eye-Witness*, op.cit.

8. In reality, however, the system of mandates was a mere device by which annexation was cloaked in morality. It was the beginning of what has been called 'constructive international colonialism'.

9. This vast territory, 275,000 square kilometres large, consisted of prongs to what are today Chad, Congo Brazzaville, Congo Democratic Republic, Central African Republic and Gabon.

10. E Ardener, 'The Boundaries of Kamerun and Cameroon' in S Ardener (ed.), *Kingdom on Mount Cameroon*, op. cit., pp. 275-278.

11. See F Serre, 'Les Revendications Marocaines sur la Mauritanie' *Revue Française de Sciences Politiques*, vol. 16, 1966, p. 320.

12. *Western Sahara*, ICJ Rep.1975, p. 12. See, also, UNGA Res.3292 of 1974 recognizing the right of the people of the Spanish Sahara to self-determination in accordance with Resolution 1514 (XV).

13. UNGA Res. 3438 of 1975 reaffirmed the inalienable right of the people of Belize to self-determination and independence, thereby rejecting once more Guatemala's claim to the territory.

14. ICJ Report, 1962.

15. For example, the Senegalese Leopold Sédar Senghor and the Ivorian Houphouët Boigny were both Government Ministers in France in the 1950s.

16. For example, the French West Indian, Felix Eboué was Governor of French Equatorial Africa.

17. See sections 4 and 7 of the *Statut, Journal Officiel de la République Française, du 18 avril 1957*. My translation: "Camerounese nationals shall enjoy the same civil, civic, and social rights as French citizens; in particular, they shall have access to all civil and military offices and may vote at elections and run for elective office throughout the French Republic." Cf. By 1960 three representatives from neighbouring Equatorial Guinea sat in *Cortes*, Madrid, Spain.

18. Genesis 41:41.

19. Daniel 3:30.

20. Daniel 6:28.

21. Esther 10:3.

Chapter Seven
Refutation of the 'Consent to Incorporation' Thesis: The Plebiscite in 1961

The incorporation thesis is strenuously canvassed by Cameroun Republic. That thesis runs like this. The Southern Cameroons was completely fused into Cameroun Republic following the results both of the 1961 plebiscite and the 1972 "referendum". Those polls were sufficient mandate for fusion and the Southern Cameroons thereafter became part of Cameroun Republic. The UN-sponsored plebiscite in the Southern Cameroons was *"un référendum de rattachement"* ('a referendum for incorporation into Cameroun Republic'), not an independence poll; and it resulted not in the association of the two countries in a federal union but in the incorporation of the Southern Cameroons into Cameroun Republic by command of the United Nations. As a result of that incorporation Cameroun Republic acquired title to the territory of, and therefore sovereignty over, the Southern Cameroons.[1]

A close examination of this thesis will show that it has only a superficial attraction and that it amounts to a facile and lame argument.

The 'incorporation' thesis completely fails to take account of the cumulative effect of Article 76b of the UN Charter, the phraseology of the plebiscite questions, the content of the pre-plebiscite agreement concluded between the Southern Cameroons and Cameroun Republic, and operative paragraph 4(b) of UN Resolution 1608 (XV). The plebiscite was a self-determination poll at which the Southern Cameroons voted first and foremost to achieve independence, which independence decision was endorsed by the UN. A dependent territory does not achieve independence, even in a nominal sense, by its incorporation pure and simple into another country (at least not without its express, free, voluntary and fully-informed decision), because in that case the territory would not cease to be a non-independent territory.

Achieving independence entails, at the very minimum, self-government and self-identity because self-determination has to do with self-preservation and not extinction. On the good authority of Professor Philips Cadbury of the University of London, speaking in November 1960:

> [U]nification does not connote absorption or loss of identity but [...] something more like the Ghana-Guinea Union [...] [I]n the absence of a third option, the second option offered in the plebiscite in February will win a substantial majority. *But this will not be a mandate for absorption, but for negotiation on equal terms.*[2]

The Premier of French Cameroun, Mr. Ahidjo, had expressed a similar view (although he would later renege on that in words and deed) on 25 February 1959 at the 849th meeting of the Fourth Committee of the UN:

> *We are not annexationists.* [...] [I]f our brothers of the British zone wish to unite with independent Cameroun, we are ready to discuss the matter with them, *but we will do so on a footing of equality.*"[3]

The Southern Cameroons could not in law have negotiated with Cameroun Republic as an equal party and then proceeded to "join" that country as an unequal party. Since when did unequal parties start concluding valid contracts? Had Cameroun Republic come out in the open and offered incorporation as the terms and conditions under which the Southern Cameroons might be expected to "join" it, it is doubtful to the extreme that the political leadership of the Southern Cameroons would have accepted that as the correct interpretation of the second plebiscite question and campaigned for that proposition. Aware of the very high probability of this happening if the prospects of absorption were to be held out to the Southern Cameroons, in 1959 French Cameroun reassured the UN that its desire for political association with the British Cameroons did not in any way mean it had a hidden agenda to annex the territory.

Throughout nearly fifty years of its union with Nigeria, the Southern Cameroons opposed any form of Nigerian domination in the Southern Cameroons. It insisted on and asserted its identity and personality, and consequently doggedly refused integration into that country even though both shared and still share a common language of public administration, a common legal and educational system, culture, value system, and administrative and constitutional history. Given this record of unyielding attachment to its identity and personality and the insistence on its political autonomy, the Southern Cameroons could not have decided either in 1961 or in 1972 to become a mere appendage, an internal colony, of Cameroun Republic. In the eyes and experience of Southern Cameroons citizens Cameroun Republic remains a *terra incognita*, a foreign country with a different "tongue", legal system, educational system, administrative system, value system, culture, attitude, history, colonial experience and constitutional development.

The Southern Cameroons did not vote, and could not have voted, for the annihilation of its personality and identity, and for the treatment of its citizens as stateless, as persons of a lesser order. That would not have been self-determination but self-destruction. There was nothing the Southern Cameroons could possibly have stood to gain by such a tragic vote, which clearly would have been an act of collective political suicide.

> We did no come cap in hand to be integrated into French Cameroun. French Cameroun people accepted the federal system [...] Ahidjo categorically declared before the UN that any policy on integration on the part of French Cameroun would sound the death knell on the hopes of the people of the British Cameroons. He further declared that they of French Cameroun were not annexationists.[4]

The plebiscite was a self-determination poll. Self-determination means self-preservation, not self-destruction. The purpose of the plebiscite was to enable the people of the Southern Cameroons to pronounce themselves, by one poll, on two matters. First and foremost, on the issue of their independence (that is, their freedom from colonial rule) and, subsidiarily, on the 'alternative', imposed by the UN, of "joining" Nigeria or Cameroun Republic. The matter of independence follows from the principles of equal rights and self-determination of peoples, from Article 76b of the UN Charter and from the phraseology of the plebiscite questions, all considered together.

A Camerounese academic and later a government minister was thus able to state that the Southern Cameroons *'a opté pour l'indépendance et la réunification avec la République du Cameroun.*[5] This evident fact is officially acknowledged by Cameroun Republic itself in one of its official publications in which it is stated as follows:

> On January 1st 1960 French Cameroun became independent under the new name of Cameroun Republic. Following agitation for independence by the then Southern Cameroons [...] a plebiscite was held on February 11th 1961 under the United Nations supervision [...] *The result of the plebiscite ... gave the Southern Cameroons automatic independence* [...][6]

In another of its official publications, Cameroun Republic concedes that the Southern Cameroons did accede to independence on 1 October 1961.

> The first of October 1961 [...] coincided with the promulgation of the new Federal Constitution *and the Independence of Western Cameroon [read: the Southern Cameroons].*[7]

The word "joining" in the plebiscite questions was understood by all concerned (the Southern Cameroons, Cameroun Republic, the United Nations, and the Administering Authority) to mean forming a federal association of two component states, legally equal in status. Equal in status because the Southern Cameroons attained statehood by its Independence vote on 11 February 1961, albeit the United Nations decided that the effective date of its independence, 1 October 1961, was also to be the date of the expected inception of the federal union. In effect therefore, the political association was that of two juridically equal partners since an independent state and a dependent territory cannot create a federal union. The reason for this is that a federal union is based on the principle of legal equality of the component states. It is precisely because that principle is not breached that two or more dependent territories, like independent states, can also create a federal union. Because they are all dependent territories they exist in the federation on a footing of juridical equality. Also, two or more dependent territories may unite and subsequently achieve independence as a single state, which then transforms itself by an act of state into a federal state. But in law, a dependent territory and an independent state cannot create a federal union.

It follows that the plebiscite was not "a plebiscite for incorporation" as Cameroun Republic erroneously claims. No United Nations document bearing on the Southern Cameroons uses the term "incorporation" or even the politically loaded term "unification" or "reunification". Cameroun Republic's somewhat addictive and obsessional use of the word "reunification" is part of its political manoeuvring in a pathetic attempt to shore up its empty " father-state" rhetoric and baseless territorial claim to the Southern Cameroons. Cameroun Republic labours under the delusion that by repeatedly using the word "reunification" it will succeed in impressing in the public mind its false claim that the Southern Cameroons is a hitherto separated part of its territory returned to it.

The terminology consistently used in UN documents on the Southern Cameroons is "join". Admittedly it is a woolly term. The UN appeared to have been alive to this. It invited the Southern Cameroons and Cameroun Republic to put an agreed meaning on the word. After several rounds of talks, it was common ground between the two parties that "joining" meant "forming a federal union". The pre-plebiscite agreement between the two countries therefore stipulated a federal union of two states on a footing of legal equality. The Federal Constitution (entirely drafted and adopted by Cameroun Republic alone, it should always be borne in mind) clinched the point about equality of status in Article 1 when it defined the Cameroon Federation as formed by two countries, the Southern Cameroons and Cameroun Republic: 'The Federal Republic of Cameroon is formed [...] of the Territory of the Republic of Cameroun, henceforth called East Cameroun, and of the Territory of the Southern Cameroons, [...] henceforth called West Cameroon.'

The Southern Cameroons therefore did not "join" Cameroun Republic in the sense of a fusion of its territory with that of Cameroun Republic so that it disappeared completely in favour of the latter. It did not become a part of that country. It did not become extinct. The Southern Cameroons expected to "join" Cameroun Republic in the sense of forming a political association with that country in the shape of a new State, the Federal Republic of Cameroon; in the same way as a man and a woman are joined in marriage and they form a new social unit, the family, but each remaining a separate person with his/her individuality and space. Since a new state emerged, even in the context of the *de facto* federation that existed, Cameroun Republic became extinct as a separate state and subject of international law. An informed author observed:

> Il y a eu réunification, dont la principale conséquence est la disparition de la République du Cameroun en tant que Etat souverain et indépendant.[8]

The emergence of the new state also meant that the Southern Cameroons forbore to assert its separate independence. As the two component states of the Federation, the Southern Cameroons and Cameroun Republic came under the sovereignty of Cameroon Federal Republic, and were replaced by the latter in the responsibility of their international relations.

The United Nations Yearbook 1961 records at page 469 that on 1 October 1961 'the Southern Cameroons joined the Republic of Cameroun as a federal state.' The same Yearbook records at page 495 the statement of Ambassador Aimé Raymond N'Thepe, Cameroun Republic's Representative at the UN at the time, that 'the Southern Cameroons had become an integral part of the territory of the Federal Republic of Cameroon.' Needless to say that Cameroun Republic had also become an integral part of the same Federation.

In regard to the issue of UN membership, however, there was an abnormality concerning the emergent Federation. The Federal Republic of Cameroon, as a subject of international law, was entitled to apply for UN membership, although it is not a condition of statehood that a state become a member of the UN. Still, for sinister reasons UN membership was not applied for and was not claimed by the Federal Republic. The India/Pakistan "jurisprudence" had enunciated the principle that when a new state is created, whatever the territory and the population that it comprises, and whether or not it formed part of a State Member of the UN, it cannot claim the status of membership unless it is formally admitted.[9] However, the Cameroon Federation's non-membership of the UN did not deprive it of its status of a subject of international law.

In theory of law the political association of the Southern Cameroons and Cameroun Republic was one of two independent states voluntarily pooling their sovereignties and thereby transforming themselves conjointly into a new State and subject of international law, the Federal Republic of Cameroon.

> Le 1er octobre 1961 est né le nouvel Etat: la République fédéral du Cameroun. Si dans les règlements des problèmes internes à la Fédération, il a pu être dit qu'il n'y avait pas de nouvel Etat, sur le plan international il y a eu une situation nouvelle permettant de parler d'un nouvel Etat souverain. D'une part en raison du fait que la fédération est basée sur le principe d'égalité entre les deux Etats fédérés: le Cameroun occidental et le Cameroun oriental. Il n'y a pas d'Etat principal ce qui aurait pu conduire à dire que la République fédérale continue cet Etat. Il y a eu réunification dont la principale conséquence est la disparition de la République du Cameroun en tant que Etat souverain et indépendant.[10]

Because the federal political association resulted in the extinction of Cameroun Republic and the emergence of a completely new State, the Federal Republic of Cameroon, diplomatic envoys that had already been accredited to Cameroun Republic had to be accredited anew, this time to the Federal Republic.[11]

Furthermore, evidence that the Southern Cameroons did accede to statehood is not lacking. The political association of the Southern Cameroons and Cameroun Republic to create the Federal Republic of Cameroon, and the resultant extinction of Cameroun Republic could only have been predicated on the fact of Southern Cameroons' de-colonisation and emergence into statehood. The legal basis of the territory's independence is the continuing right of self-determination, first exercised on 11 February 1961 and exercisable time and again, and not UN Resolution 1608 (XV). That resolution simply endorsed the Independence decision and fixed the effective date of that Independence, signified by the termination of the trusteeship agreement relating to the territory.

In the Southern Cameroons therefore, 1st October was declared an official public holiday and celebrated annually as Independence Day; the same day was commemorated throughout the Federation as 'Unification' Day. The 11th of February was Plebiscite Day, celebrated in the Southern Cameroons to mark the day on which the people of the Southern Cameroons took the decision, through a vote, to achieve independence. If the Southern Cameroons were incorporated into Cameroun Republic that continued, the latter could not possibly have two Independence dates (1st January and 1st October) since a colonial territory cannot twice be decolonised by the same colonial power.

Other evidence of achievement of independence by the Southern Cameroons can be seen from certain acts and outward symbols confirmatory of its statehood. First, the two stars placed on the top left hand corner of the flag of the Federation symbolised the political association of two states, equal in status. As an act of political compromise in a spirit of give and take (a spirit Cameroun Republic never reciprocated), the Southern Cameroons accepted as the colours of the Federal flag those of the flag of defunct Cameroun Republic. The Southern Cameroons did not cavil at that flag as its colours consisted of the pan-African yellow-green-red horizontal tricolour first used by Ethiopia as the colours of its flag and later by most African states in various combinations.

Second, there is the differently worded English text of the Federal anthem. The Southern Cameroons went along with the music of Cameroun Republic's anthem, but rejected its lyrics (which spoke of that country as having lived in barbarism and slowly emerging from savagery[12]) and came up with its own differently worded anthem (lyrics by Dr BN Fonlon). In the result, the Federal anthem adopted in 1961 consisted of two completely different anthems existing side by side, lyrically different though musically the same (as for example the national anthems of South Africa and Zambia which are lyrically different but musically the same).

Southern Cameroons anthem

First verse
    O Cameroon, Thou Cradle of our Fathers,
    Holy Shrine where in our midst they now repose,
    Their tears and blood and sweat thy soil did water,
    On thy hills and valleys once their tillage rose;
    Dear Fatherland, thy worth no tongue can tell,
    How can we ever pay thy due?
    They welfare we will win in toil and love and peace,
    Will be to thy name ever true!

Second verse
    From Shari, from where the Mongo meanders,
    From along the banks of lowly Boumba stream,
    Muster thy sons in union close around thee,
    Mighty as the Buea Mountain be their team;
    Instil in them the love of gentle ways,
    Regret for errors of the past;
    Foster, for Mother Africa, a loyalty
    That true shall remain to the last.

Refrain
    Land of promise, land of glory!
    Thou, of life and joy, our only store!
    Thine be honour, thine devotion,
    And deep endearment, for evermore!

Cameroun Republic anthem

Premier couplet
    O Cameroun berceau de nos ancêtres
    Autrefois tu vécus dans la barbarie.
    Comme un soleil tu commences à paraître
    Peu à peu tu sors de ta sauvagerie.
    Que tous tes enfants du Nord au Sud,
    De l'Est a l'Ouest soient tout amour;
    Te server que ce soit leur seul but,
    Pour remplir leur devoir toujours.

Deuxième couplet
>Tu es notre seul et vrai Bonheur,
>Le jardin que nos aïeux ont cultivé.
>Nous travaillons pour te rendre prospère,
>Un beau jour enfin nous serons arrivés.
>De l'Afrique sois fidèle enfant
>Et progresse toujours en paix,
>Espérant que tes jeunes enfants
>T'aimeront sans borne à jamais.

Refrain
>Chère patrie, terre Chérie,
>Tu es la tombe où dorment nos pères,
>Notre joie et notre vie,
>A toi l'amour et le grand honneur.

Third, in the same spirit of compromise the Southern Cameroons agreed to the adoption of Cameroun Republic's emblem and motto as those of the Federation. This was so because the design of the emblem incorporated Southern Cameroons' symbol of tied sticks, fasces, signifying unity and the motto spoke of peace and hard work, values to which the Southern Cameroons attached real importance.

The Southern Cameroons had argued that Douala, more proximate to it than Yaounde, should be the Federal capital while Buea and Yaounde continued to be the respective capitals of the two federated states. Eventually, however, the Southern Cameroons reluctantly caved in and agreed that Yaounde, the capital of the federated state of East Cameroun (erstwhile Cameroun Republic), should also double as the Federal capital.[13] That turned out to be a big mistake.

If in 1961 the Southern Cameroons was, politically speaking, absorbed by Cameroun Republic in spite of evidence of having achieved independence, then the word "incorporation" would seem to be simply political jargon for the more legalistic term colonisation. If the Southern Cameroons was indeed outrightly annexed in 1961 then that fact validates the conspiracy theory according to which a plot was hatched at the UN to deny the Southern Cameroons even qualified independence and to stage-manage a plebiscite so as to facilitate the transfer of the territory to an African successor colonialist (or "foster mother", as the British put it).

This would mean the UN and Britain acted in breach of the Charter of the United Nations. The implication would be that the Southern Cameroons is still a classic colonial territory yet to be liberated from colonial subjugation. The UN, however, maintains that the trusteeship agreement was validly terminated (i.e. substantively and procedurally) and that it has no residual responsibility over the Southern Cameroons. That being the case, the claim that the Southern Cameroons was incorporated into Cameroun Republic in 1961 would have to be construed, for it to make any sense at all, to mean that when the trusteeship agreement was terminated on 1st October 1961 the Southern Cameroons passed from the status of a trust territory (under British rule) to that of a non-self-governing territory (under Cameroun Republic rule) under Chapter XI of the UN Charter: the end of colonial rule by Britain and the beginning of colonial rule by Cameroun Republic.

Such an interpretation in effect denies that the trusteeship agreement was validly terminated, for the declared goal of the system, and the legal obligation of the administering power under it, was the progressive development of the trust territory ultimately to self-government or independence, and not its transfer to a successor colonialist.

On 25th September 1961 the British Queen issued a Proclamation 'signifying Her Majesty's agreement to the termination with respect to the Southern Cameroons of the Trusteeship Agreement of 13th December 1946.' The Proclamation recalled that the General Assembly of the United Nations had resolved on 21st April 1961 that the said Trusteeship Agreement should in agreement with the Administering Authority 'be terminated with respect to the Southern Cameroons on 1st October 1961, upon its joining the Republic of Cameroun.' Two days after the instrument by the Queen, on 27th September 1961, there was an exchange of notes between the UK Government through its Ambassador at Yaoundé and the Government of Cameroun Republic regarding the termination of trusteeship over the Southern Cameroons at midnight of 30th September 1961.[14]

Cameroun Republic's occupation of the Southern Cameroons is sometimes said to find support in this Exchange of Notes. But did the UK Government by that formal diplomatic communication purport to transfer the Southern Cameroons to Cameroun Republic? The answer of course is in the negative as borne out by the tenor of the two notes that were exchanged.

Her Majesty's Ambassador at Yaoundé to the President of Cameroun Republic

Yaoundé, le 27 septembre 1961

Monsieur le Président,
D'ordre de mon Gouvernement, et en exécution de la Résolution No. 1608 (XV) du 21 avril 1961 de l'Assemblée Générale des Nations Unies, stipulant que la Tutelle que le Royaume-Uni exerçait au Cameroun Méridional en vertu de l'Accord de Tutelle du 13 décembre 1946 prendra fin 'le 1er octobre prochain, au moment où ce Territoire s'unira à la République du Cameroun.' j'ai l'honneur de vous informer que cette Tutelle cessera de s'exercer au Cameroun Méridional le 30 septembre 1961 à minuit, étant donné que ce Territoire se joindra à la République du Cameroun le 1er octobre 1961 à zéro heure.
Veuillez agréer, &c.

C. E. KING

The President of Cameroun Republic to Her Majesty's Ambassador at Yaoundé

Yaoundé, 1e 27 septembre, 1961

Excellence,
Jai l'honneur d'accuser réception de la lettre en date de ce jour, par laquelle Votre Excellence a voulu me faire connaitre ce qui suit:
[As in Ambassador King's Note]
Je constate que, conformément à la Résolution sus-visée, le Cameroun Méridional se joindra à la République du Cameroun le 1er Octobre prochain et que par conséquent l'administration sous-tutelle britannique de ce Territoire cesse de s'exercer le 30 septembre 1961 à minuit.
Veuillez agréer, &c.

A. AHIDJO

The Note from the UK Government merely reminds Cameroun Republic of the end, in three days' time, of UK's trusteeship over the Southern Cameroons. Why was the reminder necessary? It was, because the Southern Cameroons had opted to federate with that country and the political association was billed to take effect on 1 October 1961, the date of the termination of the trusteeship and hence of British administration. The UK Government pointedly said it was acting consistent with UN Resolution 1608 (XV) and took care to reproduce that part of the Resolution, which provided for the termination of the Trusteeship Agreement 'on 1 October 1961, upon the Southern Cameroons joining the Republic of Cameroun.' The reply from Cameroun Republic simply noted the fact that UK administration would end on the date and time indicated.

There was no transfer, and in law there could not possibly have been any transfer of the Trust Territory, at least not by this document.[15] The UK Government did not say or even purport to suggest that the Southern Cameroons was to be incorporated into Cameroun Republic. It was not competent of that Government so to say just as it had no power whatsoever to transfer the Trust Territory. Nowhere did the UK Government indicate that it was going to regard the Southern Cameroons as part of the territory of Cameroun Republic. Admittedly, well before the Queen's proclamation and the Note from the UK Government, Cameroun Republic had already assumed the exercise of a colonial sovereignty over the Southern Cameroons through its annexation law of 1st September (camouflaged as the so-called federal constitution) and its military occupation of the territory by mid-September. But that is something fundamentally different from the claim that the Exchange of Notes was a basis for the incorporation of the Southern Cameroons into Cameroun Republic.

This Exchange of Notes may be usefully contrasted with the Exchange of Letters between the UK Government and the Nigerian Government regarding the incorporation, on 1st June 1961, of the Northern British Cameroons into the Federation of Nigeria[16] consistent with UN Resolution 1608 (XV) in terms of which the Northern Cameroons had to join Nigeria 'as a separate province of the Northern Region' of that country.

The High Commissioner for the United Kingdom in the Federation of Nigeria to the Prime Minister of the Federation of Nigeria

Lagos, 29th May 1961

Sir,

I have the honour to refer to the plebiscite held in the Northern Cameroons on the 11th and 12th February, 1961, which resulted in a majority vote in favour of joining the Federation of Nigeria and to Resolution No. 1608 (XV) of the Fifteenth Session of the General Assembly of the United Nations.

2. I am instructed to recall the discussions held in London in May 1960, with representatives of the Nigerian Governments at which the terms on which the Northern Cameroons would rejoin Nigeria were referred to.

3. It is the understanding of the Government of the United Kingdom of Great Britain and Northern Ireland that the Government of the Federation of Nigeria, and the other Governments in Nigeria, so far as they are concerned, agree with the Government of the United Kingdom that the Northern Cameroons should be admitted to the Federation of Nigeria and incorporated in Northern Nigeria and that the Governments concerned will take the necessary legislative action to amend the Constitutions of the Federation and of Northern Nigeria in accordance with Section 16 of the Nigeria (Constitution) Order in Council, 1960.

4. The Government of the United Kingdom further understand that it is the intention that the new system of local administration which was introduced into the Northern Cameroons on the 1st July, 1960, shall continue after the incorporation of the territory into Nigeria.

5. In accordance with paragraph 4 *(a)* of Resolution 1608 (XV) of the Fifteenth Session of the General Assembly of the United Nations the Government of the United Kingdom will regard the Northern Cameroons as being part of the territory of the Federation of Nigeria with effect from 1st June 1961.

6. I shall be grateful for your confirmation that these understandings of the Government of the United Kingdom are

correct and that the Government of the Federation of Nigeria agree that this note and your reply confirming these understandings shall constitute an agreement.

I have, &c.

HEAD

The Prime Minister of the Federation of Nigeria to the High Commissioner for the United Kingdom in the Federation of Nigeria

29th May 1961

My Lord,
I have the honour to acknowledge the receipt of your Note of today's date which reads as follows:
[As in the High Commissioner's Letter]
I have pleasure in confirming that these understandings of the Government of the United Kingdom are correct and that the Government of the Federation of Nigeria agree that your Note and this reply confirming these understandings shall constitute an agreement.

I have, &c.

ABUBAKAR BALEWA

This Anglo-Nigerian agreement clearly dealt with the fusion of the Northern British Cameroons into Nigeria: the admission of the Northern Cameroons to Nigeria by its incorporation in the Northern Region of Nigeria; and the British recognition of the Northern Cameroons as part of Nigeria with effect from 1 June 1961. In the law of state boundaries the critical date of Nigeria's territorial framework became 1 June 1961 and not 1 October 1960, the date of that country's independence, as would normally have been the case in the absence of the Anglo-Nigerian agreement. Nigeria's sovereignty over the Northern Cameroons is grounded in: the pre-plebiscite constitutional offer of integration into Nigeria made to the Northern Cameroons, the Northern Cameroons vote at the plebiscite accepting that Nigerian offer, UN Resolution 1608 (XV) operative paragraph 4(a) directing that the Northern Cameroons shall on 1 June 1961 join Nigeria as a separate province of the Northern Region of that country, and the Anglo-Nigerian Exchange of Letters. The situation regarding the Southern Cameroons is, by contrast, very different from that of the Northern Cameroons. No legal basis exists for Cameroun Republic's assumption of sovereignty over the Southern Cameroons.

Cameroun Republic did take over the Southern Cameroons. But that was a forcible, and not a consensual, takeover. The consent of the Southern Cameroons based on participation by voting, at the plebiscite, first and foremost for independence and then subsidiarily for federal political association with Cameroun Republic did not suggest that prior consent authorised any action by Cameroun Republic at all without limitation. One may draw a parallel with an elected government. It is well known that sometimes even elected governments betray their election promises and acquire repressive habits or interfere with the working of the existing system by which they were elected. That is why in any given government by consent, the idea of consent to be governed embodies by necessary implication checks and balances, including the right to vote. The idea and possibility of popular resistance to unjust laws and a tyrannical political system is implicitly written into every country's political and constitutional system.

Notes

1. See Cameroun Republic's Application Instituting Proceedings in the case *Land and Maritime Boundary between Cameroun and Nigeria*, 29 March 1994, and that country's Oral Arguments in February 2002; AD Olinga, 'La Protection des Minorités et des Populations Autochtones en Droit Public Camerounais,' 10 *Revue Africaine de Droit International et Comparé* (1998), p. 271.

2. *The Guardian Newspaper* (London), 25 November 1960. Emphasis added.

3. Statement of the Premier of French Cameroun on 25 February 1959 at the 849th meeting of the Fourth Committee of the United Nations. Quoted in JN Foncha, *An Open Letter Addressed to the Government of Republic of Cameroun*, (pamphlet) 1993, p. 8. Emphasis added.

4. JN Foncha, *An Open Letter Addressed to the Government of the Republic of Cameroun*, published in pamphlet form (35 pages) in January 1993, pp. 9 and 12. The late Dr JN Foncha was the Premier of the Southern Cameroons (1959-1961), Prime Minister of West Cameroon (1961-1964) and Vice President of the informal Cameroon federation (1961-1970).

5. Njoya, op. cit., p. 174. My translation: "The Southern Cameroons opted for independence and reunification with Cameroun Republic."

6. Ministère de l'Information et de la Culture, *L'Essentiel sur le Cameroun*, Yaounde, [undated], p. 24. Emphasis added.

7. Commissariat Général à l'Information, *Institutions et Constitution de la République Fédérale du Cameroun*, Imprimerie Meyerbeer, Nice, 1962, p. 13. "Le premier Octobre 1961... coïncida avec la promulgation de la nouvelle Constitution Fédérale *et de l'Indépendance du Cameroun Occidental*." Emphasis added.

8. Ibid., p. 173. My translation: 'Reunification took place, the major consequence of which is the extinction of Cameroun Republic as a sovereign independent State.' Camerounese politicians and academics are pathologically obsessed with the term 'reunification'. But the fact of the matter is that there was no such alternative or option as "reunification" (whatever that meant) at the plebiscite.

9. Opinion of the UN Secretary General and accepted by the General Assembly. See Roberts-Wray, op.cit. pp. 272-273.

10. Ibid. My translation: 'A new State emerged on 1 October 1961: the Federal Republic of Cameroon. Although in addressing certain internal problems of the Federation it was claimed that there was no new State, at the international level a new situation had been created such that one is entitled to speak of a new sovereign State. First, the Federation is based on the principle of equality between the two federated states: West Cameroon and East Cameroun. There is no principal State, which could have prompted one to say that the Federal Republic is a continuation of that principal state. Reunification took place, the major consequence of which is the extinction of Cameroun Republic as a sovereign independent State.'

11. Ibid., p.198.

12. Until it was modified in the mid-1960s, the first verse of the national anthem of Cameroun Republic ran thus: "*O Cameroun berceau de nos ancêtres / Autrefois tu vécus dans la barbarie. / Comme un soleil tu commences à paraître / Peu à peu tu sors de ta sauvagerie. / Que tous tes enfants du Nord au Sud / De l'Est à l'Ouest soient tout amour; / Te server que ce soit leur seul but, / Pour remplir leur devoir toujours.*"

13. The town of Douala was a nest of insurgents of the UPC political party and the nerve centre of the UPC insurgency in Cameroun Republic. It was also the hotbed of other political opponents of Ahidjo. The thought of making Douala the Federal capital was simply unacceptable to the French and of course to Ahidjo who feared being assassinated or overthrown by a coalition of UPC and other forces opposed to his French-imposed rule in Cameroun Republic.

14. This Exchange of Notes is published in 166 B.F.S.P. 102 and is here reproduced from I Brownlie, *African Boundaries: A Legal and Diplomatic Encyclopaedia*, C Hurst, London, 1979, p. 581.

15. Whenever there has been a cession or transfer of territory from one owner-state to another clear legal language has always been used. An example of cession of territory is the transfer of sovereignty over Gibraltar by Spain to Britain under Article X of the Treaty of Utrecht 1714. The cession reads: 'The Catholic King does hereby, for himself, his heirs and successors, yield to the Crown of Great Britain the full and entire property of the town and castle of Gibraltar, together with the port, fortifications, and forts thereunto belonging; and he gives up the said property to be held and enjoyed absolutely with all manner of rights for ever, without any exception of impediment whatsoever.' 28 *Commonwealth Treaty Series* 325. Quoted in DJ Harris, *Cases and Materials on International Law*, Sweet and Maxwell, London, 2004, p. 227.

16. This Exchange of Letters is published in 166 B.F.S.P. 115; 478 U.N.T.S. 3; Cmnd. 1567. The agreement entered into force immediately. See Ian Brownlie, *African Boundaries: A Legal and Diplomatic Encyclopaedia*, C. Hurst, London, 1979, p. 580.

Chapter Eight

Refutation of the "Consent to Incorporation" Thesis: The Pretended "Referendum" in 1972

The other "incorporation" line of argument canvassed by Cameroun Republic is that by "voting in favour" of "the institution of a unitary system" in the 1972 "referendum", the Southern Cameroons thereby gave the mandate for its own incorporation into Cameroun Republic and cannot thereafter be heard to deny that it is part of that country.[1] The 1972 "referendum", it is further contended by Cameroun Republic, was a purely internal act of the Federal Republic of Cameroon and is beyond the reach of international scrutiny. This line of argument rests on the concept of constitutional autonomy enjoyed by a state and assumes that recourse to the referendum procedure was constitutional and that the "referendum" itself, as conducted, was a valid poll. These matters call for closer examination.

In relation to international law, every state enjoys constitutional autonomy as an incidence of its sovereignty. The state is thus not subject to any other earthly authority, except, of course, for the limitations imposed by international law, and the presumption of international regularity applies to internal acts it performs. Furthermore, the governmental structure of a state and the form of its political regime do not concern the international legal order as there is no rule of international law requiring that the state must have a given structure. Further still, it is trite learning that the existence of a state is exposed to the flow of things and times, among which are change in the form of government and loss or increase of territory.

However, constitutional autonomy is necessarily subject to international law because that concept cannot be a licence for any rule, policy, structure of state, or form of political regime, in violation of peremptory norms of general international law such as prohibitions on the use of force or aggression, genocide, racial discrimination, and slavery, the denial or suppression of self-determination, and the suppression of fundamental human rights.

International law may be indifferent to the structure and political regime adopted by a state. But it does not follow that those matters may not have repercussions at the level of international or domestic politics. Neither does it follow that those matters are completely within the domestic jurisdiction, since the principles of democracy, international election standards, peaceful co-existence of states, and human and peoples' rights, for example, cannot be ignored.

Again, while the structure of a state and its political regime might well be matters outside the concern of international law, it does not follow that they are also matters outside the concern of the municipal legal order. Thus, under domestic law the legitimacy or even the legality of a particular constitution may be challenged; and a particular structure of the state may be validly impugned.

A Nazi-type Anschluss

History shows that the referendum (or plebiscite) is the common fare of despots whenever they wish to confirm or rubber stamp a foregone state of affairs. In France, for example, Napoleon III who had risen to power by the principle of the plebiscite used it in 1859 to whitewash Piedmont's reluctant transfer of Savoy and Nice to France. In 1938, Adolf Hitler, after entering Austria with his troops and secret police and annexing it, held a "genuine" plebiscite with the customary totalitarian results approving the *Anschluss*. In 1958, Charles de Gaulle, who became President of France during a crisis over Algeria, used the referendum procedure to rubber stamp his dictatorial constitution that ushered in the Fifth French Republic.

Ahidjo's 1972 "referendum" was thus mere imitation, and a poor and farcical one at that, because it was a pretended referendum in more ways than one. Ahidjo characterised his dictatorial scrapping of the Federation as a 'peaceful revolution'. In the context in which that phrase was used, "annexation" is the apposite terminology for what was euphemistically termed "revolution". Every revolution is illegal in terms of the constitution valid until then. Whether the revolution is characterised as peaceful or bloody (in fact a revolution need not involve bloodshed just as force need not involve a clash of arms), its effect remains the same. The existing constitutional order and government are overthrown. A junta (which may include members of the ousted government) installs itself, deriving its poisoned power from force or threat of force.

Refutation of the 'Consent to Incorporation' Thesis: The Pretended "Referendum" in 1972

On 6 May 1972, after a massive deployment of more troops in the Southern Cameroons and putting them on high alert, Ahidjo stunned the Federation with the announcement that he had decided to scrap and was scrapping the Federation.[2] Aware of what this grave decision portended, he said he was taking full responsibility for it before history. In the one-party highly authoritarian State that Ahidjo had established his word was the law. The announcement practically meant that the Federation was effectively dead on that fateful day of 6 May 1972. The "referendum" was merely a pseudo-legal gimmick. And the so-called Constitution of 2 June 1972 was the attendant "legal" window dressing.

Ahidjo passed himself off as a political wizard. Could he and his political coterie have been so politically naïve as not to realise that they were introducing a new form of imperialism and thereby exciting Southern Cameroons' worst fears of colonial subjugation by Cameroun Republic? Or was it just a case of coffin-like narrowness of vision? For it was clearly foreseeable that they could not destroy the Federation without putting asunder the political association between the Southern Cameroons and Cameroun Republic.

Neither the four legislatures of the Federation (the Federal National Assembly in Yaounde, the state House of Assembly in Buea, the state House of Chiefs in Buea, and the state Chamber of Deputies in Yaounde) nor the Governments of the two constituent states of the Federation nor even the Federal Government (as distinct from Ahidjo and his confederates) had by resolution or otherwise expressed any desire to end the Federation. Nor was there a groundswell of antagonism against federalism in any of the two component states. In no party committee, political bureau, or cabinet meeting was it debated and agreed that the Federation was inappropriate and should be dissolved. In no sitting of the Federal National Assembly was the matter discussed and a resolution adopted after a full and informed debate. Indeed, there was no public, governmental, ministerial, parliamentary, or party debate on the matter.

Ahidjo tried his hand at a piece of legitimising rhetoric by advancing three main reasons for scrapping the Federation. First, he said the Federation had served its purpose of "facilitating" what he called "reunification." Thus, for the Camerounese political rulership, the Federation was a mere temporary expedient to enable the Southern Cameroons to swallow the bitter pill of what was in effect its annexation. This hitherto unarticulated view could not have contrasted more with that of the leaders of the Southern Cameroons for whom the Federation was meant to be perpetual, as indeed the Federal Constitution itself so provided in its Article 47 which prohibited any constitutional revision that would impair the unity and integrity of the Federation. There was nothing in the Federal Constitution to suggest, even remotely, that federalism was a mere temporary form of state to be dealt away with at any time at the whims and caprices of the incumbent Federal President and his political confederates.

Second, Ahidjo pleaded "consolidation" of so-called "national unity" as a justification for his autocratic and peremptory decreeing of the Federation out of existence. But there is no necessary incompatibility between "national unity" and federalism. National unity does not mean national uniformity. Moreover, since national unity is not a legal concept, it is doubtful that it can be juridically effective. It is a purely political or moral expression, which may be persuasive within an enabling political order. In Cameroun Republic, where the political order has always been very disabling, national unity is a myth. The term is used verbally but has no existential content. It is no more than a mobilising and emotively compelling slogan. It has far less to do with any national cause than with demands of a political nature and content. In any case, national unity can never be achieved by decree or horsewhip.

The "national unity" discourse of Cameroun Republic conceals pathologically obsessional efforts at ensuring the complete extinguishment of the Southern Cameroons as a politically, culturally, legally, geo-politically and historically distinct territorial unit. And so when Cameroun Republic talks of moving to a higher level of "national unity" it is speaking in a coded language that means further tightening the noose around the neck of the Southern Cameroons so as to ensure its total destruction.

In the mouth of Cameroun Republic, the idiom of national unity has never meant promoting and securing within Cameroun Republic itself a sense of common belonging, cohesion and harmony among its disparate, refractory, and antagonistic ethnic groups. The

Camerounese understanding of national unity has always been that the Southern Cameroons must be destroyed identity-wise, personality-wise, culturally, as a unitary territory, and as a political unit and be completely fused into and under the boot of Cameroun Republic.

Ahidjo himself provided the evidence that unity had nothing to do with the forced dissolution of the Federation. In 1961 he espoused the existence of unity within federal states in these terms:

> As you know, during our earlier discussions with the representatives of the Government party in the Southern Cameroons, we agreed on the broad outlines of a reunification in the form of a federation adapted to the specific conditions of our respective Territories. Some of our compatriots, either out of ignorance, or often with the aim of creating confusion, claim that a Federal State is not based on true unity. These people do not know, or pretend to forget, that citizens of countries such as the USA, Switzerland, West Germany and USSR, which are Federal States, are as united as citizens of other nations of the world.[3]

It would seem that Ahidjo remained a proponent of federalism, at least judging from his statements on the subject, right up to about 1971. In the face of strong and persistent rumours from 1966 onwards of impending secession by the federated state of West Cameroon (i.e., the Southern Cameroons) and the consequential collapse of the Federation, a journalist directly asked Ahidjo in 1969 about the future of the Cameroon Federation. He once more defended the Federal State and pointedly said national unity is not necessarily an incidence of a unitary state:

> We have a strong centralized Federation [...] I repeat, national unity does not necessarily mean that you must have a unitary state. There are examples of very solid unity in Federal States or even Confederations.

Obituarists of the Cameroon Federation contend that it had failed, and that unitarism was inevitable. Admittedly, the Federation was seriously at risk of demise by the fact that the autonomy of the

Southern Cameroons was systematically being eroded by the despotic imposition of a centrally organised one-party system and its accompanying system of patronage and policy of divide and rule; by Ahidjo's atavistic absolutism; by Cameroun Republic's slavish Francophonity, its legal and political hegemony, and its culture of duplicity, violence and excessive centralisation. Nevertheless, the Federation existed in law and in fact, however distorted it had become; otherwise it would not have been dissolved since what does not exist cannot be dissolved.

In any case, historically, whenever federalism has failed the result has always been disintegration, never integration. In other words, a failed federation (e.g. the Mali Federation, the Federation of Rhodesia and Nyassaland, the USSR, the Yugoslavia Federation) inexorably leads to the break-up of the federal state, not its transformation into a unitary state because if federalism fails then, *a fortiori*, unitarism will also ineluctably fail, as unitarism is incompatible with the basic philosophy that informs entities in settling for a federal system. Examples of failed federations and their resultant break-up are many.[4] The only known instance where a unitary state supplanted a federal state is the case of Hitler's Germany in 1934. But even then, after World War II the Germans lost no time in reinstating the German Federation.

Ahidjo's third excuse for the dissolution of the Cameroon Federation was the claimed high cost of running the Federation and the claimed poverty of the Southern Cameroons. This is a familiar line repeated by Cameroun Republic since the 1960s (as a result of the dubious claim in Sir Phillipson's 1959 highly controversial report that the Southern Cameroons would not be economically viable as a separate independent state). In 1967 a foreign journalist made the following observation that included an echo of the poverty thesis:

> British West Cameroon, about twice the size of Maryland, had been an adjunct to the sprawling colony of Nigeria. French Cameroun [...] was part of France's equatorial empire. With different official languages and currencies [...] and with entirely different administrative, political, judicial and educational systems, about the only thing the two territories appeared to have in common was a brief period [...] under German colonial

rule, which ended after World War I [...] Some complain that Ahidjo's recent move to extend the eastern single-party system into the west marks the beginning of the end of any effective western autonomy. They are probably right [...] [Ahidjo's] policy throughout has been to bring the west into full alignment with the eastern system. Defenders of this policy point out that the west represents less than one fifth of the total population, less than one twelfth of the total areas and *generates only one-tenth of overall economic activity. And they note that the western government, which has been teetering on the brink of bankruptcy, is now dependent on subsidies from the federal center.*[5]

Ahidjo's excuse based on the cost of the federal system is not borne out by the evidence. The bloated and ossified bureaucracy, the overlapping duplication, the slowness, the opacity, the corruption and the agonising waste inherent in the Jacobin unitary system instituted by Ahidjo compares very unfavourably with what obtained under the federal system. If cost were really a critical consideration then that concern could easily have been taken care of by adopting the Tanzanian model of two governments, a Union Government, and a Government for the Southern Cameroons so as to allay fears of a new form of imperialism.

The claimed poverty of the Southern Cameroons does not even stand up to a cursory examination. If the Southern Cameroons were worthless, why would Cameroun Republic desperately be holding on to it? No one ever grabbed and held tenaciously on to a thing that is worthless! The bitter truth, the disagreeable truth, is that the Southern Cameroons is a huge economic bonanza for Cameroun Republic. Without the Southern Cameroons, Cameroun Republic would long ago have been a failed state like its neighbours Chad and Central African Republic. The British Government opposed sovereign statehood for the Southern Cameroons on the ground that Britain would have 'nothing to gain from an independent Southern Cameroons.' Well, Cameroun Republic continues to have everything to gain from the Southern Cameroons and its resources which continue to ensure the development of that country and to enrich beyond imagination its political elite.

To deprive the Southern Cameroons of its autonomy, Ahidjo, the Federal President, had by decree seized and vested in the Federal Government (which he tightly controlled) all of Southern

Cameroons' revenue-generating agencies and departments. One would have thought that a system of revenue allocation would then have been put in place. But Ahidjo was opposed to such a system. Consequently, neither the Constitution nor any federal law provided for revenue allocation to the Southern Cameroons federated state.

To increase his already enormous powers Ahidjo had decided to bring the Federal purse under his personal tight control, making money available to the federated states and to federal ministerial departments when and how he saw fit. This was a system of patronage known as *'enveloppes budgétaires octroyées par la Présidence'*. The Southern Cameroons federated state was therefore embarrassingly forced to go cap in hand begging for subsidies from the Federal President to run the state. It became dependent on an annual Presidential subsidy, erratically granted, to balance its state budget. Without economic and financial autonomy, Southern Cameroons' political and legal autonomy became more and more illusory.

Ahidjo's aim was to procure the bankruptcy of the Southern Cameroons government, which would then trigger off calls by the government and people of the Southern Cameroons for Cameroun Republic to take over the Southern Cameroons and "save" it from its "perdition". Ahidjo would then pass himself off as "saviour" of the Southern Cameroons and Cameroun Republic's takeover of the territory would be presented as a so-called colonialism or annexation by "consent." But ten years into this economic strangulation of the Southern Cameroons there was no sign that its government was ever going to be bankrupt any time soon. The expected revolt by the people of the Southern Cameroons against their own government never came. The expected calls for Ahidjo to "liberate" the Southern Cameroons by grabbing it never came.[6] The Southern Cameroons government had found ingenious ways of generating income and was very prudent in its financial management. In fact by 1972 when Ahidjo declared, in imperial fashion, the formal annexation of the Southern Cameroons, a major economic development plan launched by the state was already well underway.

One fact Ahidjo feigned not to know and dishonestly concealed is that the Southern Cameroons is rich in natural resources, minerals (e.g., diamond and bauxite), gas, crude oil, timber, bananas and food crops. The French Oil Company, Elf, had discovered oil offshore from the Rio del Rey estuary in the late sixties but, for political and business reasons, asked Ahidjo to delay an official announcement of the discovery until after the formal takeover of the Southern Cameroons. That announcement was only made in February 1973, eight months after the takeover of the Southern Cameroons. So, even as he spoke on that day of 6 May 1972, Ahidjo knew he was lying through his teeth. He had deliberately distorted the functioning of the Federation. He had purposefully deprived the Southern Cameroons of taxing powers and of control over its economy. Ahidjo had his predatory eyes on the oil and gas just discovered in the Southern Cameroons.

The Southern Cameroons had quickly become disillusioned with its political association with Cameroun Republic, which it considered a huge prison. Ahidjo was aware of this fact. He feared the oil might provide the needed catalyst for the Southern Cameroons to withdraw from the Federation in exercise of the right of self-determination as any component state in a constitutive federation is entitled to. He believed the formal annexation of the Southern Cameroons under the thin disguise of unitarism would remove that perceived looming threat of withdrawal.

Politically, the imposition of what was presented as no more than a unitary system, confirmed Southern Cameroons' worst fears of colonisation by Cameroun Republic. It heightened Southern Cameroons' awareness of its specificity, personality and identity. It intensified the cleavage between the Southern Cameroons and Cameroun Republic. It aggravated the antagonism and mutual distrust between citizens of the two countries. Ahidjo's ill advised decision achieved the very opposite of what he claimed he set out to achieve: disunity rather than unity, an end to a political association that was asunder even before it began.

Lately, the Government of Cameroun Republic and its ruling political party (RDPC) have found no greater abuse for the hated people of the Southern Cameroons than resorting to hate speech and demonising them as *les Biafrais* ("Biafrans"), *les Nigerians* (Nigerians), *les Anglofools* ("stupid Anglophones" *)*, and *les enemies dans la maison* ("enemies within the house"). They consistently call on the people of the Southern Cameroons to 'leave and go elsewhere' (*'qu'ils aient ailleurs'*), yet they continue to hold them in bondage, even as Phaoah held the Israelites captives.

The [...] mayor of Yaounde, Emah Basile, referred to [citizens of the Southern Cameroons] as 'enemies in the house'. As such, they should either voluntarily 'go across our borders' as Mbombo Njoya, minister of territorial administration and present sultan of Foumban, once remarked or be chased away. [Citizens of Cameroun Republic] tend to refer to [citizens of the Southern Cameroons] as 'Anglofools', Biafrans or Nigerians. By using the term Biafran, they are expressing their strong belief that [citizens of the Southern Cameroons] are inclined to be secessionists. By using the term Nigerian, they point to the colonial link between the Southern Cameroons and Nigeria. We recently heard the story that when told by a visitor that he hailed from Kumba [in the Southern Cameroons], the Cameroun [Republic] Ambassador to Belgium, Isabelle Bassong, exclaimed: 'Oh, Kumba, donc vous êtes moitié Nigérien et moitié Camerounais.'[7]

For the people of the Southern Cameroons the Francophonity imposed on them and the ubiquity, brutality and rapacity of the *gendarme*, the *préfet*, the *gouverneur*, the *commandant* and the *commissaire* in their territory are living symbols of alien domination and daily reminders of their shameful status as a colonised and oppressed people. Indeed, for Cameroun Republic's civil and military functionaries sent on tours of duty in the Southern Cameroons, the territory provides a prime opportunity to gain upward mobility and more privileges; to revive flagging careers or to launch new careers through zealousness in bloody repression and other forms of oppression; to make fortunes through various forms of extortion and corrupt practices; and to lead a life of debauchery and extravagance, with complete impunity.

In the *gendarme, préfet, gouverneur, commandant* and *commissaire*, living symbols of tyranny and colonialism, wickedness and iniquity are combined. Their appointment to the Southern Cameroons is virtually a licence to kill, torture, maim, imprison, rob and cheat any and every citizen of the Southern Cameroons. As the terror has spread and intensified, it has branded people with memories that remain raw for the rest of their lives. The longer the appointee stays, the more animalised he is, and the more his rapacious, brutal and violent nature is emboldened to commit with impunity any crime he chooses to against Southern Cameroons citizens. And the more brutal he is the greater the chance of being rewarded with promotion or appointment to higher office.[8]

The entire Cameroun Republic colonial system in the Southern Cameroons is militarised. Even the uniforms of the colonial *gouverneurs* and *préfets* are like those of regimental commanders complete with khaki and *kepi*. These viceroys are themselves appropriately called *chefs de terre* (ground chiefs). They form part of a chain of the fascist-like centralised administrative hierarchy known as *commande* or *commandement*.

But what makes it possible for the *gouverneurs, préfets, militaires* and *gendarmes* sent to the Southern Cameroons to so blithely and routinely deal out pain and death with sadistic pleasure and impunity? First, brutal repressive behaviour is one of the extremely bad habits Cameroun Republic inherited from France. State-sponsored and/ or condoned violence has since become part of its national character. Second, the reign of terror can be regarded as *de facto* national policy of Cameroun Republic: a pre-emptive strategy meant to dissuade any contemplated revolt against colonial rule. The rulers of Cameroun Republic have not declared extra-judicial killing, maim, torture, abduction and arbitrary imprisonment as official government policy. Nevertheless, they are not unaware of the reign of terror unleashed by their agents and minions in the Southern Cameroons. What is more, the terrorisation is allowed to go on. None of the civil or military functionaries involved in acts of brutality, terrorisation and other forms of human rights abuse have ever been prosecuted for any of these crimes.

Third, there is the cultural factor. To Cameroun Republic and its French mentors the "Anglo-Saxon" culture of the Southern Cameroons inherited from British colonialism is a threat to the Latin culture of Cameroun Republic inherited from France and so must be destroyed and the 'Anglophones' forcibly assimilated. Because in any system of terror, the functionaries must first of all see the victims as inferior, Cameroun Republic's viceroys in the Southern Cameroons consider themselves riders and the local people horses, a foundation psychologically reinforced by their impulsive Francophile prejudice and mindset.

Fourth, the Yaounde government can be taken to authorise the terror in the Southern Cameroons; at least it turns a blind eye. No

Cameroun Republic functionary in the Southern Cameroons has the moral courage to question the terrorisation of the population because that would mean challenging the system that provides his livelihood. Besides, everyone around them is participating in the system, doing the same thing: the *gouverneur* next door, the *préfet* next door, the *militaire* or *gendarme* next door. By going along with the system the official is paid, promoted, uplifted in status, and awarded medals for '*services rendus dans la zone Anglophone.*' With time these officials have become used to it like the commanders of the Nazi death camps became used to mass killings. And like those commanders, Cameroun Republic's viceroys in the Southern Cameroons might well claim that they themselves never do it, only low-level functionaries. But that is a mere attempt to put a symbolic distance between themselves and the physical act of terror itself. Terrorising the local people is part of colonial subjugation, as is having someone else to do the terror.

Finally, as terror is the unquestionably enforced order of the day in the Southern Cameroons, Cameroun Republic's functionaries regard wielding it efficiently as a manly virtue, *la manière forte* beloved of the regime. So ultimately, the official becomes used to the system of terror he is required, expressly or impliedly, to enforce.

A historical and political swindle

The fact that Cameroun Republic builds its expansionist case on the so-called "referendum" of 1972 indicates the level of desperation in which it finds itself. That "referendum" was so seriously flawed that it did not meet minimum international voting standards. On that account it did not qualify as a valid poll and so cannot be said to have enabled the people to express their wishes.

There was no published list of voters and polling stations. The exact number of registered voters and actual voters was therefore not ascertainable or verifiable. What purported to be the results of the "referendum" were published, but, as is the well established tradition in Cameroun Republic, those results were fixed; the figures were cooked. Election rigging, even up to this day, is a well known and officially-sanctioned practice in Cameroun Republic. Besides, one may point to a number of easily detected discrepancies in the published "referendum" results. Two sets of results on the same "referendum" were published within an interval of one week.⁹ That time interval enabled the doctoring of the results in the light of detected incongruities and improbabilities in the results earlier published.

The first results gave only global figures for the Federation as a whole. The second gave no such figures but only figures for each of the two component states of the Federation. These figures for each of the two states were clearly arbitrarily assigned because all the supposed vote counting was centralised in one place, in the Ministry of Territorial Administration, and "results" were computed for the Federation as a whole rather than for each of the two component states of the Federation. What emerges from a comparison of the two sets of results speaks volumes about the "referendum."

The first results gave the total number of votes cast, but in the second this is significantly omitted. In the first results the sum of the 'yes', 'no' and 'void' votes does not tally with the number of votes cast as ought normally to be the case, but exceed it by some 670 votes. According to the first results there were 846 'no' votes, but in the second results the figure was revised downwards to a mere 176 'no' votes, 846 nays being considered too high for comfort. In the second results, the sum of the 'yes', 'no' and 'void' ballots from the two states does not tally with the figure given as the total number of those votes. The arithmetic just did not tally. To brush aside these discrepancies as *de minimis*, as small and inconsequential, will miss the whole point. The fact is that these discrepancies, from just a quick look, actually betrayed and confirmed a systematic pattern of official electoral fraud.

There is another piece of evidence that points to this pattern of fraud. It relates to what might be called census politics, that is to say, the manipulation of population figures for political and other ends.[10] At the time of the "referendum" the combined population of the Southern Cameroons and Cameroun Republic was put at 6,450,000 and broken down as follows[11]: Southern Cameroons, 1,100,000; Cameroun Republic, 5,350,000. This means the ratio of the population of the Southern Cameroons to that of Cameroun Republic was roughly 1:5. But only ten years earlier the population of the Southern Cameroons was stated to be 800,000 and that of Cameroun Republic 3,200,000, that is, a ratio of 1:4.[12]

If these figures were to be believed, it means that within ten years the population of Cameroun Republic increased by a staggering 67%, while that of the Southern Cameroons increased by a mere 37%. And yet there had been no war or epidemic in the Southern Cameroons to account for its stated 'poor showing'. Moreover, the reproductive health map of Cameroun Republic showed and still shows most of that country as areas of endemic infertility. This is borne out by a 1978 fertility study in the country. Going by the above population figures the population of Cameroun Republic would today be something like 25 million (but in fact it is slightly less than half that number) and that of the Southern Cameroons a mere 2.8 million (in fact it is about two times that number). There is no country in the world with a phenomenal population explosion of 67% within ten years.[13]

Clearly, there was here a case of cooking census figures. This is another dimension of psychological conditioning by Cameroun Republic. Its purpose is to induce in the people of the Southern Cameroons a sense of smallness, "nobody-ness", insignificance, and therefore irrelevance in decision-making. It is part of the malevolent design aimed at fostering the idea that only the people of Cameroun Republic matter and the people of the Southern Cameroons an irksome and expendable "linguistic minority" in the francophone Cameroun Republic house. Since population census is commonly used for administrative, research, business, industrial and political purposes, Cameroun Republic has for a very long time been in the dishonest business of census manipulation for suspect administrative and political ends. Whereas as early as 1953 the British had made an assessment of the population of the Southern Cameroons (population at that date was 750,000 and by 1961 estimated as at least a million people), the French never conducted any general census in French Cameroun. At the time of its independence therefore Cameroun Republic did not even know the number of its inhabitants and so resorted to exaggerated estimates.

> Les premiers recensements statistiques, malheureusement isolés, remontent à la période 1955-1959 et concernent les cinq villes suivantes: Douala (1955), Edea (1956), Yaounde (1957), Ebolowa (1958) et Mbalmayo (1959). Au moment de son accession à l'indépendance, le Cameroun ignore donc

l'effectif exact de sa population et devait se contenter d'estimations quelquefois grossières.[14]

There are edifying examples of instances in which Cameroun Republic has been guessing and exaggerating its population. The constitution of Cameroun Republic, enacted a few months following its independence on 1 January 1960, contained no provision stating the population of that country; nor did any other official document in that country.[15] But a year later, in anticipation of its political association with the Southern Cameroons in a federal setup, Cameroun Republic arbitrarily declared its population to be 3,200,000 and had that figure written into the Federal Constitution.

In the Second Five Year Development Plan (1966-1971), however, Cameroun Republic declared that in 1959 its population was 3,700,000 (forgetting the figure it had written into the Federal Constitution), and that in 1965 it was 5,200,000 (this was about the same figure it gave seven years later, in 1972, as its population). No population census had been carried out before 1959 or either in that year or in 1965. Cameroun Republic then made a projection of its population as follows: 5,800,000 in 1970 (the 1972 "referendum" gave the figure 5,350,000) and 7,000,000 in 1980.

That is not all. According to the second published "referendum" results, of the 1.1 million people of the Southern Cameroons, 717,916 people voted. This meant an extremely high voter turnout of 70%. That is very improbable because it would mean that every single adult citizen of the Southern Cameroons (including the sick and the disabled, and possibly a significant number of children) participated in the so-called "referendum". Those disqualified from voting on account of age, crime or infirmity of mind or body could not have constituted a mere 30% of the population. It is common knowledge that there was very high voter apathy due to disillusionment, dejection and a sense of powerlessness. Because of that, a very significant percentage of voting-age adult citizens of the Southern Cameroons did not participate in the 1972 fraud.

The claimed 70% voter turnout in the Southern Cameroons is all the more improbable when it is considered that the voter turnout in Cameroun Republic was given as only about 50%. If these figures are to be believed, it means the people of the Southern Cameroons were more eager to offer themselves for formal annexation than were the people of Cameroun Republic to annex them. These figures must be taken with at least a pinch of salt. If the voter turnout in the Southern Cameroons was 70% of the population of the Southern Cameroons, then the active electorate must have been at least 80%; an impossibility. Even during the very critical UN-sponsored plebiscite in the Southern Cameroons, on 11 February 1961, the active electorate was only 44% of the population of the Southern Cameroons and the voter turnout was just 41%.[16]

The so-called "referendum" is assailable on other grounds. It did not present the electorate with alternative choices. There was only a single question. It was loaded, long-winded and ambiguous. It read:

> Do you approve, so as to consolidate national unity and to accelerate the economic, social and cultural development of the nation , the draft constitution submitted to the Cameroonian people by the President of the Federal Republic of Cameroon and instituting a Republic, one and indivisible, under the name of United Republic of Cameroon?[17]

Instead of a simple and clear question capable of eliciting a straight 'yes' or 'no' answer, there was framed and presented a circumlocutory and vague question. Either the framers of the question were so foolish that they could not frame a simple question or they deliberately chose to make it vague for self-serving political purposes. Worse, the people were asked to pronounce themselves on a document they had not actually seen, less still studied and publicly or privately debated. Under the circumstances, there was no choice and the electorate made none, less still a free and informed choice. The people of the Southern Cameroons dismissed the whole exercise as a charade in which the "choice" was between "oui" and "yes."[18]

There can be no real choice under an authoritarian government, which no one denies Ahidjo's regime was. Even his handpicked successor as republican president, Paul Biya, felt able to admit that his predecessor's government was despotic, although he has himself been unable or unwilling to move Cameroun Republic away from that dreadful legacy.

Refutation of the 'Consent to Incorporation' Thesis: The Pretended "Referendum" in 1972

The environment in which the "referendum" was conducted was a very disabling one. It was neither permissible nor tolerable to campaign against what Ahidjo had decided. Voters were intimidated and coerced to go to known polling stations and to cast the 'yes' ballot paper. There was no secret ballot. Gun-trotting and whip-cracking gendarmes maintained an intimidating presence at polling stations. There, the polling officer openly handed each voter the 'yes' ballot paper to openly cast in the ballot box. The famous "referendum" was neither free nor genuine nor fair nor safe. It was a sham "vote" devoid of any free expression of the will of the people.

One would have thought that the people of the Southern Cameroons alone ought to have been consulted, since it is they alone who voted affirmatively in the 1961 plebiscite for a federal form of political association, and without their vote there would not even have been the informal political association that came into being. But Ahidjo chose to make his "referendum" a countrywide affair. This was an insurance policy that guaranteed automatic "success" since, even if every single Southern Cameroons citizen voted 'no' that vote would have been overwhelmed by the predictable crude majoritarian 'yes' vote of the people of Cameroun Republic. It is also for this reason that Ahidjo rejected separate polls for each of the two federated states.

Clearly, the lessons of the UN plebiscites in Togo and in the Northern Cameroons were not lost on Ahidjo. The "referendum" score was the customary 99.999% "affirmative vote" that is always fixed well in advance by the government itself. One is only too familiar with "elections" in one-party authoritarian regimes of the Cameroun Republic type where the ruler, desiring to legitimise his terror and caprices, stage-manages 'elections' in which the 99.999% results are pre-arranged by the government agency mandated to do so.

Ahidjo's 1972 "referendum" was therefore a parody of the ballot box, a huge political comedy and a gigantic exercise in self-deception. It was choreographed (including the so-called motions of "indefectible attachment" and "unalloyed support" attributed by the regime to the people) from start to finish by the Ministry of Territorial Administration. That government ministry is the department of government responsible for administering all public "elections", fixing the results thereof, and manufacturing (with the complicity of the central committee of the *parti unique*) "motions of support" supposedly from the masses, to the claimed "father of the nation." The purported "referendum" was an elephantine historical and political swindle, a treachery most foul. It was, moreover, a legal fraud and a treasonable violation of the Federal Constitution.

A treasonable legal fraud

The Federal Constitution laid down a special procedure for its amendment. In disregard of this special procedure, Ahidjo chose to forcibly scrap the Federation and to organise a purported "referendum" for the purpose of validating his controversial decision. The so-called "referendum" was also a ploy to alter the very basis of the political association between the Southern Cameroons and Cameroun Republic. The referendum" ' was illegal insofar as its aim was not only to impair the Federation's unity and integrity but also to abolish the very Federation itself. The whole exercise was a treasonable violation of Articles 2(1), 8, and 47(1)(2)(4) of the Constitution.

The decision to impose what was presented as a mere change from a federal to a unitary form of state was taken by Ahidjo and his confederates, all of them citizens of Cameroun Republic: Ahmadou Ahidjo (Federal President), Moussa Yaya Sarkifada (Deputy President of the Federal National Assembly), Paul Biya (Secretary General at the Presidency), Charles Onana Awana (Minister of Finance), François Sengat Kuo (Deputy Secretary General at the Presidency and Ahidjo's speech writer), Ousmane Mey (Federal Inspector of Administration for the North). This same political coterie, aided by a Frenchman, Professor Maurice Duverger,[19] produced a secretly drafted "unitary constitution."

Throughout these proceedings, the Southern Cameroons was purposefully kept completely in the dark. The action was therefore a sectional enterprise. And inasmuch as the Southern Cameroons was not privy to it and was made to submit to it, the action amounted to an assumption of the exercise of "national sovereignty" by a "section of the people" in league with foreign intellectual mercenaries. This violated Article 2(1) of the Federal Constitution which provided: 'National sovereignty shall be vested in the Cameroonian people, who shall exercise such sovereignty either through its deputies in the Federal Assembly or by way of referendum. No section of the people, nor any individual, may assume the exercise thereof.'

The Federal President, sworn in to defend the Federation in accordance with the Constitution of the Federal Republic of Cameroon, failed to uphold the said Constitution and purposefully subverted it. In pursuance of a treasonable conspiracy to that effect, he destroyed the very Federation he was under oath to maintain and preserve. This was a treasonable violation of Article 8 of the Federal Constitution. That article enacted: 'The President of the Federal Republic of Cameroon, Head of the Federal State and Head of the Federal Government, shall uphold the Federal Constitution and shall ensure the unity of the Federation and the conduct of the affairs of the Federal Republic.'

Article 47 of the Federal Constitution gave the majority of Federal Members of Parliament (MPs) representing each of the two federated states power to veto any constitutional revision that violated state interest. The same article rendered inadmissible any proposal for the revision of the Constitution that would impair the unity and integrity of the Federation. This prohibition was an absolute bar admitting of no exception or derogation whatsoever. The same article 47 also empowered the President of the Federation to initiate a revision of the Constitution, but only after he or she had consulted with the Prime Ministers of the two Federated States. These provisions were designed to safeguard the rights and interests of the spatially and demographically smaller Southern Cameroons compared to Cameroun Republic. Article 47 read:

(1) Any proposal for the revision of the present Constitution which impairs the unity and integrity of the Federation shall be inadmissible.
(2) The power to initiate the revision of the Constitution shall belong equally to the President of the Federal Republic, after consultation with the Prime Ministers of the Federated States, and the Deputies of the Federal Assembly.

(3) Any proposal for revision submitted by the Deputies must be signed by at least one-third of the Members of the Federal Assembly.
(4) Proposals for revision shall be adopted by simple majority vote of the Members of the Federal Assembly, provided that such majority includes a majority of the representatives in the Federal Assembly of each of the Federated States.
(5) The President of the Federal Republic may request, under the same conditions as for a federal law that a second reading be given to a law revising the Constitution.

The provisions of Article 47 dealt specifically with "revision of the Constitution". They were therefore special provisions. In theory of law, these special provisions overrode the somewhat parenthetical reference to referendum in Article 2(1), a general provision of the Constitution. The legal maxim is *lex specialis derogat generali*. The conditions and procedure for conducting any referendum contemplated by Article 2(1) were laid down in Law No. 69/LF/15 of 10 November 1969. Was this yet another special law on the subject and to which Ahidjo therefore properly had recourse in disregard of Article 47 of the Constitution? This is extremely doubtful. In terms of the doctrine of the hierarchy of norms that piece of legislation was an ordinary law hierarchically inferior to the Constitution and could not therefore override a constitutional provision. Besides, the said piece of legislation, a procedural law, had no independent existence divorced from the general constitutional provision in pursuance of which it was enacted. It follows that that statute and its parent constitutional provision were general provisions on the matter of referenda and could not override the special provisions of the Constitution bearing on the same subject.

A referendum has, of course, always been a legitimate method of consulting a people on an issue of great political importance to a country. It is based on sound political theory. But it must be legal. In the Federation, the matter of a referendum derived its legality from the Federal Constitution, the supreme law of the land. A referendum was therefore a principle subordinate, and not superordinate, to the Constitution. For that reason, it could not be used to circumvent the Constitution. Nor could it be used to override norms in the Constitution superordinate to other norms therein, such as the norm which prohibited any impairment of the Federation. That absolute bar was based on the sensible political consideration that impairing the federal structure of the State would be tantamount to altering the very basis of the political association between the Southern Cameroons and Cameroun Republic. Since it was illegal to alter the basis of the political association between the two countries that taint of illegality could not be cured by a referendum.

In a Federation, sovereignty is divided. While the Federal State may monopolise the enjoyment of external sovereignty, internally, the Federal Government and the governments of the component Federated States share personal and territorial sovereignties. Federal internal sovereignty is vested in the people of the Federation as a whole who exercise it themselves either directly or through the Federal President and Federal MPs elected by them. Member-state internal sovereignty is vested in the people of each component state of the Federation who exercise it themselves either directly or through members of the state legislature elected by them. Dissolution of the Federation was a grave matter. It was bound to have profound repercussions on these two levels of sovereignty. This imposed a political and legal obligation to consult at the two levels of sovereignty.

Thus, even if recourse to a referendum had been legal, it would still have been open to the serious political objection that it was not enough to have consulted only those in whom Federal sovereignty vested, in complete disregard of those in whom member-state sovereignty vested (the people or parliament of each federated state). Besides, the Federal Constitution was never adopted by referendum. There was thus no compelling reason, even political, why it was necessary to resort, asymmetrically, to a so-called "referendum" in order, ostensibly, to seek to validate its abrogation. Ahidjo could therefore not, either legally or politically, transfer the responsibility for any decision regarding the revision of the Federal Constitution from the Federal National Assembly and the Prime Ministers of the Federated States to the nationwide electorate exclusively.

Certain norms within the framework of a constitution are superordinate to others by virtue of the fact that in terms of their material content they occupy a special position. They are entrenched and may not be revoked or altered, except after a stringent procedure that normally includes a full and informed debate leading to an informed vote. In some cases, such norms are so vital to the body politic that they are unalterable. For example, Article 79(3) of the Fundamental Law of the Federal Republic of Germany forbids any modification thereof that might impair the federal structure of the Republic. This provision is intended to ensure that Germany is never again transformed into a unitary state as it was by Hitler in 1934. Article 47(1) of the Constitution of the Federal Republic of Cameroon had the same mischief in mind. It was also meant to prevent the transformation of the structure of the State from federal to unitary, so as to avoid the impression of a new form of imperialism in the shape of the larger state colonising the smaller one.

Article 47(1) in effect declared sacrosanct the federal form of state. It was a safeguard against Cameroun Republic unconscionably using its crude majority to impose on the Southern Cameroons the Jacobin unitary form of state it had slavishly adopted under its 1960 constitution. The first and foremost approach to statutory interpretation is the literal or plain meaning rule. That rule ordains that the legislator's intention must be found in the ordinary, natural and literal meaning of the words used because those words themselves best declare the intention of the lawmaker. In the case at hand, therefore, the word "federation" must be given that sense which is its natural import. A federation is a form of political and administrative organisation of a state or community. In Article 47(1), the word "Federation" was not used to denote the state itself, because if the draftsman intended to convey that meaning he would have used, as in other parts of the Federal Constitution, the expression "Federal Republic" or "State,"

Certain constitutional norms are of such fundamental significance for the perennity of the State and the protection of peoples and sub-national entities that they may not be eliminated from the constitution. The federal structure of the State was one such guarantee entrenched in the Cameroon Federal Constitution. It was of such fundamental importance that it could not be invalidated by any constitutional revision whether through Parliament or a referendum. In Nigeria when General Ironsi embarked on transforming the political structure of that country from a federal to a unitary state, he thereby unwittingly signed the death warrant both of himself and of his government.

It is sometimes said that one parliament cannot bind another and that a form of state is not cast in stone. But this is true only to a certain extent. First, while a state may change its form, such a change must be constitutional. Second, the very existence of the modern state is founded on certain core principles so fundamental that they may not be altered even by a later parliament. Supposing a state is founded on republicanism, may the republic be transformed into a monarchy without doing serious violence to the state? And supposing further that a state is founded on freedom, religious tolerance, and racial equality; may a later parliament introduce tyranny, slavery, religious intolerance and racial discrimination? May Cameroun Republic be transformed into a kingdom or a dependency of another state without any challenge? May it unquestioningly accept to be fused, say, into Nigeria or into Chad for whatever reason?

The concept of 'sovereign people' (in whose name so many crimes are committed by rogue rulers) has meaning only in a democracy (which Ahidjo's Cameroun definitely was not) and, moreover, refers to supreme, rather than absolute, power.

It follows from the foregoing critique that Ahidjo did not act within his legal powers but within the logic of his imperialistic politics. He must have known that he could not impair the federal structure of the State without breaking the Constitution and putting asunder the informal political association between his native country and the Southern Cameroons. And because Biya is no fool, subject to proof to the contrary, he too knew that the revival of his native Cameroun Republic as a political and legal expression would necessarily entail the symmetrical revival of the statehood of the Southern Cameroons unlawfully suppressed. The action taken by Ahidjo in May 1972 was a legal nullity. First it was the fruit of a poisoned tree, a criminal conspiracy. Second, it impaired the federal structure of the State. Third, it was unilateral and unconstitutional. Fourth, it was imperialistic in character. Fifth, it amounted to a suppression of the self-determination of the people of the Southern Cameroons; and that cannot be accepted.

Clearly, what Ahidjo did was not a constitutionally valid exercise of his powers as Federal President. Since his resort to a referendum was unconstitutional, the referendum exercise was itself null and void *ab initio*. The issue at hand was of course political. But the procedure for the referral of that political issue to a vote was an imminently legal matter that had to conform to the law. Besides, it is clear, except of course to the tyrant or the megalomaniac, that political decisions and actions must always be taken within the law otherwise there would be absolute chaos internally and externally. If Cameroon were a democracy Ahidjo and all his accomplices would have been impeached and jailed for their treasonable conduct.

Even if the "referendum" was constitutionally valid, even if it was properly conducted without any rigging, and even if the people of the Southern Cameroons clearly and knowingly voted in favour of the institution of a unitary state in place of the Federation (these points not being conceded, of course) that could not by any stretch of the imagination have been a licence for the military seizure and occupation of the Southern Cameroons, for the suppression of its autonomy[20] and legal personality, for its dismemberment, for the imposition therein of rule from Cameroun Republic, and for oppression.

Notes

1. J Owona, 'La Nouvelle Constitution Camerounaise du 20 Mai 1972: de l'Etat Fédéral à l'Etat Unitaire,' *RJPIC*, 1973, No. 1, p. 3; E Mbarga, 'Evolution Politique du Cameroun en 1972: Le Référendum du 20 Mai 1972 et la Formation de la République Unie du Cameroun,' *RJPIC*, 1973, No. 3, p. 363. For very serious doubts as to the constitutional validity of the 1972 so called 'referendum', see JM Breton, 'De la Tutelle à la République Unie: Réflexion sur la Dynamique Unitaire dans l'Evolution Institutionnelle du Cameroun Indépendant,' *Penant*, 1979, p. 209; F Mbome, 'L'Expériences de Révision Constitutionnelle au Cameroun,' *Penant*, 1992, p. 31.

2. For details on how the Federation was overthrown, see C Anyangwe, *Imperialistic Politics in Cameroun: Resistance and the Inception of the Restoration of the Statehood of the Southern Cameroons*, Langaa Research & Publishing, Bamenda, 2008, chapter 8.

3. Statement of Ahidjo made at a public function in May 1961. My translation.

4. For example, the Central African Federation, the Colombia Federation, the Czechoslovakia Federation, the Ghana-Guinea Union, the Indian Federation, the Mali Federation, the Malaysia Federation, the Senegambia Confederation, the Soviet Union, the United Arab Republic, the Yugoslavia Federation.

5. Donald H Louchheim, 'A Loveless African Marriage is Doing Surprisingly Well', *The Washington Post*, 12 March 1967. See www.dibussi.com (visited 6 November 2007). Emphasis added.

6. But this did not prevent Ahidjo and his minions from putting out the big lie that it was Minister Nzo Ekanghaki, a citizen of the Southern Cameroons, who put into Ahidjo's head the idea of the take over of the Southern Cameroons and pleaded with him to do so, and Ahidjo did him the favour of acceding to that request! See Gaillard, *Ahidjo: Patriote et Despote*, op. cit., p. 134.

7. N Jua & P Konings, 'Occupation of Public Space: Anglophone Nationalism in Cameroon', (2004), *Cahiers d'études africaines*, http://etudesafricaines.revues.org/document4756.html.

8. Take for example the following Cameroun Republic viceroys in the Southern Cameroons: Lowe Bell Luc René (nicknamed 'Grenade' for being the one who infamously gave orders to the military to use grenades against protesters in Bamenda in 1990), Essoma Massoma, Koumpa Issa, Bonda Thomas Ejake, Bilai Okalia, and Oben Ashu. For the killings, brutal repressions or other forms of repression in which these 'distinguished' *gouverneurs* and *préfets* specialised, barbarities they and the Yaounde regime found so triumphant and so congenial, they were promoted to ministerial or other higher office.

9. The results were first published on 30 May 1972 and then on 7 June 1972. See *Bulletin Quotidien de l'Agence Camerounaise de Presse*, No. 118 du 30 juin 1972, pp. 3-4; *Bulletin de l'Afrique Noire*, No. 694 du 7 juin 1972.

10. GO Ehusani, *The Politics of Population Control*, Ahmadu Bello University Press, Zaria, 1994.

11. Owona, op. cit., p. 5.

12. See Constitution of the Federal Republic of Cameroon, article 60.

13. According to the *Cameroon Yearbook 1973-1974*, Presbook, Victoria, p. 103, the annual growth rate of the population of Cameroon was 2.1%. The publication puts Cameroon's population at 5 million in 1963, and 6 million in 1973, and puts the estimated population at 6.4 million in 1975 and 7.9 million in 1985.

14. E Ngwe, & G Tati, *L'Utilisation des Résultats des Recensements en Afrique: Le Cas du Cameroun*, Yaounde, Cahiers de l'IFORD, No. 12, 1996.

15. For example, the *Premier Plan Quinquennal de Développement Economique et Social*, 1961, by the *Ministère des Finances et du Plan de la République du Cameroun* is strangely conspicuously silent on the country's population.

16. These plebiscite figures are consistent with the published voting population of the Southern Cameroons during the internationally monitored presidential

elections of October 1992 and municipal elections of January 1996 in Cameroun Republic..

17. See *Journal Officiel de la République Fédérale du Cameroun*, 9 mai 1972, No. 2 (Supplémentaire), p. 364. My translation.

18. "Pris de court [...] les anglophones ont été incapable de concevoir une réplique. Ils ne prendront même pas la peine de contester sérieusement les résultats invraisemblables de la consultation [...] De toute façon, commentera-t-on de Bamenda à Victoria au soir du 20 mai 1972, 'le choix était entre oui et yes'." Gaillard, op. cit., p. 165. My translation: "Taken unawares [...] anglophones [i.e. the people of the Southern Cameroons] were unable to think of a response. They did not even bother to seriously challenge the improbable results of the poll [...] The comment from Bamenda to Victoria on the evening of 20 May 1972 was that in any case, 'the choice was between yes and yes'."

19. He is the same esteemed Professor hired some ten years previously by Ahidjo to review the Constitution of Cameroun Republic (1960) and, again, the Constitution of the Federal Republic of Cameroon (1961), both of which were drafted by a Mr. Jacques Rousseau, Ahidjo's French technical adviser on administrative and institutional matters. See, Gaillard, op. cit., pp. 108, 122, 165.

20. The observation may be made that unitarism is not necessarily incompatible with regional identity and personality, and regional self-rule or autonomy as the examples of Great Britain, Italy, Tanzania, South Africa and many other countries clearly demonstrate.

Chapter Nine

The Bakassi Equation

In March 1994 Cameroun Republic filed an Application in the Registry of the International Court of Justice (ICJ) instituting proceedings against Nigeria in respect of a dispute, which, according to the averments of Cameroun Republic, 'relates essentially to the question of sovereignty over the Bakassi Peninsula.' Cameroun Republic's recital of the background facts, especially in paragraph 6 of its Application, and its account of the toponymy of Bakassi, particularly in paragraphs 15-17, contained significant distortions and portrayed a deliberate attempt at obfuscation. Paragraph 6 recited as follows:

> Pursuant to the relevant provisions of the Treaty of Versailles and then of the United Nations Charter, Cameroon was placed successively under the mandate and trusteeship systems, the mandatory powers and thereafter the administering authorities being in both case France and the United Kingdom. These two regimes embodied international recognition of the frontier between Cameroon and Nigeria and Camerounese sovereignty over the Bakassi Peninsula. The 'Camerounity' of the Peninsula was confirmed by the results of the plebiscite conducted under the auspices of the United Nations on 11 and 12 February 1961, on the occasion of which the nationals of the former Southern Cameroons chose to be incorporated into Cameroon.

This passage invites a number of observations. First, "Cameroon" is used deceptively as a polysemous denotation, in an effort to obfuscate the identity of the territory being referred to.

Second, the erroneous impression is given, to anyone who is not aware of the true situation, that a certain unitary colonial territory known as "Cameroon" was placed under joint Anglo-French international tutelage. As already shown in an earlier chapter, the truth is that by mid-1916 German *Kamerun* had ceased to exist as a unitary colonial territory following its conquest by British and French forces and its subsequent partition between Britain and France along the Simon-Milner Line. The partition was confirmed by the League of Nations when separate mandates were granted to Britain and France over their respective parts, namely British Cameroons and French Cameroun. It is the British Cameroons, not French Cameroun that has a frontier to the west with Nigeria from Lake Chad to the Atlantic Ocean. The Bakassi Peninsula is located in the British Southern Cameroons where it shares a maritime border with Nigeria.

Third, there is an attempt by Cameroun Republic to befog the identity of two separate territories, the Southern Cameroons, of which the Bakassi Peninsula is geographically, legally and politically an integral part; and French Cameroun Republic, which has no border at all with Nigeria at the Bakassi Peninsula. Sovereignty is not acquired through myths, such as the myth of a so-called "camerounité" (whatever that actually means), or through homophones, such as the similarly pronounced but differently spelt names of the two distinct countries, the Southern *Cameroons* and *Cameroun* Republic.

Fourth, the UN-sponsored plebiscite in the Southern Cameroons took place on 11 February 1961. The plebiscite did not "confirm", and could not have "confirmed", Cameroun Republic's alleged title to the Bakassi Peninsula because that country never at any time had title to it in the first place. Only that which already exists can be confirmed.

Fifth, citizens of the Southern Cameroons never voted for incorporation into Cameroun Republic. There was no such political status option available at the plebiscite. The people could therefore not have opted for what was not available. The plebiscite vote was primarily a vote to achieve independence and secondarily a vote to *join* Cameroun Republic in a federal political association. Had the Southern Cameroons declined to go along with the "joining" that fact would not have entailed the invalidation of the Independence vote and the indefinite continuation of the trusteeship. Cameroun Republic may have wished that the Southern Cameroons be incorporated into its territory. But wishes are not horses.

The averments in paragraphs 15-17 were a strenuous attempt by Cameroun Republic to claim indirectly a purported historic sovereignty over the Bakassi Peninsula. A very strained effort is made to link the Peninsula with a locality in the territory of

Cameroun Republic some 300 kilometres away. The fantastic claim is made that the ancestry of the native inhabitants of Bakassi Peninsula is traceable to a native community in Cameroun Republic called "the Sawa", that the place names of the different localities in the Peninsula are in the Duala-language (a dialect spoken by a small coastal tribe in Cameroun Republic), and that 'the Douala [*sic*] had been exploiting' fish in the Bakassi Peninsula 'since the fifteenth century.' Theses are incredible assertions!

There is no shred of evidence to support them. The concentrated scholarly studies of Dike and Ardener on the Niger Delta and Ambas Bay do not mention them; nor does anthropological material or the history books of Engelbert Mveng, Abbé Ketchoua, or Victor Julius Ngoh.[1] German, British and French colonial records make no mention of any connection between the natives of Bakassi and the natives in Cameroun Republic identified as "Sawa.". Further, natives of Duala are not known seafarers. There is no historical evidence that they ever were. Even today they are not known to be a people with nautical experience. It is therefore extremely doubtful that in the 15th century they navigated the Gulf of Guinea some 300 nautical miles westwards to the Bakassi Peninsula on mere fishing expeditions. Nor is there any evidence that they ever came in contact with the neighbours of the Bakassi natives, the Calabaris or Ibibios, with whom they would definitely have interacted had they ventured into the waters around the Bakassi Peninsula. Even the notorious letter of the Duala chiefs pleading with Britain to take over their territory does not mention any contact with the Calabaris but speaks of the Douala natives "hearing" about good English laws in Calabar.

Besides, it is strange that these same natives of Duala who, one would suppose, wondrously paddled in dugout canoes regularly during a fantastic period of over six centuries as far as to the Bakassi Peninsula in search of fish, and who supposedly named all the various localities of the area, never even attempted to settle the Peninsula teeming with the very fish they so badly needed for their gastronomic pleasure. Even more curious is the fact that the Bakolle who actually settled the Peninsula chose, as it is claimed, to give the various localities of the Peninsula Duala rather than Bakolle native names. Whatever the case, the mere fact that the place names could have some meaning in the Duala dialect might well be a fortuitous happening and does not, without more, conclusively attest to a Duala connection with the area. Furthermore, the Negroid peoples of central and southern Africa are Bantus and speak a language with a common root. That being the case similarities in names, words and expressions would not be surprising. But that is as far as it goes, and there is no sense in trying to read more meaning into that phenomenon than is reasonably warranted.

At the end of its Application, "Cameroon" requested the World Court to adjudge and declare, inter alia, 'that sovereignty over the Peninsula of Bakassi is Camerounese, by virtue of international law, and that that Peninsula is an integral part of the territory of Cameroun.'

This was a strange request in view of Cameroun Republic's admission in paragraphs 6 and 17 of its Application that the Bakassi Peninsula is part of the territory of the Southern Cameroons and the Court's acknowledgement in paragraph 210 of its Judgment that 'the peninsula was recognized by the United Nations as being a part of the Southern Cameroons.' Given the hard fact that Bakassi is part of the territory of the Southern Cameroons how does it then also become part of the territory of Cameroun Republic? The boundaries of that country ossified on the date of its independence (1 January 1960), consistent with the customary international law principle of *uti possidetis* and Article 4(b) of the Constitutive Act of the African Union. The Applicant sought to explain away this contradiction with a piece of syllogistic reasoning. Applicant made the fantastic claim that the results of the plebiscite of 11 February 1961 decided the "incorporation" of the Southern Cameroons into Cameroun Republic and that therefore Bakassi 'appertain[s] to Cameroun Republic.'

The logic thus runs like this: Bakassi is unquestionably part of the territory of the Southern Cameroons. The Southern Cameroons decided to be incorporated into Cameroun Republic and was so incorporated. Therefore, Bakassi is part of the territory of Cameroun Republic. *Quod Erat Demonstrandum*. The fallacy in this syllogism lies in the unproven assertion that the Southern Cameroons decided to be incorporated into Cameroun Republic. That deductive reasoning stands to collapse upon a showing that the claim by Cameroun Republic is false.

The Bakassi Peninsula is not some chattel or personalty that was physically taken away from the Southern Cameroons and supposedly handed over to Cameroun Republic after the plebiscite. The Peninsula was, is, and will ever remain part of the territory of the Southern Cameroons. Its geographical appurtenance to the Southern Cameroons was not and could not have been affected by Southern Cameroons' political association with another state.

What is more, the plebiscite was never about incorporation into Cameroun Republic. There was no such political status option at the plebiscite. The Southern Cameroons could therefore not have decided to be incorporated into Cameroun Republic and it did not, on 1st October 1961, fuse into Cameroun Republic. There was a Federation of which both the Southern Cameroons and Cameroun Republic were component parts. 'A federal society involves a dovetailing rather than a supersession of legal orders. The competence to transact and the competence to perform exist conjunctively in the total legal order at the international level, but exist disjunctively in the instrumentalities of government at the constitutional level.'[2]

During the Cameroon Federation territorial sovereignty over the Bakassi Peninsula vested jointly in the Federation and in the Federated State of the Southern Cameroons. The dissolution of the Federation removed any obligation of association. The subsequent revival of the statehood of Cameroun Republic necessarily entailed the restoration of its colonially-defined frontiers existing on the date of achievement of its independence from France on 1st January 1960; for independence was achieved within the area of the French trusteeship.[3] The acceptance of the post-colonial nation-state and the assumption of sovereignty over that territorial framework meant acceptance of the legacy of the colonial partition. No part of those frontiers of Cameroun Republic is anywhere near the Bakassi Peninsula. Cameroun Republic does not and has never shared a maritime boundary with Nigeria. It is therefore hard to see how the Bakassi Peninsula can possibly be an 'integral part of the territory of Cameroun Republic.'

That country's annexation and armed occupation of the Southern Cameroons is an internationally wrongful act and cannot found its claimed sovereignty over Bakassi. Cameroun Republic's sovereignty claim over the Bakassi Peninsula was a ploy designed to obtain a favourable ruling from the International Court of Justice (ICJ) for use politically to shore up its pathetic claim that the Southern Cameroons voted at the plebiscite to be, and was, incorporated into Cameroun Republic as part of its territory. Cameroun Republic had tried a similar trick in 1961 in regard to the Northern British Cameroons in a case it brought against Britain (*Cameroun v. UK, a.k.a. Northern Cameroons Case*), but at that time a more perspicacious ICJ quickly saw through the ruse and dismissed the case as without object.[4]

Both Nigeria and Cameroun Republic were laying conflicting claims to territory that indubitably belongs to the Southern Cameroons as evidenced by various applicable international boundary treaties and the international tutelage agreement relating to the Southern Cameroons. Professor Malcolm Shaw rightly pointed out during the oral pleadings in the "Bakassi case" that Bakassi Peninsula falls firmly within the Southern Cameroons. This fact is affirmed by the March 1913 Anglo-German Treaty respecting the settlement of the frontier between Nigeria and Kamerun. It is also confirmed by the British Order in Council (Definition of Boundaries Proclamation, 1954) determining the boundary between the Eastern Region of Nigeria and the Southern Cameroons.

Furthermore, the map of the United Nations illustrating the plebiscite voting districts in the Southern Cameroons clearly shows the Bakassi Peninsula as part of the Southern Cameroons, a territorial framework confirmed by UN Resolution 1608 affirming the results of the plebiscite which itself took place within the agreed territorial delimitation. A *Note Verbale* from the United Nations Secretary General dated 8 January 1971 confirmed the notorious fact of the Rio del Rey district, the Enong and Bakassi Peninsula being part of the Southern Cameroons under British Trusteeship.[5]

A further request that was made by Cameroun Republic was for the Court to declare and adjudge "that the Federal Republic of Nigeria has violated and is violating the fundamental principle of respect for frontiers inherited from colonization (*uti possidetis juris*)." Cameroun Republic saw the mote in Nigeria's eyes, but does not see the log in its own eyes. It is as much guilty of having violated, and of violating, the fundamental principle of *uti possidetis juris* as

Nigeria was. That principle ordains that colonial territories become independent within their colonial boundaries, forfeiting any historical claims they might aspire to regarding territories now held within the old colonial boundaries of others.[6]

Uti possidetis juris implies the continuity *ipso jure* of boundary and territorial treaties. Once a people achieve independence, the principle of *uti possidetis* freezes the territorial titles, thereby delimiting the newly independent state's entitlement to territorial integrity, sovereignty and independence.[7] The critical date for the photograph of the territorial situation is the date of national independence. Decolonised states are therefore obligated under international law to respect frontiers inherited from colonisation as of the date of their achievement of national independence.[8]

The territorial boundaries of Cameroun Republic became frozen on the date of its achievement of its national independence from France on 1 January 1960. Its territory devolved upon it as successor to French Cameroun on the basis of the pre-existing colonially-defined territorial framework within which it achieved independence. Cameroun Republic cannot therefore run away from or conceal its independence date as it has been trying to do over the years. It is within the four walls of its frontiers as they stood on the date of its independence that Cameroun Republic is entitled to assert its independence, its territorial integrity and its domestic jurisdiction. It follows that Cameroun Republic's claim to sovereignty over the territory of the Southern Cameroons or any part thereof is misconceived and can find no justification under the principle of *uti possidetis* or under any other known principle or rule or doctrine of law. A trespasser *vi et armis* may be in control of land but he has neither lawful possession nor legal title; nor can a right usurped be validated by the effluxion of time.

Boundaries are of course not sacrosanct. Permissible alteration of state frontiers may take place in a number of ways.[9] For example, it may take place politically, following an informed decision freely taken by a people as a whole within its defined boundaries, for its territory to be completely fused with the territory of another state. This is what happened in the case of the Northern British Cameroons. In a UN-sponsored plebiscite held in that territory on 12 February 1961, the people there voted to achieve independence by "joining" Nigeria *as a separate province of the Northern Region'* of that country consistent with the pre-plebiscite constitutional offer Nigeria had made to the people of that trust territory.[10] The UN validated the vote and decided in operative paragraph 4(a) of General Assembly Resolution 1608 (XV) that the Trusteeship Agreement concerning the British Cameroons shall be terminated with respect to the Northern Cameroons "on 1 June 1961 upon it joining the Federation of Nigeria *as a separate province of the Northern Region of Nigeria.*"[11] The resultant joinder indeed took place on 1 June 1961. The fusion of that territory into Nigeria entailed an *adjustment* of Nigeria's colonial-inherited frontiers at that point. Then 1 June 1961 became the critical date of the photograph of Nigeria's territorial framework.

By contrast, the Southern Cameroons did not "join" Cameroun Republic as a part of that country, but as an equal partner in the joint creation of a new subject of international law of which both became parts. The Southern Cameroons did not fuse into Cameroun Republic. Its personality and identity did not become extinguished. By common agreement, the two countries formed a federal political association of two states, equal in status.

Following the emergence of the Federal Republic of Cameroon as an international person and the consequential extinction of Cameroun Republic as a subject of international law, no question arose of frontier adjustment for Cameroun Republic since it was extinct and became a federated state within an overarching Federal State. The hitherto international boundary between the Southern Cameroons and Cameroun Republic seemingly changed status from frontiers to mere administrative boundaries separating the two component states of the Federation, but otherwise remained unchanged. The Federal Republic succeeded to all territorial treaties relating to the frontiers of the Federation: to the west, the Anglo-German Agreement of 11 March 1913 respecting the settlement of the frontier between Nigeria and the Cameroons, from Yola to the Sea; and to the east, the frontier between the French Cameroun trust territory and French Equatorial Africa.

1st October 1961 is the critical date for the photograph of the territorial situation of the Federal Republic of Cameroon (extinct since 1972), not of Cameroun Republic revived as a legal and political expression in 1984. The Federal Republic of Cameroon was not identical with Cameroun Republic to permit of the argument that Cameroun Republic was the mere continuation of the Federal Republic of Cameroon. Nor was the Federation legally based or could legally have been based on a principle of principal and minor component states. Such an arrangement, had it existed, would not have been a federation at all.

The federal political association between the Southern Cameroons and Cameroun Republic was a constitutive federation. It did not entail any alteration in the inherited colonially-defined frontiers between the two countries. Moreover, since the political association was a *de facto* federation the boundary between the two federated states was a mere *de facto* internal boundary. The demise of the Cameroon Federation and the subsequent revival of Cameroun Republic as a legal and political expression *ipso jure* confirmed as an international frontier the hitherto *de facto* internal boundary between the Southern Cameroons and Cameroun Republic. In fact, the frontier line between the Southern Cameroons and Cameroun Republic has always been a *de jure* international boundary.[12]

Regrettably, in its ruling of 10 October 2002, in *Case Concerning the Land and Maritime Boundary between Cameroon and Nigeria (Cameroon v. Nigeria: Equatorial Guinea Intervening)* (so-called 'Bakassi case'), the International Court of Justice (ICJ) did not go into all this learning. It decided that sovereignty (what kind of sovereignty?) over the Bakassi Peninsula belongs to Cameroun Republic and not to Nigeria, the other competing claimant of the Peninsula. This case invites closer scrutiny for one to decipher the true meaning of the ruling.

The ruling in the case cannot be interpreted to mean that the Court decided that Cameroun Republic has sovereign *title* to the Peninsula. Sovereignty over territory is not necessarily the same thing as sovereign title to the territory. A colonial power has sovereignty over its colonial territory but sovereign title to the territory vests in the people of the territory. The UN mandated and superintended plebiscite in the Southern Cameroons meant, in international law, a recognition that the inhabitants of the territory constitute a people and thus are entitled to the inalienable right of self determination. The plebiscite was also an acknowledgement that the people of the Southern Cameroons have sovereign title to the territory of the Southern Cameroons. Sovereignty over ther Southern Cameroons was never transferred to the mandatory/administering authority.

Colonial sovereignty is always a precarious sovereignty because it is provisional in terms of status in that it is fundamentally limited in its object (confined to mere administration and certain responsibilities). Thus, if Cameroun Republic indeed has sovereignty over the Bakassi Peninsula it can only be a colonial sovereignty.

Contrary to what Cameroun Republic has since been saying, the ICJ ruling did not *establish* the boundaries of Cameroun Republic. What the Court did was to *specify* the frontier between Nigeria and a conflated entity acting in that case simply as "Cameroon" (French: 'Cameroun'), rather than as "Republic of Cameroun" (French: 'la République du Cameroun'). That conflated entity consisted of occupied Southern Cameroons subsumed under the occupying state of Cameroun Republic. It cannot credibly be asserted that the ruling in the case delimited the frontiers of Cameroun Republic because that would contradict all historical facts. Cameroun Republic was a trust territory administered not by Britain but by France. It could therefore not inherit, from its colonisation, boundaries other than those of French Cameroun. French Cameroun never had and does not have a common boundary with Nigeria at the Bakassi Peninsula.

Furthermore, the ruling could not have been based, and was not based, on the determination of the boundary inherited by Cameroun Republic from its colonisation. At the time of that ruling, Cameroun Republic had ceased being a colonial territory for 42 years. Its western frontier with the Southern Cameroons is on the Mungo River, along the alignment described in the Anglo-French boundary treaty known as the Milner-Simon Declaration of 1919 and more particularly the Anglo-French (Graeme-Marchand Declaration) boundary treaty of 1931. Cameroun Republic could not inherit boundaries other than those of French Cameroun, and its boundary in relation to the Southern Cameroons is at the Mungo River and not at Bakassi. Therefore, the ruling of the International Court of Justice specified, not the boundary inherited by Cameroun Republic from its colonisation by France but, the boundary inherited by Nigeria from its colonisation by Britain.

Cameroun Republic is the political and legal entity which, as the former United Nations trust territory under French administration, gained independence from France on 1 January 1960 and inherited, consistent with international law, the boundaries of French Cameroun. When consumed by delusions of grandeur, Cameroun Republic speaks of itself variously as *'état du Cameroun'*, *'unicité du territoire'*, *'Kamerun'*, *'camerounité'* and *'re-unification du Cameroun'*. These are labelling tricks meant to convey to the unwary inquirer the idea that colonising Cameroun Republic and colonised Southern Cameroons constitute one country. The fact of the matter is that those labels do not correspond to any known legal entity; they are mere political expressions and sloganeering.

Cameroun Republic came up with the self-coined word *'camerounité'* for the first time in the case whose ruling is the subject of the present scrutiny. There, Cameroun Republic hid under the cloak of a nebulous entity known as 'Cameroon', appearing as the party suing Nigeria. That country could not appear under its official name and style of *la République du Cameroun* and argue credibly that it has a frontier with Nigeria at the Bakassi Peninsula. It needed to find some basis on which to defeat Nigeria's physical presence (military and administrative) in, and control of, the Peninsula. It found that in the polysemous, if not vague, name 'Cameroon' (as vague as if someone spoke simply of Congo or Guinea or Korea or Georgia) and in the equally vague word *'camerounité'*, coined in imitation of the Ivorian *ivoirité*. The Court was, in the final analysis, confronted with deciding simply on the *'camerounité'* or the *'nigerianité'* of the Bakassi Peninsula. Mindful of the boundary alignment as delimited in the Anglo-German boundary treaty of 11 March 1913, the Court was satisfied that Bakassi fell on that side of the alignment that had the character of 'cameroon-ness' (*'camerounité'*) rather than 'nigerian-ness' (*'nigerianité'*). That was the true basis of the ICJ ruling. And in a sense it was a decision which, though correct in holding that the Peninsula does not appertain to Nigeria, nevertheless was obtained by Cameroun Republic through misrepresentation.

Nowhere in the ruling does the Court say Cameroun Republic has legal title to the Bakassi Peninsula and to the rest of the Southern Cameroons. The Court could not have said so because there is absolutely no legal basis for it. In international law an existing state can acquire additional territory only by occupation, conquest, accretion and avulsion, or cession. None of these modes of territorial acquisition applies in this case and Cameroun Republic never argued that any applied; not even cession.

Cession of state territory is the transfer of sovereignty over state territory by the owner-state to another state. There is no evidence at all that either Britain or Nigeria at any time transferred the Bakassi Peninsula and/or the rest of the Southern Cameroons to Cameroun Republic. Neither of those countries could have done so for the simple reason that none of them was the owner-state either of the Peninsula or of the rest of the Southern Cameroons.

Further, it cannot even be contended that the plebiscite vote in the Southern Cameroons in favour of a plotical association with Cameroun Republic amounted to a cession of the Southern Cameroons to Cameroun Republic. The plebiscite was organised in pursuance of the international law right of self-determination as a mode of decolonisation not cession of territory. It was never intended that sovereignty over independent Southern Cameroons would pass to Cameroun Republic. The vote in favour of a political association with Cameroun Republic only involved the acquisition of certain governmental powers by the new body (the federal government) that was going to represent the two countries in association. The acquisition of such powers, even had it been exclusive, without the intention to cede territorial sovereignty (and there was no such intention), does not suffice. In any case, a non-state entity (e.g. a colonial territory such as the Southern Cameroons was at the time of the plebiscite) cannot, unlike a state, cede territory because cession involves transfer of sovereignty over state territory by the owner-state and a dependent territory not being sovereign state is not an owner-state.

The case did not involve testing a purported title by Cameroun Republic against the title of the people of the Southern Cameroons to their territory. Further, title to disputed property is always examined only relatively to the proofs presented by the disputing parties and not against all the proofs and claims in the world. What this means is that all claims to ownership can always be contested by any party with a better title. For, there is always the possibility of evidence of superior title over territory emerging in the course of justice and in the course of time. And when that happens there is bound to be opportunity for any claimed title to be tested against the new evidence. Territory over which sovereignty was previously recognised or simply assumed as lying with one state may subsequently be found, when better title is presented and examined, to actually lie with different peoples. In the meanwhile, however, the whole world might have been assuming the illegal occupier to be the rightful owner.

It is trite to stay that occupied territories are always temporarily subsumed under the personality of the occupying power. The phenomenon of hiding a distinct legal entity in a party before an international jurisdiction is a historical fact common in all situations of occupation. When, therefore, the occupying power is a party to litigation before any international jurisdiction, there is no severance of the occupied territory from the territory of the occupying power. And no judicial notice is taken of the composite and illegal nature of the party. Thus, when Nigeria was in occupation (contested) of the Bakassi Peninsula, no court in which Nigeria appeared as a party severed the Peninsula from the rest of Nigeria. The same could be said of Imperial Ethiopia with regard to Eritrea. That is exactly the phenomenon that occurred in the ICJ case at hand.

There, the 'Cameroon' party consisted in fact of Cameroun Republic and occupied Southern Cameroons treated *as if* they were a conflated entity. The matter before the Court was not whether the party called 'Cameroon' included more than one legal entity (and on behalf of which the 'Bakassi case' was instituted) or whether the tactical lumping together of the Southern Cameroons and Cameroun Republic into the nebulous party called 'Cameroon' had any legal basis. Courts are especially careful not to take up any matter which has not been specifically put before them for adjudication. They will not decide any matter not specifically pleaded. So doing would not be the proper discharge of the judicial function. Unless a court is specifically seized of it, it will not scrutinise the legality or legitimacy of the composition of the political entity that has standing to sue and be sued as a party to a case before it.

The law makes a clear distinction between a *de facto* and a *de jure* situation. While the territory of the Southern Cameroons, because of its colonial occupation by Cameroun Republic, appears *de facto* to be part of that country, it is *de jure*, distinct and separate from the territory of the colonising state. The situation is on all fours with that which obtained when the Southern Cameroons, even though a mandated or trust territory, was administered for over 45 years by Britain as an integral part of Nigeria. Maps of the time showed the Southern Cameroons as part of Nigeria. The long period of cohabitation with Nigeria engendered the perception that the people of the Southern Cameroons were Nigerians, so much so that when the Southern Cameroons' political leadership in Nigeria left that country in 1953 and established a government in Buea, capital of the Southern Cameroons, the withdrawal of the Southern Cameroons from Nigeria was characterised as 'secession' from Nigeria. It took the ruling of the International Court of Justice in the above case to recall the legal position that according to international law, the territory of the Southern Cameroons had all along remained a separate and distinct territory from that of Nigeria and that the Southern Cameroons-Nigeria border had all along remained an international, not an internal, boundary. It is submitted that by parity of reasoning the Southern Cameroons-Cameroun Republic boundary has, *de jure*, always remained and will always remain an international boundary, notwithstanding Cameroun Republic's occupation of and baseless sovereignty claim over the territory.

Under international law, the attainment of independence involves the replacement of one sovereign by another and thus gives a derivative title to territory. Cameroun Republic, the new sovereign that took over from French Cameroun, could therefore inherit no other boundaries from its colonisation but those of French Cameroun. Under the mandates/trusteeship agreements, France exercised over that territory powers of administration and various responsibilities, and was duty-bound to promote the territory's development and ultimate independence. Independence was achieved within the limits of the principle of *uti possidetis juris*.

The boundary alignment of the territory of French Cameroun in relation to the territory of the Southern Cameroons is at the River Mungo to the east of the Southern Cameroons, about 300 kilometres from the Bakassi Peninsula which is located on the southwest border of the Southern Cameroons with Nigeria. The Peninsula lies deep in the Southern Cameroons. It is therefore a historical, a geographical and a legal impossibility for Cameroun Republic to have inherited boundaries which were not those of French Cameroun on 1 January 1960. It is also a legal impossibility, under Article 4(b) of the Constitutive Act of the African Union, for Cameroun Republic to have inherited both the boundaries of French Cameroun and those of British Southern Cameroons.

On 1 January 1960, the date on which Cameroun Republic inherited its frontiers, that date being also that on which its frontiers became frozen, consistent with Article 4(b), the Southern Cameroons was still a United Nations trust territory under British administration with its own internationally-defined boundaries. The Southern Cameroons had never at any time been part of French Cameroun and has never been a legal part of Cameroun Republic. The trust over the Southern Cameroons was not terminated until 1 October 1961, nearly two years after the ossification of the frontiers of Cameroun Republic following its achievement of independence. One then wonders by what miracle Cameroun Republic inherited, on 1 January 1960 and from French Cameroun, the boundaries of the Southern Cameroons at the Bakassi Peninsula.

It is submitted that the preceding legal and historical facts establish conclusively the following: (1) That the ICJ ruling did *not* determine the boundaries inherited by Cameroun Republic from colonisation at the time of its independence; (2) That the ICJ ruling specified only the boundaries between the Federal Republic of Nigeria, on the one hand, and the illegally conflated 'two Cameroons' assumed and treated in that case *as if* they were one, on the other hand; thus leaving the boundary between the 'two Cameroons' *inter se* unspecified, since that was not the issue before the Court; (3) That the ruling, however, specified by necessary implication and on the basis of the Anglo-German Declaration of 11 March 1913, the common boundary alignment inherited at independence by Nigeria and the contiguous territory of the Southern Cameroons at the Bakassi Peninsula; but not the boundary inherited by Cameroun Republic because it did not and could not in law inherit the British Southern Cameroons boundaries; (4) In essence therefore, the true meaning of the 'Bakassi' ruling is that it specified the common boundary between the Federal Republic of Nigeria and the Southern Cameroons from the sea through the Bakassi Peninsula right up to Nkambe; and from there the common boundary between Nigeria and Cameroun Republic up to Lake Chad.

The 'Bakassi case' was fought between two parties laying claim to territory that belonged to neither of them and so naturally each side, in the hope that it would win the case, had every reason, not only to suppress evidence which could reveal that the territory belonged to a third party, the Southern Cameroons, but to proffer only arguments that would give itself victory and not the true owner. This naturally implies that all the vital evidence and facts that could reveal the true owner of the territory were suppressed. Both parties had a mutual interest in suppressing the Southern Cameroons' voice in the hope of stealing its territory.

It follows that the ICJ ruling of 10 October 2002 puts nothing to rest as regards the title of the people of the Southern Cameroons over their territory asserted against Cameroun Republic's present and continuing illegal occupation of the territory of the Southern Cameroons. The ruling concerned only the parties in that case; and even then the scope of what the Court decided appears vague. Whatever the case, the Court was not requested to decide who had legal title to the Peninsula; nor was it requested to pronounce itself on the assumption of sovereignty over the Southern Cameroons by Cameroun Republic. The ruling of the Court cannot therefore be taken as having decided any of those matters. Further, that ruling does not exclude the possibility of there being at stake the right of a third party over the contested territory. The decision in the Bakassi case, like any other decision of the ICJ in contentious matters, has no binding force except between the parties to it and in respect of that particular case.[13] This means that the 'Bakassi decision' has no force of law in the relations between the Southern Cameroons and Cameroun Republic.

Since the Court was not requested to decide who had legal title to the Peninsula, it did not decide, could not have decided, and cannot be taken to have decided that legal title to the Peninsula vests in Cameroun Republic. Legal title to any territory or part thereof vests in the people of the territory. Accordingly, legal title to the Bakassi Peninsula, which is unquestionably an integral part of the Southern Cameroons as attested by relevant international boundary treaties, necessarily vests in the people of the Southern Cameroons. It is significant that while the ICJ ruled that "sovereignty" over the Peninsula belongs to Cameroun Republic it studiously did not pronounce itself on the legality of Cameroun Republic's claimed sovereignty over the Southern Cameroons, especially in light of the two principles, self-determination and *uti possidetis juris*.

Notes

1. Dike, op.cit.; S Ardener (ed.), op.cit.; E Mveng, *Histoire du Cameroun*; VJ Ngoh, *Constitutional Development in Southern Cameroons 1946-1961: From Trusteeship to Independence*, Ceper, Yaounde, 1990; Abbé T Ketchoua, *Contribution à l'Histoire du Cameroun de 450 avant Jésus Christ à nos Jours*, Yaounde, 1962.

2. DP O'Connell, *State Succession in Municipal Law and International Law. II. International Relations*, Cambridge University Press, Cambridge, 1967.

3. Whiteman, *Digest of International Law. II.* 1963, pp. 142-145.

4. See DHN Johnson, 'The Case Concerning the Northern Cameroons' *International and Comparative Law Quarterly*, vol. 13, 1964, p. 1143.

5. B Ate, 'Nigeria-Cameroon Boundary Dispute' *Nigerian Institute of International Affairs*, 1987, p. 23. In a brief historical note on Bakassi posted on the Internet on 30 November 2007, Mola Mbua Ndoko wrote: 'During the British colonial administration [of the Southern Cameroons] [...] the area that is presently called Bakassi was known as Bakolle Clan. The area was and is still known for [...] large quantities of fish [...] [T]he administrative Division to which Bakolle Clan originally belonged is the then Victoria Division (known now as Fako Division). Bakolle Clan is precisely one of the clans that constituted the then Victoria Native Authority of the Honourable Chief Johannese [sic] Manga William (Manga ma Nambeke), Member of the Legislative Council of Nigeria in Lagos [...] After [...] 1961 when Balondo clans were created an administrative Division known as Ndian Division with headquarters in Mundemba, Government detached Bakolle Clan from Fako Division and made it part of Ndian Division. Bakolle Clan was subsequently created an administrative sub-division of Ndian Division. Bamuso was named the headquarters town of Bakolle Clan.'

6. R Higgins, 'Postmodern Tribalism and the Right to Secession: Comments,' in Brolmann et al. (eds), *Peoples and Minorities in International Law*, Martinus Nijhoff, Dordrecht, 1993, p. 34.

7. Ibid.

8. See the 1964 Cairo resolution on border disputes adopted by African states by which they pledge "to respect the frontiers existing on their achievement of national independence." See also the opinion of the ICJ in *Burkina Faso v. Mali*,

1986 ICJ Rep. para. 25. Article 4 of the Constitutive Act of the African Union (AU) declares as one of the AU's core principles binding on Member States, 'the respect for borders existing on achievement of independence.'

9. It may take place consensually, for example, by consensus in a mixed demarcation commission or by agreement between limitrophic states on, say, cession of territory or a boundary adjustment. It may take place judicially following adjudication by an arbitration tribunal or the International Court of Justice.

10. *Plebiscite Commissioner's Report,* op. cit., paragraphs 83-96. Emphasis added.

11. Emphasis added.

12. See, chapter 14.

13. See Article 59 of the Statute of the International Court of Justice.

Chapter Ten

The Matter of Secession

Cameroun Republic repeatedly declares that the on-going self-determination struggle by the people of the Southern Cameroons is a secessionist bid. In its view international law and municipal law proscribe secession and sanction its suppression by force of arms. In reality, the secession rhetoric of Cameroun Republic is simply a piece of propaganda – a policy manoeuvre, a bogey, a scarecrow – conjured in an attempt to prevent righteous internal challenge and lawful external scrutiny of the colonisation of the Southern Cameroons by Cameroun Republic.

Domestic law

The Southern Cameroons and Cameroun Republic constitutionally contracted to federate and to remain in a federal union. Federalism was the condition *sine qua non* of the envisaged political association. The political rulership of Cameroun Republic breached this contractual engagement when it unilaterally dissolved the Federation and revived Cameroun Republic as a legal and political expression. That fundamental breach entitled the Southern Cameroons, as injured party, to consider the contract as terminated and to take the reciprocal action of reviving its statehood as well. No question arises of a continuing obligation of political association since the type of union agreed on had been decreed out of existence. Circumstances had substantially changed. The former rules, the former framework, and the former underpinnings relating to federalism became inapplicable. The obligation of political association lost its effect and ceased to be binding.

The union was of course not condemned to endure until the end of time. No union is. It is the case that when one country unites with another, it is free subsequently to opt out of the union and restore its former status or try another union with some other country in exercise of the continuing right of self-determination. History affords many instances of this.[1] The entitlement to pull out is based on sound theory. A right to contract in implies a right to contract out, a power of entry implies a power of exit, a power to opt in implies a power to opt out. A party is even at liberty to rescind a contract unilaterally. However, the rescission amounts to a breach of contract redressible by appropriate remedy.

As concerns municipal criminal law, insecure states – states whose foundations are weak – commonly criminalise what they consider as secessionist bids. In the case of the defunct Federal Republic of Cameroon, s.111 of the Federal Penal Code on "secession" punished 'whoever undertakes in whatever manner to infringe the territorial integrity of the Republic.' The crime was conceived as an offence against the territorial integrity of the 'Republic' and therefore as a species of the crime of treason which is based on breach of the duty of allegiance to the state. 'Republic' referred to the territories comprised in the State formed by the political association of the Southern Cameroons and Cameroun Republic on 1 October 1961 under the name and style of the Federal Republic of Cameroon. The protected territorial integrity under s.111 is thus that of the Federal Republic of Cameroon. In relation to the Southern Cameroons, s.111 lapsed with the forcible dissolution of the Federation in 1972. Additionally, the dissolution of the Federation and revival of Cameroun Republic as a legal and political expression *ipso facto* revoked Federal Republic citizenship and terminated the duty of Federal Republic allegiance.

For the time being and because of the unfortunate circumstances in which they find themselves, citizens of the Southern Cameroons are forced to yield obedience to Cameroun Republic. That country's forcible occupation of the Southern Cameroons and maintenance of an administration in the Southern Cameroons of paramount force compels obedience from citizens of the Southern Cameroons as a matter of necessity. In the absence of any true and genuine duty of allegiance owed by the people of the Southern Cameroons to Cameroun Republic, a citizen of the Southern Cameroons is incapable of committing treason against the State of Cameroun Republic.

In sum, the crime of secession under s.111 of the Federal Penal Code was an offence against the Federal Republic, and Cameroun Republic is not that State. Further, the Southern Cameroons has never legally been part of Cameroun Republic notwithstanding the many fraudulent attempts by its rulers to so make the Southern

Cameroons. The authorities of Cameroun Republic thus lack the necessary valid sovereign power in the Southern Cameroons to sustain a charge of treason. Nor do courts of that country have under international law competence to try a citizen of the Southern Cameroons for an alleged offence of treason. Agents of Cameroun Republic routinely kidnap alleged criminal suspects from the Southern Cameroons to that country for "trial". In law, the courts of that country lack competence to try them because of the illegality of their arrest under international and human rights law.

In any event, secession *per se*, as distinct from the use of unlawful methods to bring it about can never be a crime for the simple reason that state frontiers are not sacrosanct. If secession *per se* were to be an offence on the reasoning that it impairs territorial integrity, then union, incorporation, or cession of territory would also offend against the criminal law for in either case territorial integrity is impaired, the international boundaries of the state are affected. The fact of the matter is that a state may, consistent with the law of nations and its constitution expand, shrink, or become extinct, depending on the vicissitude of its history and the political actions of those in charge of it. Secession is not illegal *per se* and indeed is, and has been, politically possible.

Some deny that there is a right to secessionist self-determination. Even if that contention were to be correct that does not mean that secession is illegal in international law, nor, for that matter impossible. Secession can be achieved through use of force (e.g., Ireland from the UK, Eritrea from Ethiopia, Bangladesh from Pakistan, Kosovo from Serbia) or peacefully as in the velvet division of Czechoslovakia into two states – the Czech Republic and the Slovak Republic –, the secession of Singapore from Malaysia, the secession of Senegal from Mali, and the secession of Pakistan from India.

The "secession" or "separatist" [2] rhetoric by Cameroun Republic is deeply flawed in another critical way. While the Southern Cameroons was part of the defunct informal Federal Republic of Cameroon, it is not, and has never been, part of Cameroun Republic. The territory of the Southern Cameroons was not carved out of the territory of Cameroun Republic and the boundaries (both international and internal) of the Southern Cameroons were not determined by Cameroun Republic. The Southern Cameroons' struggle for statehood is an anti-colonial struggle aimed at freeing the land from the colonial subjugation of Cameroun Republic. That struggle does not involve any claim to any of the peoples that make up the tribal mix of Cameroun Republic. It does not involve any claim to an inch of land outside the boundaries of the Southern Cameroons as defined in the relevant boundary treaties referred to under the mandates and trusteeship agreement relating to the territory. The territorial framework of Cameroun Republic remains exactly the same as it was on the date of its achievement of independence from France on 1 January 1960. Southern Cameroons' assertion of its statehood does not impinge on any proper interest of Cameroun Republic be it legal, territorial or political. The territorial integrity of Cameroun Republic is in no way infringed.[3] There is no dismemberment of its territory. There is no loss of part of its population. There is no impairment of its national unity. There is no impairment of its territorial integrity. There is therefore no secession of territory from Cameroun Republic. The territory of the Southern Cameroons is well delimited by international boundary treaties.

The Southern Cameroons was previously under British rule and was "decolonised" on 1 October 1961 following a UN plebiscite organised seven months earlier in recognition of the right of the people of the territory to self-determination. The plebiscite also amounted to recognition that the people of the Southern Cameroons have sovereign title to their territory. The territorial titles of the Southern Cameroons became frozen on 1 October 1961 since the right of self-determination was exercised within the limits of the principle of *uti possidetis*. Cameroun Republic, as a colonial power in relation to the Southern Cameroons, cannot assert the principle of territorial integrity in answer to the continuing right of self-determination of the people of the Southern Cameroons and their sovereign title to their territory. It could not, in 1961, obtain sovereignty over the Southern Cameroons by cession: there is no instrument attesting to the cession of the Southern Cameroons by either the UN or the UK or the people of the Southern Cameroons themselves to Cameroun Republic. It could not, in 1972, obtain sovereignty by conquest either by pen and ink or by rifle and machine gun: conquest is no longer a valid method of acquisition of territory, and besides, since there was neither treaty of cession nor war between the Southern Cameroons and Cameroun Republic, the question of conquest does not even arise. The people of the Southern Cameroons are therefore fully entitled to free themselves from the foreign and colonial occupation of Cameroun Republic, and by any means recognised under international law.

International law

International law adopts a neutral attitude on the debate whether there is a right to secede or not. It neither concedes nor denies a right to secede, whether "unilaterally" or "consensually". It is common learning that territory can be lost through revolt followed by secession of a part of the territory concerned. The UN Charter neither confirms nor denies a right of rebellion. The matter is purely domestic and is left within the purview of municipal law.[4]

Recognition of a seceding entity is essentially a political rather than a legal act. There is no duty under international law to grant recognition to any entity. However, once the reality of secession has occurred and been made effective, international law usually eventually recognises that fact. In the event of a successful secession, attested by the "effectivity" of the new state, it is doubtful that the status of the emergent state may still be questioned.[5] Indeed, some authors argue that, 'although rebellion is treason in the eyes of municipal law, it results [...] in a duty of other states to recognize the change and treat the new government as representing the state in international sphere.'[6]

Other commentators go further by arguing that self-determination encompasses the "unilateral" right to secession. They argue that there is no need to restrict the right and no need to fear the proliferation of new states, because no existing state has after all occupied its present borders for over 160 years, and states have been historically, and are constantly being, created, changed or wiped off the surface of the earth.[7] In fact keeping a people within borders not determined by them against their wishes even though the state occupying these borders is itself independent amounts to a new form of colonialism.

Third states are notoriously reluctant to make public their dealings with territorial units, the international personality of which still remains a matter of open controversy. While they may wait indefinitely before according recognition, the actual state of affairs cannot be denied and recognition is usually eventually accorded, *de jure* or *de facto*. After all, according to the weight of academic and judicial opinion, recognition is cognitive, not constitutive. Historically, state formation and transformation have occurred, and will continue to occur, through a process of fusion or fission. In the contemporary period the process has been more of fission than fusion.

Most of today's 194-odd states came into existence through a process of state fission, that is to say, by seceding from an existing Power, colonial or non-colonial.[8]

International law does not concede a right to secession. But that does not mean the United Nations has a mandate to take on the mantle of an omnipotent knight-errant roaming the world to combat threatened secession. It does not mean that secession does not occur. It does not mean that state practice does not recognize secession. A state may suffer a part of its territory to secede. In fact some states give their component territorial units a constitutional right to secede.[9] A state may even cede part of its territory. History affords many instances of cession of territory.[10]

When it is posited that a part of a state has no right under international law to secede, all what is meant is that unlike decolonisation which contemporary international law deals with, secession is a pure fact situation, a meta-juridical phenomenon which eventually international law merely acknowledges as a matter of realism. It is precisely because secession is a meta-juridical phenomenon that writers on international law refer to it in passing only and merely as a derivative right from the norm of self-determination, available in a colonial context and even in a non-colonial context such as that of a constitutive federal union. 'It is of the essence of federalism, which is a voluntary union, that two or more units choosing to federate retain the right to withdraw from the federation in accordance with agreed constitutional processes'.[11]

Some writers are even prepared to argue that a genuine enjoyment of human rights must include a right to secede.[12] For, in the words of Judge Dillard in his separate opinion in the *Western Sahara Case*, 'it is for people to determine the destiny of the territory not for the territory to determine the destiny of the people.'[13]

A survey of state practice attests to the neutrality of international law in the matter of secession. The evidence shows that the attitude of states is eminently v-ariable. More often than not the attitude bears the hallmark of pragmatism dictated by political considerations and calculations.[14] In the Katanga case (1960), for example, the wording of the various UN Security Council resolutions on the matter clearly showed that rabid cold war politics and righteous hostility towards mercenarism were critical in swaying the attitude of states against Katanga's secession.

In the "Biafra" case (1968), the UN Secretary General overstated the legal position when he declared at a press conference that 'the UN has never accepted and does not accept and [...] will [never] ever accept the principle of secession of a part of its member state.'[15] Significantly, and in spite of that overzealous statement, the political organs of the UN never pronounced themselves on the "Biafra" case, no doubt considering the matter as a purely internal affair of Nigeria. Five states did recognize "Biafra." And those that formally did not appeared to have been influenced by political rather than by legal considerations. A good many states studiously refrained from condemning the "Biafran" claim to secede, and adopted a "wait and see" attitude. Some states, like France, for example, were clearly sympathetic and actively gave aid and comfort to "Biafra", an attitude that could be considered a *de facto* recognition.

In the case of Bangladesh (1971), the UN Security Council was paralysed by a series of successive vetoes. Even in the General Assembly where the matter was deferred, no consensus emerged for or against the claim of Bangladesh to secede. The various resolutions of that organ mentioned nothing about the territorial integrity of Pakistan, which incidentally had also seceded from India on 15 August 1947. And once the Chinese opposition was overcome, Bangladesh was admitted to membership of the UN in 1974. In the view of one author, the people of Bangladesh asserted their independence and established their own sovereign state in exercise of their right of self-determination.[16]

Contrary to what has sometimes been claimed, African states have never unanimously subscribed to the view that self-determination applies only to peoples under European colonisation and domination. First, of the five states that recognized "Biafra", four were African.[17] Second, the African Charter on Human and Peoples' Rights significantly makes no mention, even in its preamble, of the affirmation of territorial integrity. Third, after thirty years of armed struggle, Eritrea eventually imposed a "consensual secession" on Ethiopia. The Organisation of African Union (OAU), which had all along ritualistically affirmed Ethiopia's sovereignty and territorial integrity, lost no time in admitting Eritrea to membership of the Organisation. This did not prevent a bitter Eritrean Head of State from mounting the OAU rostrum and severely criticising that Organisation for playing the ostrich throughout Eritrea's long armed struggle.

Fourth, the OAU collectively recognised and admitted to its membership the self-declared Saharawi Arab Democratic Republic (SADR) against continuing Moroccan opposition. This is significant in view of the territory's continuing armed occupation by Morocco. It is also significant in view of the fact that the Saharawi Government is in exile. Further, it is again significant because the UN paradoxically considers the territory as one yet to be decolonised through the holding of a self-determination referendum at which one of the choices would be, so it seems, incorporation into Morocco. How can the Saharawi Arab Democratic Republic be both an independent sovereign state, recognised by many states and admitted to membership of a regional organisation (the AU), and a colonial territory still to be decolonised?

Just as international law is neutral in the matter of secession, it is also neutral in the matter of mergers although it will, of course, eventually recognize the reality when union has taken place and been concretised. The two ideas, separation and union, would appear to be inconsistent with the norm of territorial integrity of states. A blind adherence to the principle of territorial integrity would mean that neither secession nor union is permissible, an absurdity. What that apparent inconsistency suggests is that the principle of territorial integrity is not etched on stone tablets.

International law is not so silly to insist that state frontiers must remain sacrosanct at all cost. Of course, it would be a good thing for international order if states could remain constant and unchanging. An unqualified right of secession could lead to disruption of state systems. Equally, unrestrained state expansionism would revive imperial order, long rejected, and would imperil the Westphalian state system. These two concerns go in tandem. The principle of territorial integrity is designed to take care of both. It represents a repugnance to both unbridled secession and unbridled territorial aggrandizement. It aims at securing respect for the preservation of the territorial *status quo* of states. Contemporary international law does not encourage secession, just as it rejects annexation as invalid and inimical to international peace and security.

Yet international law cannot prevent state fission (whether consensual or unilateral) any more than it can oppose consensual fusion. It cannot because the modern state is a living organism and its territory may expand or shrink. Like every human creation, the state, in its existence, is exposed to the flow of things and times, 'to the slings and arrows of outrageous fortune.' Much depends upon its historical fortunes. And if the facts of history are reckoned with, many reasons may be found to account for the likely growth, decrease, or even extinction of a state. To prevent disorder, international law has had to develop a series of rules regulating such territorial changes.

Some legal scholars suggest that since the creation of the United Nations in 1945, state practice has evolved towards non-recognition of "unilateral secession."[18] They do not deny that there have been successful secessions even after 1945. But they posit that these have been "consensual" and, presumably for that reason, accepted in state practice. It is submitted that the distinction between "unilateral" and "consensual" secession may well be a fine one in many cases. Clearly, the so-called consensual secession is but the tail end picture of a unilaterally inspired and initiated secessionist process.

There is not a single recorded case in history where a state, on its own volition, without internal or external pressures of some kind, decided to become extinct by liquidating itself or by dismembering itself into two or more states. The evidence in the matter of secession shows that a secessionist process is always triggered by something, usually some historical wrong or injustice, some unlawful act such as usurpation of a fundamental right or a festering grievance or a long train of unbearable wrongs and injustices. The process then develops. It gathers momentum. And it eventually imposes on the holding authority the necessity to let go. This "let go" is erroneously characterized as "consensual secession." In fact, however, it is merely the penultimate stage of a creeping "unilateral secession." The "consensual secession" is in reality one imposed on the holding authority.

The expression "consensual secession" masks the pressures, more or less covert or subtle, that a powerful state, a group of states, or an inter-governmental organisation may bring to bear on the holding authority to let go of the seceding entity. Several examples come to mind. These include the role of the UN in the decolonisation process, the role of the British in the Pakistani secession from India, the role of the USA in the dissolution of the USSR. They also include the role of the European states in the velvet dissolution of Czechoslovakia and the violent break-up of Yugoslavia, the role of the European Union and the United States of America in the secession of Kosovo from Serbia, and the role of India in the Bangladeshi case. There is again the role of the Gulf States in the Eritrean case, the role of Algeria in the Western Sahara case, and the role of Portugal and Australia in the East Timor case. Every seceding entity has its guardian angel.

The term "consensual secession" also disguises the fact that here too there is an exercise in diplomacy and international relations designed to provide a face-saving route for the holding state. This credibly explains why there is always resort to such "consensual" expedients as legislation sanctioning the secession or a bilateral/multilateral accord validating the secession.

All this window dressing is meant to make "unilateral secession" palatable and thus maintain the fiction that part of a state can break off and assume a separate existence only by and with the concurrence of the holding state. In the final analysis the so-called consensual secession resolves itself into an exercise in public relations intended to massage the ego of the holding state. "Unilateral" and "consensual" secession – that is merely a semantic game, a veritable pun. The distinction between the two terms is tenuous and does not correspond with reality. In fact there is no legal or practical interest in making the distinction at all. It is submitted that secession is secession, *tout court*.

It is doubtful that there has been, since 1945, only one example of successful "unilateral secession" (as distinct from the dissolution of a state). When the British Southern Cameroons was separated from Nigeria in 1960 after 45 years of enforced "administrative union" with that country, the matter was considered as a case of secession from Nigeria and the views of that country regarding the secession were considered as of no moment.[19] In December 1962 Nyasaland (Malawi) seceded from the 10 years' old Central African Federation[20] and in February 1963 Northern Rhodesia (Zambia) also seceded therefrom.[21] These two cases of secession were not the result of agreement to that effect by the component entities of that Federation.

In August 1960 Senegal seceded from the Mali Federation formed by Senegal and French Soudan in January 1959 and independent on 20 June 1960. The fact that French Soudan (later retaining the name Mali) subsequently acquiesced in the Senegalese *fait accompli* does not change the reality that secession was procured by act of Senegal alone (with France acting as guardian angel in this case).

In 1958 Egypt and Syria unified to form the United Arab Republic and thereafter continued their membership of the UN as a single Member. But in 1961 Syria seceded from the Union in protest of Egyptian domination.[22] Egypt (maintaining the name "United Arab Republic" until 1971 when it was changed to the "Arab Republic of Egypt") and Syria restored their respective sovereignty and resumed their respective status of independent States. They were allowed to re-occupy their respective UN seats without having to apply for readmission. The UN studiously declined to pronounce itself on whether the Egypto-Syrian divorce was a case of secession or not, although clearly it was. On 10 August 1998 Nevis (population 10,000) seceded from the Island State of St. Kitts & Nevis and became a separate independent state.

There is also the rather bizarre case of the Comoros Islands, which comprises the islands of Grande Comore, Anjouan, Moheli, and Mayotte. These islands became a French protectorate in 1886 and were administered from Madagascar from 1912. On 6 July 1975 Ahmed Abdallah unilaterally declared the Comoros Islands independent. The Unilateral Declaration of Independence (UDI) notwithstanding, the independence was recognised by the UN and the OAU and the Republic of Comoros was admitted to membership of these organisations. In either case the Comoros was admitted to membership as an integrated unitary territory, that is, including Mayotte. Yet the French held on to Mayotte (because of the French naval base on the island at Dzaoudzi) and have since refused its inclusion in the Comoros Republic. The French argue that in a French-organised referendum on 8 February 1976 (seven months after Abdallah's UDI) the inhabitants of Mayotte voted to secede from the Comoros and to become and to remain French forever.

Where the government of the State concerned maintains its opposition to "unilateral secession", such opposition may or may not prevent international support or recognition for the seceding entity. On 24 September 1973, PAIGC,[23] which was in control of only liberated areas in Guinea Bissau, declared the whole of that Portuguese territory an independent sovereign state. That was a "unilateral secession". The secession was opposed by Portugal, the parent State of Guinea Bissau. The UN[24] and, a year later, Portugal itself recognised the secession notwithstanding the earlier Portuguese opposition. In 1976 POLISARIO[25] proclaimed the Western Sahara the independent Saharawi Arab Democratic Republic (SADR) against Moroccan opposition. The SADR has since been recognised by many States and is a member of the African Union in spite of the fierce opposition of Morocco, the power claiming sovereignty over the territory and militarily occupying it.

More recently, in 2008, the tiny Serbian province of Kosovo declared its independence from Serbia. Despite Serbia's (and Russia's) stiff opposition to the Kosovar secession the United States of America and European powers lost no time in recognising Kosovo's independence. In the mid-1990s two provinces of the Republic of Georgia, Abkhazia and Ossetia broke away and each asserted its separate independence. In 2008 Georgia made a determined bid to retake these provinces by force. Russia intervened with overwhelming force, expelled the Georgian forces from the breakaway provinces, occupied Georgia itself for several months and formerly recognised Abkhazia and Ossetia in the face of strong opposition from Georgia, the European Union and the United States of America.

On the other hand the fact that the parent State allows part of its territory to separate and become independent is no guarantee that rapid admission to membership of the UN will follow the "achievement of independence" or that recognition by third states will necessarily follow. By various Acts of its Parliament between 1977 and 1981, apartheid South Africa decided to "decolonize" its homelands: Transkei, Bophuthatswana, Venda, and Ciskei. These were granted "independence". But the UN adopted a number of resolutions calling for the non-recognition of these "Bantustan states". Consequently, no state ever recognized them. What this negative state practice suggests, if any thing at all, is that mere grant of independence without more by the parent state does not necessarily guarantee recognition by third states and that the matter is eminently one of politics rather than law. The policy and practice of apartheid and racial discrimination in South Africa conspired to invalidate the grant of independence to the "Black Homelands." [26] An additional reason for the non-recognition of the "Bantustan states" was the perception that the creation of those "states" amounted to territorial changes brought about by the use of force contrary to the UN Charter.[27]

One might go further and say that in the case of Rhodesia, what invalidated its claim to statehood were not so much its unilateral secession (UDI) and Britain's apparent opposition to independence. Rhodesia's UDI failed because of the policy of systematic and institutionalised racial discrimination in that country, a policy that had excited worldwide condemnation and opprobrium.

Another case of "decolonisation" of sorts by the parent State but which was opposed by the UN is that of French Togo. On 28 October 1956 the people of French Togo voted in a plebiscite to become an autonomous Republic within the French Union, but the UN refused to end the territory's trusteeship status.

The Francophone province of Quebec has made sustained efforts to "unilaterally secede from Canada." Quebec, be it noted, though French-speaking, is an integral part of Canada. The French settled Quebec and Montreal in 1608 and 1642 respectively, and in 1663 declared both areas New France. However, through military victory over French forces in Canada, the British captured Quebec in 1759 and took control of the rest of New France in 1763. According to the international law of the time and up to the early twentieth century, title to territory could validly be acquired by subjugation (conquest followed by occupation). Quebec therefore became part of the British Dominion of Canada. In 1931 Canada was proclaimed a self-governing Dominion within the British Empire, which later became the "British Commonwealth of Nations" and today has been transmuted into the Commonwealth (shorn of 'British' and 'Nations').[28]

Canada has a federal system of government. It has two 'territories' and ten provinces. Quebec is one of the ten provinces and, in spite of its minority position, has supplied most of Canada's Prime Ministers. The Meech Lake Agreement signed in June 1987 and subject to provincial ratification, gave constitutional protection to Quebec's French language and cultural specificity. It was however heavily criticized for giving Quebec too much political power. As a result the Agreement died in 1990. This sparked a separatist revival in Quebec that culminated in the Charlottetown Agreement of August 1992.

In October that year a referendum on the secession of Quebec was defeated. The Quebecois themselves voted, by a narrow margin, to remain part of Canada. However, the premier of the provincial government of Quebec promised yet another referendum on secession. The basis of these referenda is the belief or assumption that a vote in favour of secession would, by giving the government of Quebec the popular mandate, adequately expressed, entitle it to lawfully effect the secession of Quebec from Canada. Such a vote, it is also assumed, would incapacitate the national government from taking such measures as it sees fit, if it so wishes, to thwart the secession.

This brief recital of the facts relating to the Quebec case is sufficient to distinguish it, both on the facts and in law, from the Southern Cameroons case. As was earlier argued, the territory of the Southern Cameroons is not, and has never been, part of the territory of the colonising State of Cameroun Republic. The implementation of the plebiscite result aborted. Cameroun Republic simply annexed the Southern Cameroons arguing, dishonestly, that the plebiscite vote was mandate for the annexation of the territory. The UN did not even react as it had done in the case of French Togo in 1956 where the French claimed that a plebiscite they organised in the trust territory decided the incorporation of French Togo into the French Union. And yet the only territorial integrity Cameroun Republic is entitled to protect under international law is the integrity of the colonial territory to which it succeeded when it achieved independence on 1 January 1960. Any territorial claim outside that territorial framework is necessarily expansionist and is impermissible under international law.

It is submitted that the ongoing struggle in the Southern Cameroons is a case of revolt against annexation and colonial oppression in order to restore the territory's independence unlawfully suppressed by Cameroun Republic. That struggle hardly qualifies as a secessionist struggle, as has been erroneously suggested in some quarters. What Southern Cameroons is claiming is exactly the freedom French Cameroun Republic claimed from colonial occupation and what, only a few decades ago, French Cameroun claimed from France, and France itself from Nazi Germany.

There is only one sense in which the Southern Cameroons could possibly be considered a part of Cameroun Republic. It could be deemed a part of that country only in the same way in which a colonial possession used to be considered a part of the territory of the colonial power. However, the 1970 Declaration on Friendly Relations declares that a colonial territory has a separate and distinct status from that of the colonising state. What this means in concrete terms is that a colonial power cannot plead the principle of territorial integrity in an attempt to defeat the unquestionable right to self determination of the colonial territory. Moreover, it is now well settled in international human rights law that every colonial territory has a right in international law to free itself from colonial yoke by resorting to any internationally recognised means.

Conclusion

By way of concluding remarks on the subject of secession a number of points may be highlighted.

There is no general prohibition of secession from an independent state. The evidence in support of this proposition consists of the many cases of successful secessions before and after the creation of the United Nations. However, the fact that there is no international law rule that territorial units may not secede from an existing state does not suggest that territorial entities necessarily have a *right* under contemporary international law to secede from an independent state, although some commentators argue that the right of self-determination includes the "unilateral" right to secede.

The attitude of states on the matter of secession remains conditioned by politics and therefore continues to be variable. The question of right or wrong, legality or illegality, is hardly decisive.

A claim to secession need not be, and has not always been, derived from the right of self-determination, a norm of comparatively recent origin. Before the articulation of self-determination as a norm of international law, wars of independence were, and are still, conceived as just wars based on the natural law doctrine of the inherent right of peoples to free themselves from oppression and subjugation. That is why wars of national liberation are considered legitimate. Even when, in theory of law, a national liberation struggle was characterised as a secessionist bid, the separation was justified as a "remedial secession", in other words, a secession dictated by the categorical imperative of remedying a fundamental wrong, the just correction of which could not otherwise be procured. The same is still true today. Self-determination as a fundamental norm in international law is a distinct right from the inherent right of all people to freedom from tyranny, oppression and servitude.

Secession therefore has two sources. To begin with, it is a derivative right from the continuing right of self-determination applicable in a situation of colonisation, whether by a neighbouring power or a power from across the seas, and also applicable in a non-colonial context. Furthermore, secession also derives from the inherent right of all peoples, even in a non-colonial context, to liberate themselves from oppression, subjugation and exploitation. There is no small number of writers on international law who posits that there are exceptional situations in which reasons for secession, by a people, from an existing state are particularly compelling.[29] The exceptional situations include the following: a legitimate claim to territory wrongly annexed by another state; systematic oppression and domination, as well as gross and consistent violations of human rights (extreme and unremitting persecution with no reasonable prospect for peaceful change); the dissolution or breakup of a constitutive federation; powerlessness to freely determine internal political status (i.e., internal self-determination is absolutely beyond reach); unlawful suppression of self-determination (independence); a people having come under the domination of a controlling State by way of an unjustifiable historical event such as annexation or occupation; the legally suspect assumption of jurisdiction by the controlling State.

The Southern Cameroons case is indubitably not a case of secession. But even if the fantastic assumption is made that it is "secessionist" it would strongly qualify as one of those situations in which secession could be said to be legitimate; that is, a case of remedial secession based on the law of nature. For, not only did the exercise of self-determination in the Southern Cameroons misfire, it was also forcibly suppressed and the people of the territory have been languishing for decades under the oppression of Cameroun Republic. Any state that does not conduct itself in compliance with the principle of equal rights of all peoples and that of self-determination of peoples cannot invoke the prohibition against impairment of territorial integrity.[30] Nor can it rightfully appeal to force. The legitimacy of the struggle against colonial oppression or domination implies that any use of force to suppress the exercise of the right of self-determination would constitute a forbidden use of force and would qualify as aggression under international law. Any retaliatory action by the freedom fighters to repel such aggressive force would be a permissible measure of self-defence, and outside assistance to that end may be sought consistent with Article 20 (3) of the African Charter on Human and Peoples' Rights and paragraph 5 of Principle 5 of the 1970 Declaration on Friendly Relations.

Self-determination was originally conceived purely as a political rather than as a legal concept. It was included in the UN Charter seemingly as an optional principle of international law. It was therefore initially a controversial principle and its legal status and reach much disputed by academics and politicians. But it is now well settled that self-determination is a right in international law, in fact a norm of *jus cogens*. It is no longer just a process of decolonisation. It is also a human right, a right of peoples, and is thus a continuing right exercisable from time to time even within post-colonial independent states[31] and cannot be forfeited by a colonial people once they have chosen to end their state of political tutelage.³² This development occasioned little surprise. The UN itself did not confine the right of self-determination to the classic colonial situation but extended it to two non-colonial contexts: cases of foreign occupation (e.g., the occupation of Palestinian territories by Israel) and cases of racial discrimination (e.g., Rhodesia and apartheid South Africa). The justification for these extensions rested upon the "exceptional and specific" nature of those cases. But the categories of cases that are "exceptional and specific" cannot be closed.

Notes

1. Some examples of 'opting out': the Netherlands from Spain in 1579, Belgium from the Netherlands in 1830, Ecuador from the Great Colombia Republic in 1830, Greece from Turkey in 1830, Venezuela from the Colombia Union in 1830, Texas from Mexico in 1836, Zanzibar from Muscat in 1856, Panama from Colombia in 1903, Mongolia from China in 1911, Finland from Russia in 1917, Iceland from Denmark in 1918, Ireland from the United Kingdom in 1919, Pakistan from India in 1947, Senegal from the Mali Federation in 1960, Syria from the United Arab Republic in 1961, Nyasaland (Malawi) from the Central African Federation in 1963, Singapore from the Malaysia Federation in 1965, Somaliland from Somalia in 1990, the Baltic States from the USSR in 1991, Eritrea from imperial Ethiopia in 1991, and Macedonia, Slovenia, Croatia, Bosnia and Herzegovina all proclaimed their independence from Yugoslavia in 1991. As recently as 2008 Kosovo proclaimed its independence from Serbia and was recognised by many States; and two Georgian provinces (Abkhazia and Ossetia) broke away from the Republic of Georgia and declared their respective independence (recognised only by Russia). Monténégro also proclaimed its independence.

2. Cf. M Kamto, 'La montée de séparatisme au Cameroun,' *Génération*, Hors Série, No. 1, 1995, p. 10; A Kom, 'Conflits interculturels et tentative séparatiste au Cameroun,' *Cahier Francophone d'Europe-Centre-Orientale*, 5-6, tome 1, 1995, p. 143. Maurice Kamto and Ambroise Kom are serious academics and some of Cameroun Republic's foremost thinkers. But I would suggest that on this issue of what they call 'separatism' they have disappointingly failed to demonstrate intellectual rigour, allowing the imperialistic politics of their native Cameroun Republic and their French cultural prejudice to get the better of them.

3. Reiterating the principle *uti possidetis juris* the Organisation of African Union (OAU) Resolution on Border Disputes adopted in 1964 declares that 'the borders of African States, on the day of their achievement of independence, constitutes a tangible reality" and it solemnly calls on OAU Member States "to respect the frontiers existing on their achievement of national independence.' This principle of respect for borders existing on the date of achievement of independence is emphasised in key documents of the African Union (AU), which replaced the OAU in 2002, such as the Constitutive Act of the AU, the AU Solemn Declaration on a Common African Defence and Security Policy, and the Protocol Relating to the Establishment of the Peace and Security Council of the AU.

4. Shaw, op. cit., p. 796.

5. But cf. Rhodesia, Somaliland, and the Bantustans of Apartheid South Africa, unrecognized (for certain critical reasons) in spite of effective control over territory.

6. H Lauterpacht, *Recognition in International Law*, 1947, p. 407.

7. Prince Hans-Adam II of Liechtenstein, 'Self-Determination and the Future of Democracy', Paper presented at the Institute of Strategic Studies, 25 January 2001.

8. See, for example, the cases mentioned in footnote 164.

9. For example, the USSR did, and Ethiopia does. At the Bamenda All-Party Conference (26-28 June 1961) which met to adopt a common position on proposals to be included in the federal constitution, a very interesting proposal which was discussed at some length was that there should be a clause in the federal constitution providing for the legal secession of the Southern Cameroons should that become necessary. Although the Conference appeared to have shelved the proposal, it was a prescient sentiment which was never abandoned. (See, Benjamin, op. cit., p.109.) For, at the Foumban constitutional meeting in July 1961 the Southern Cameroons delegation while accepting the characterisation of the would-be new country as "one" , successfully opposed the idea that it would also be "indivisible", thus serving notice of an eventual pull-out should any future event or circumstance impose such a course.

10. For example: the cession to the USA, of Alaska by Russia, of Louisiana by France, of Texas by Mexico, and of certain islands in the West Indies by Denmark.

11. N Jayawickrama, *The Judicial Application of Human Rights Law*, Cambridge University Press, 2002, p. 228.

12. See for example, Deborah Z. Cass, 'Rethinking Self-Determination: A Critical Analysis of Current International Law Theories' 18 *Syracuse Journal of International Law* (1992) 21; Aureliu Cristescu, *The Right to Self-Determination: Historical and*

Current Development on the Basis of United Nations Instruments, UN Publication, E/CN.4/Sub.2/404/Rev.1.

13. 1975 ICJ Rep 12, 114.

14. Dinh, Daillier et Pellet, *Droit International Public*, LGDJ, Paris, 1980, p. 431.

15. UN Monthly Chronicle, February 1970, p. 40.

16. N Jayawickrama, *The Judicial Application of Human Rights Law*, p. 232.

17. The African States that recognised "Biafra" were: Cote d'Ivoire, Gabon, Tanzania, and Zambia; the non-African State was Haiti.

18. See for example J Crawford, op. cit.

19. Mazrui & Tidy, op. cit., p. 78.

20. Ibid., p. 111.

21. Ibid., p. 113.

22. Ibid., p. 52.

23. The acronym stands for *Partido Africano da Independancia de Guine e Cabo Verde* (African Party for the Independence of Guinea and Cape Verde).

24. See UNGA Resolution 3061(XXVIII).

25 Acronym for People's Front for the Liberation of Sequiet el-Hamra and Rio de Oro.

26. J Dugard, *International Law. A South African Perspective*, Juta & Co., Johannesburg, 1994, pp. 77-81.

27. JG Starke, *Starke's International Law* (11th Edition by IA Shearer), Butterworths, London, 1994, p. 143.

28. 'The word "Commonwealth" has come to be accepted as the new name for the British Empire. The parts of the Commonwealth are called "Commonwealth countries" and the self-governing Commonwealth countries are called "Members of the Commonwealth." KC Wheare, *The Constitutional Structure of the Commonwealth*, Clarendon Press, Oxford, 1960, p. 1.

29. For example, A Cassesse, *Self-determination of Peoples*, Cambridge University Press, Cambridge, 1995, p. 120; JE Stromseth, 'Self-determination, Secession and Humanitarian Intervention by the United Nations' *American Society of International Law Proceedings*, 1992, pp. 370-371; CN Okeke, *The Theory and Practice of International Law in Nigeria*, Fourth Dimension Publishers, Enugu, 1986, p. 276. And see also, L Brilmayer, 'Secession and Self-determination: A Territorial Interpretation' 16 *Yale Journal of International Law* 177 (1991); M Haile, 'Legality

of Secession: The Case of Eritrea' 8 *Emory International Law Review* 479 (1994); V Nanda, 'Self-determination under International Law: Validity of Claims to Secede,' 13 *Case Western Reserve Journal of International Law*, 257 (1981).

30. The prohibition is contained in paragraph 7 of Principle 5 of the 1970 Declaration on Principles of International Law Concerning Friendly Relations and Co-operation Among States in Accordance with the Charter of the United Nations.

31. VP Nanda, 'Self-determination Outside the Colonial Context: the Birth of Bangladesh in Retrospect' in Alexander & Friedlander (eds), *Self-determination, National, Regional and Global Dimensions*, 1980, p. 193; Klabbers & Lefeber, 'Africa: Lost between Self-determination and Uti Possidetis' in C Brolmann et al. (eds), op.cit, p.47; TM Franck, 'Postmodern Tribalism and the Right to Secession' in Brolmann, op.cit., p. 3; M Reismann, 'Coercion and Self-determination: Construing Charter Article 2(4)' 78 *American Journal of International Law*, 1984, p. 64; M. Nowak, 'The Right of Self-determination and Protection of Minorities in Central and Eastern Europe in the Light of the Case Law of the Human Rights Committee' 1 *International Journal on Group Rights*, 7 (1993); GH Tesfagiogis, 'Self-determination: Its Evolution and Practice by the United Nations and Its Application to the Case of Eritrea' 6 *Wisconsin International Law Journal*, 1987, p. 75; R Higgins, op. cit.; R Higgins, 'Africa and the Convention on Civil and Political Rights During the First Five Years of the Journal: Some Facts and Some Thoughts' 5 *Revue Africaine de Droit International et Comparé*, 1993, p. 55.

    For the old view, canvassed in the 1970s and 1980s, that self-determination is available only in a colonial context, see, for example, F Ermacora, 'Human Rights and Domestic Jurisdiction' 124 *RdC*, 1968, p. 375; K Satpal, 'Self-determination in International Law' 10 *Ind. JIL*, 1970; R Emerson, 'Self-determination' 65 *AJIL* 459, 1971; MC Smouts, 'Décolonisation et Sécession: Double Morale à l'ONU?' *Revue Française de Science Politique*, vol. 22, 1972, p. 832; Prakash Sinha, 'Has Self-determination become a Principle of International Law Today?' 14 *Ind. JIL* 332, 1974; Franck & Hoffman, 'The Right of Self-determination in Very Small Places' 8 *New York University Journal of International Law and Politics*, 1976, p. 331; G Haile, 'The Unity and Territorial Integrity of Ethiopia' 24 *The Journal of Modern African Studies*, 1986, p. 465.

32. Jayawickrama, op. cit., p. 231.

Chapter Eleven
Determination not by the "Self", but by the "Other"

Decolonisation of the Third World occupied a major part of the activities of the United Nations during the first three decades of its existence. The decolonisation efforts of the UN derived from (i) Chapters XI, XII and XIII of its Charter devoted to the interests of dependent peoples, and (ii) two distinct but interrelated rights under international law, the equal rights of peoples, and the right of self-determination of peoples.[1] Since 1960 the UN has also been guided in its decolonisation efforts by the Declaration on the Granting of Independence to Colonial Countries and Peoples[2] by which UN Member States proclaimed the necessity of bringing colonialism to a speedy end.

The UN was thus able to use self-determination as the basis for decolonisation even before the normative status of that principle became generally recognised. Self-determination quickly became the battle cry of colonial peoples in their struggle for independence. While some colonial territories achieved independence consensually others did so through armed struggle.[3] In the vast majority of cases of consensual decolonisation[4] sovereignty was simply transferred to the new state and devolution agreements providing for the inheritance of certain treaties were concluded between the departing colonial power and the new state.

In a few cases of consensual decolonisation the plebiscite procedure was employed for the purpose of ascertaining the wishes of the people of the colonial territory on the question of independence. One example is the popular consultation organised by Belgium in the Trust Territory of Ruanda-Urundi, the outcome of which was the division of the territory into two, one half achieving independence as the Republic of Rwanda and the other as the Republic of Burundi. The UN itself used the plebiscite in some cases to ascertain the freely expressed wish of a given population,[5] whenever it was satisfied that the population in question constituted *a people* within the meaning of the legal right to self-determination.[6] It appeared therefore that the plebiscite was considered a legitimate method of the exercise of that right.[7]

More often than not the exercise of that right resulted in the establishment of a sovereign independent state. It was not the case though that independence had always to be the result of the exercise of the right. In terms of relevant United Nations resolutions, termination of colonial status may result in any of the following political status options: (i) independence, (ii) internal autonomy within a freely formed association, (iii) integration in an independent state, or (iv) emergence into any other political status freely determined by the people.[8] It therefore stands to reason that to be meaningful a self-determination plebiscite has to avail the people concerned with all the above-mentioned political status options. Whenever independence has been included among the available options, the people concerned have invariably opted for it.

A free and informed choice from the various options would amount to a full exercise of the right to self-determination and would result in complete decolonisation. Dependent status (annexation, occupation, or recolonisation) cannot possibly be a permissible mode of implementing the right to self-determination. If a colonial territory is transferred to another state for occupation, annexation or colonisation *de novo* it cannot, by any stretch of the imagination, be said that the territory in question has thereby been decolonised. The termination of colonial status, even where it results in integration with an independent state, must, at the very minimum, result in autonomy or internal self-government for the territory in question.[9]

The "decolonisation" of the Southern Cameroons is a compelling case study of a self-determination process marred throughout by serious defects and controversy, to the extent that any informed person would readily argue that the exercise was so deeply flawed that it never resulted in the real decolonisation of the territory.

The plebiscite in the Southern Cameroons did not avail the people of the territory with all the political status options provided in relevant United Nations resolutions on decolonisation. The so-called "two alternatives" were not alternative status options. There was only one political status option: dependent status The people of the Southern Cameroons were simply required to choose between becoming a dependency of either of its two neighbours, Cameroun Republic or Nigeria The idea of "two alternatives" was thus a grievous misrepresentation and one that went to the very root of the plebiscite. That being the case it can hardly be said that the people of the territory freely decided their political status.

This misrepresentation was further compounded by the use of the vague term "join". The expressions free association, integration, and independence appear in relevant UN resolutions on the subject of decolonisation and already had a settled meaning. These terms or some other clear and simple language ought to have been used rather than the rather woolly word "join". It may thus be said that in the circumstances there was a constructive denial of the full exercise of the right to self-determination and that the plebiscite seemed to have been more of an officially organised procedure to enable the unlawful transfer of the Southern Cameroons to a willing successor colonialist. One Plebiscite Supervisory Officer remarked many years later:

> I saw the whole plebiscite as a cynical public relations exercise, designed to demonstrate to the world at large that the people of the Southern Cameroons were being given freedom of choice, whereas in fact the only choice they really wanted was denied to them.[10]

The decolonisation of the Southern Cameroons was beset with problems right from the outset. At the Nigerian Constitutional Conference in London in 1957, Mr. Alan Lennox-Boyd, the British Secretary of State for the Colonies declared that there could be no question of obliging the Southern Cameroons to remain part of an independent Nigeria contrary to its own wishes. He further stated that before Nigeria became independent the people of the Southern Cameroons would have to say freely[11] what their wishes were as to their own future. But he hastened to add ominously:

> Among the options open to them would be to continue under the Trusteeship Administration of the United Kingdom. I must in fairness add the warning that *you would not thereby be given the golden key to the Bank of England!* But many of the best friends of the Southern Cameroons do not foresee a destiny more likely to promote her happiness and prosperity than in continued association with Nigeria.[12]

Between late October and early November 1958, a UN Visiting Mission was despatched to the Trust Territories in West Africa.[13] On 5 December 1958, the UN General Assembly adopted Resolution 1282 (XIII) in which it noted, inter alia, the statement by the Representative of the United Kingdom that the Cameroons under British Administration was expected to achieve in 1960 the objectives set forth in Articles 76b of the UN Charter.[14]

The United Nations Visiting Mission sent to West Africa was composed of Georges Salomon (Haiti), Rikhi Jaipal (India), W.G. Thorp (New Zealand) and Benjamin Gering (USA), chairman. Its mandate, as specified by the Trusteeship Council, was to report as fully as possible on the steps taken towards the realisation of the objectives set forth in Article 76b of the UN Charter.[15] As part of its terms of reference it was also requested to include in its report on the Cameroons under United Kingdom administration, its views on the method of consultation that should be adopted when the time came for the people of the Territory to express their wishes concerning their future.[16]

In the Southern Cameroons the Mission found among the political parties a marked division of opinion. According to the Mission's report, one group of parties favoured staying with Nigeria; another group favoured separation therefrom and subsequent union with an independent French Cameroun. Given the clear division between these approaches, the Mission came to the conclusion that only the people of the Southern Cameroons, consulted by means of universal suffrage, could determine where the majority lay.[17]

Between the Mission's visit and the completion of its report, elections were held to the Southern Cameroons House of Assembly in January 1959. The party favouring separation from Nigeria, the KNDP, came to power with fourteen seats, against twelve won by the two parties standing for permanent federation with Nigeria, the KNC and KPP. The Mission considered that a new political situation had thus been created which had to be given the necessary time to evolve further. It was felt that the new political situation could produce general agreement on the future of the Southern Cameroons or, failing that, it could allow the "practicable choices" confronting the people to be precisely formulated.[18]

The Mission concluded that if general agreement should develop in the newly elected House of Assembly concerning the future of the Southern Cameroons, a formal popular consultation might prove to be unnecessary; but if no such agreement emerged, it might only be through a consultation, probably a plebiscite, at some appropriate future date that it would be possible to resolve the basic issues. In that event, the Mission considered that the conditions for such a consultation, including its timing and the question(s) to be put to the people, would have to be determined by the General Assembly and the Administering Authority in consultation, and as far as possible in agreement, with the political parties in the Southern Cameroons.[19]

At the request of the General Assembly, the Trusteeship Council examined the report of the Visiting Mission on the Cameroons under United Kingdom administration. After doing so the Council transmitted it back, with the observations of the Administering Authority and the records of its discussions, to the General Assembly for appropriate action in accordance with Article 76b of the United Nations Charter.

On 13 March 1959, the Assembly adopted Resolution 1350 (XIII). The resolution recommended that Britain, in pursuance of Article 76 b, take steps, in consultation with a United Nations Plebiscite Commissioner, to organise, under the supervision of the United Nations, a plebiscite in the Southern Cameroons in order to ascertain the wishes of the people of the territory concerning their future.[20] The Assembly expressed the hope that all concerned in the territory would endeavour to reach agreement, before the opening of its 14th session, on the alternatives to be put in the plebiscite and the qualifications for voting in it.[21]

At the 14th session the Administering Authority informed the General Assembly, incorrectly, that a plebiscite conference held in Mamfe for two days and presided over by an "independent" chairman, Sir Sidney Phillipson, had failed to reach agreement either on the alternatives to be put to the people or on the qualifications for voting. In truth, however, the outcome of the Mamfe Plebiscite Conference, held from 10-11 August 1959, clearly showed that the delegates wanted integration into or secession from Nigeria to be the choices to be put to the people, it being clearly understood that secession from Nigeria necessarily meant emerging as a sovereign independent state.

During the Conference the *Fon* (King) of Bafut expressed the sentiment of the day when he made the following prescient observation:

> We rejected Dr Endeley because he wanted to take us to Nigeria. If Mr Foncha tries to take us to French Cameroun we shall also run away from him [...] French Cameroun is 'fire' and Nigeria is 'water'. I support secession [from Nigeria] without unification [with French Cameroun].[22]

Since the UN bought Britain's incorrect information on the plebiscite alternatives to be put to the people, the Southern Cameroons Premier, Mr. Foncha, and the Leader of the Opposition, Dr Endeley, issued an agreed statement to the General Assembly.[23] They agreed on the voting qualifications as put forward in a draft resolution submitted by Ghana, Guinea, Liberia, Libya, Mexico, Morocco, Sudan, Tunisia, United Arab Republic and the United States of America. But they suggested that in view of the failure of the political parties (as distinct from the majority view that emerged from the all-stakeholders conference at Mamfe) to reach agreement on the plebiscite alternatives, it would be wise to defer consultation with the people until sometime in 1962 and that the Trusteeship Agreement 'should be terminated not later than 26 October 1962, in accordance with Article 76 of the United Nations Charter'.

The draft resolution was approved by the Fourth Committee on 9 October 1959. It was adopted by the General Assembly on 16 October 1959 as Resolution 1352 (XIV). In terms of this resolution the arrangements for the plebiscite in the Southern Cameroons had to begin on 30 September 1960, and the plebiscite had to be concluded not later than March 1961. The Assembly recommended that only persons born in the Southern Cameroons or one of whose parents was born in the Southern Cameroons should vote in the plebiscite. It decided that the two questions to be put at the plebiscite should be:

(a) Do you wish to achieve independence by joining the independent Federation of Nigeria?
(b) Do you wish to achieve independence by joining the independent Republic of the Cameroons?

The "decolonisation" process of the Southern Cameroons was thus set in motion. That rocess was plagued throughout by misfortune and various "sins" of omission and commission.

First, Resolution 1352 (XIV) left out a critical self-determination status option: emergence as an independent sovereign state. Second, the Administering Authority suppressed the emerging clear, substantial and vocal body of opinion in the Southern Cameroons in favour of outright separate independence for the territory. Third, the Southern Cameroons electorate in December 1958 / January 1959 failed to vote to the House of Assembly a substantial number of Members of Parliament (MPs) in favour of independence either then or deferred. In extenuation it may be said that separation from Nigeria, and not independence, was the issue on which that election was fought.

Fourth, the political leaders failed to reach agreement on a common stand regarding the issue of independence; they failed to insist on separate independence for the Southern Cameroons, in part because of the incorrect view put out by the Administering Authority that the territory was not economically viable. They failed to insist on deferment of consultation with the people to 1962. The political elite of the Southern Cameroons at the time must therefore bear some degree of responsibility for the continuing shameful status of the Southern Cameroons as a colonial territory.

Fifth, had British Southern Cameroons not been a practising democracy the stand of the Opposition that the territory be permanently federated to Nigeria would have been disregarded. The ruling party's position that the Southern Cameroons should first achieve independence before considering the question of possible association with Cameroun Republic would have been the only one on the table and would have prevailed.[24] Thus, in a perverse way the democratic culture of the Southern Cameroons worked, at a critical juncture of its history, against its very interest; because in the absence of democracy there would have been no alternative views to those of the ruling party with which to contend and, conceivably, there would have been no need for a plebiscite. Separate independence would have been achieved, notwithstanding the jaundiced view of the Administering Authority that the territory was not economically viable.

Sixth, by administering the Southern Cameroons as a dependency of Nigeria, rather than directly from London as a distinct and separate territory, the United Kingdom Government created an environment that tended to eclipse the issue of separate independence for the Southern Cameroons. It is therefore hardly surprising that much of the political struggle in the territory was about securing its separation from Nigeria. Had there been no forced administrative union with Nigeria the issue of outright independence would have been the primary focus of Southern Cameroons politicians. There would have been no question of "joining" either Nigeria or Cameroun Republic.

Seventh, even though the "administrative union" provision in the various trusteeship agreements came in for much criticism by the Trusteeship Council the UK Government nevertheless used the provision to constitute British Cameroons into an administrative union with the adjacent British non-self-governing territory of Nigeria. The UN did resolve that such unions must remain strictly administrative in nature and that they should not impede separate development of the territory.[25] But it took no further action on this matter. The constitution of British Cameroons into an administrative union with Nigeria did impede, and very much so, the separate development of the Southern Cameroons. It impacted negatively on the territory.

Eighth, it was unseemly of the UN to have stampeded the Southern Cameroons into a plebiscite. Foncha and Endeley had requested its deferment to 1962. The UN studiously ignored that paper request and went ahead to impose a plebiscite to be concluded 'not later than March 1961'. This *diktat* deprived the Southern Cameroons of much-needed breathing space, and time for cogitation on a very serious matter. The interest of the people of the territory and their country called for full information on the plebiscite, for cool and mature reflection, and for thoughtful action rather than precipitated action and a hurried decision. The Southern Cameroons was not drowning; and the plebiscite was not a God-ordained life jacket for rescuing the territory from a perceived perdition. Since Britain was being selfishly tight-fisted, the UN should have taken direct administration of the territory for a year or so pending a well informed and mature decision on its future. Had the plebiscite been deferred just to 1962 as the political leadership of the territory had requested there would certainly have been the third option of separate independence, consistent with the 1960 Declaration on Decolonisation, and the vote would have gone in favour of that option!²⁶

Ninth, the unjustifiable refusal to defer the plebiscite to 1962 was not the only gross injustice committed by the UN. Not only was the status option of separate independence denied to the people of the territory, deceptive language was used in the formulation of the plebiscite questions.

Tenth, the so-called "two alternatives" were in fact not status options at all but an unwarranted imposition on the Southern Cameroons to "join", willy-nilly, one or the other of its two contiguous neighbours, which was the imposition of a new colonial power on the Southern Cameroons.²⁷ Neither the option of "joining" Nigeria nor that of "joining" Cameroun Republic made any sense at all. In 1954 the Southern Cameroons had advisedly refused to be involved in Nigerian politics and in 1960 achieved the separation from Nigeria it had long wanted. How then could going back to Nigeria have become a politically correct "alternative"? Cameroun Republic is an alien land and was, at that time, awash with blood and literally in flames. How then could anyone who meant well for Southern Cameroons have made "joining" that country a sincere "alternative"? The Southern Cameroons was never pro-Nigeria. It was emphatically not pro-Cameroun Republic. It desired statehood, and if it was pro anything it could only have been pro-British.²⁸

The plebiscite campaign, in January/February 1961, confirmed the fact, known at least one year previously, that the Southern Cameroons found neither of the claimed "two alternatives" acceptable. The people of the territory questioned why the option of emergence as a sovereign independent state was denied them. Recently declassified British secret files on the Southern Cameroons throw a great deal of light on this matter. Field reports on the plebiscite enlightenment campaign filed by the Plebiscite Supervisory Officers stated that the general reaction of the people to the plebiscite was one of *'interested bewilderment'*.²⁹ Even some Plebiscite Supervisory Officers saw the plebiscite as "a fraudulent exercise."³⁰

According to field reports the Plebiscite Supervisory Officers were repeatedly asked the following painful questions everywhere they went:[31] 'Why have we not a third choice?', 'Why should a poor man sell his independence to join with bigger and richer men?', 'What should we do if we do not like either choice?' These nagging questions, to which the officers frankly confessed they had no answers, clearly indicated that the people did not relish the prospect of "joining" either Nigeria or Cameroun Republic. They wanted separate independence so as to be able to manage their own affairs and control their own lives and destiny, like all free peoples of the world.

The field reports were unanimous in their conclusion that, 'There was widespread ignorance of what exactly Cameroun Republic was' and that 'villagers have very little idea of what the outcome of the plebiscite may mean.'[32] Indeed, because the plebiscite question talked of 'the independent Republic of *the Cameroons*', a significant number of people construed the second plebiscite question as meaning, 'Do you wish to achieve independence by becoming the independent Republic of the Cameroons?'[33]

A strong majority of the people clearly did not want to revert to the *status quo ante* of integration into Nigeria. They did not want to go back to Nigeria, largely because of fear of Ibo domination. But at the same time they also had very strong misgivings about "joining" Cameroun Republic, a *terra incognita*, a foreign country profoundly different in language; history and culture; political and constitutional development, attitudes and loyalties; administrative and legal systems; educational and social culture; a country in the throes of a horrid terrorism and steeped in a culture of intolerance and violence. The Southern Cameroons Premier and his colleagues in Government clearly stated that they wanted a continued period of trusteeship administration to be followed by full independence, after which the people would then be asked to decide whether they wished to "join" Nigeria or Cameroun Republic.[34]

Notwithstanding its awareness of the openly ventilated sentiments of the people and the publicly stated stance of the Premier and his ministerial colleagues, the Administering Authority, eager to keep its 'golden key to the Bank of England', presumptuously claimed that 'many of the best friends of the

[Southern] Cameroons do not foresee a destiny more likely to promote her happiness and prosperity than in continued association with Nigeria'.[35] The Administering Authority then decided on applying sustained pressure on the Government of the Southern Cameroons to hush up its stated view and prevent the emergence of any movement in the territory in favour of sovereign statehood.[36] The British Government acted unconscionably and shirked its responsibilities. One of the Plebiscite Supervisory Officers had no doubt the British Government abnegated its responsibilities in the Southern Cameroons.

> I felt increasingly disenchanted with the while [plebiscite] process, because I still felt that the British Government had abnegated its responsibilities, forcing the people to make a difficult decision, with far-reaching consequences, without adequate preparation. Many Southern Cameroonians continued to plead for the colonial administration to be prolonged for a little longer, to give them a chance to make informed decisions about the future, but both the UN and the colonial authorities had refused to countenance this option. On the contrary, with Ian MacLeod as Colonial Secretary, I knew that the British Government of the day was only too eager to wash its hands of the Cameroons and every other colonial territory it could possibly consider 'ready' for independence, as quickly and painlessly as possible. [...] Whenever the cost of running the territories exceeded the revenue from taxation, which was certainly the case in the Cameroons, the British were only too pleased to dump them as soon as they decently could.[37]

The status option of separate independence is one of the three modes of implementing the exercise of the right to self-determination. This is provided for in UN resolutions 648 and 742 of 1952, and 1541 (XV) of 15 December 1960. This option was left out at the behest of the British Government. The pretext was that the Southern Cameroons would not be economically viable as an independent state.[38] This malicious myth was invented to serve Britain's pro-Nigerian interest. Britain feared that if the Southern

Cameroons were allowed to become independent, the Northern Cameroons would choose a similar path and that, the British reasoned, would upset Britain's relationship with Nigeria as a whole for a long time to come.[39] Britain was therefore more interested in the British Cameroons as mere infill at the eastern border of Nigeria[40] Moreover, Britain believed that an independent Southern Cameroons would make a lot of demands on its coffers by way of requests for aid and this, in the eyes of the UK Government, was an abomination since the territory, as was believed, had no resources of benefit to the UK

During debates in the Fourth Committee of the UN, on the future of the Southern Cameroons, uninformed views (based on the 'non-viability' smear peddled by the UK Government) were expressed about the territory being economically unable to stand on its own as a sovereign independent state.[41] These views were simply an echo of the jaundiced view expressed by one person, Sir Phillipson, in a 1958 British-commissioned one-man economic report on the Southern Cameroons,[42] as already mentioned in chapter four. The report was commissioned to be ready in time for use at the 1959 meeting of the Trusteeship Council and the General Assembly. Its purpose was to provide to UN Members "the evidence" of the UK Government's self-serving opposition to independence for the Southern Cameroons.

As it happened the full report could not be ready by its expected date of completion. But Sir Phillipson did put together a hasty draft the conclusion of which was that an independent Southern Cameroons would not be economically viable. Sir Andrew Cohen repeated this line over and over at the UN and the trick was done. The view stated in the final and completed Report that was eventually produced was, however, not as categorical as the view earlier stated in the draft despatched for use by the British UN Mission. It was qualified. It concluded, of course, that the Southern Cameroons 'could only exist as a separate entity on a precarious hand to mouth basis and would not be viable as a completely independent sovereign state.'[43] But the sting of that conclusion was tempered with the following rider: 'The Southern Cameroons would not *at its present state of development*, be viable. *A further period of Trusteeship, if adequate, might afford the Southern Cameroons the time it needs to develop and test its financial strength.*'[44]

But this learning no longer mattered. The earlier draft, evidently skewed to allay the political and financial concerns of the UK Government, had served its intended purpose at the UN. The British Government thus succeeded in distorting the meaning of the right of self-determination. In terms of that right it is the people that determine the destiny of the territory; but according to the British Government it is the territory that determines the destiny of the people.

At the time of the plebiscite in February 1961, Sir Phillipson's Report was about two years out of date. There was no further assessment of the economic self-reliance of the territory either by the UK Government or the UN itself. In *News Relay* No.16 of 12 December 1960, Jesco Manga William's Cameroons Indigenes Party (CIP) commented:

> The experts had apparently made it clear that the Southern Cameroons can stand on her own feet and, in practice, Sir Phillipson's Report which advised against independence for the Southern Cameroons because of its poor economy was now out of date.

The CIP's statement was corroborated by a 1963 report on the territory. In 1963 Professor D.E. Gardinier of the London Institute of Race Relations undertook an economic survey of the Southern Cameroons. The Report on the survey made this pertinent observation:

> Before 'reunification', the Southern Cameroons progressed peacefully both economically and politically. The balance of trade from 1956 to 1961 for exports and imports of the Southern Cameroons as presented by the Secretary of State for Finance (Hon. A.N. Jua) to the West Cameroon House of Assembly as from the 9th to 13th July, 1962, showed that the balance of trade for the Southern Cameroons was consistently favourable.[45]

This Report debunked the economic non-viability smeared on the Southern Cameroons by the UK Government.

The Southern Cameroons was, and still is, self-sufficient in food and an important producer of petroleum, rubber, palms (oil and kernel), tea, coffee, cocoa, bananas and timber. It has commercial quantities of oil and gas, production of which officially started in the mid-1970s. It is extremely unlikely that the British did not know of the existence of petroleum in the Rio del Rey and Bakassi Peninsulas in the Southern Cameroons. By 1959 Nigeria was known to have commercial quantities of hydrocarbon reserves in the "Bight of Biafra", a geographical area that includes the coastal stretches of the Southern Cameroons. The British petroleum company, BP, was very active drilling oil in the Nigerian delta area abutting on Southern Cameroon's Bakassi and Rio del Rey maritime areas. The British could not therefore have been unaware of oil reserves offshore in British Southern Cameroons. The so-called economic non-viability of British Southern Cameroons would therefore seem to have been a self-serving fable and a hoax.

That misinformation and disinformation about "economic non-viability" had the additional effect of weakening the bargaining power of the Southern Cameroons in its negotiation with Cameroun Republic. Even discounting the oil equation, the territory is blessed with adequate natural resources sufficient to ensure its steady economic growth and development. Less economically endowed colonial territories in Africa and elsewhere have acceded to independence as sovereign states. Economic self-sufficiency is not a pre-condition for political emancipation. With substantial economic resources, a current indigenous population of about 6 million inhabitants, and a land area of 43,000 square kilometres, the Southern Cameroons would not answer the description of a "mini-state".[46] At any rate, in international law, even the smallest territories are entitled, in exercise of the right to self-determination, to attain independence.[47]

Moreover, the exercise of that right is not conditioned upon the attainment of economic self-reliance. 'Inadequacy of political, economic, social or educational preparedness should never serve as a pretext for delaying independence.'[48] While economic viability can be used to support a claim to entitlement to independence, economic non-viability cannot be used as an excuse to deny a colonial territory the right to emerge as a sovereign independent state.

The story does not end with the red herring about economic non-viability. Trusteeship Council Resolution 2013 (XXXVI) of 31 May 1960 left it to the various concerned parties, acting jointly or severally, to put whatever meaning they wished on the vague term "to join" used in framing the plebiscite questions. That again was yet another travesty of the right of self-determination. Nigeria and Cameroun Republic were each invited to offer the constitutional terms and conditions under which each expected the Southern Cameroons to join her. What this meant was that the decision on the destiny of the people of the Southern Cameroons was not allowed to remain exclusively within the hands of the people of the territory themselves and to be taken by them alone. Outsiders were brought in to participate in a most significant manner in deciding the destiny of the Southern Cameroons.

One therefore finds a most anomalous situation whereby (i) the UN imposed on the Southern Cameroons the dead-end option of joining Nigeria or Cameroun Republic: that was determination by the UN rather than by the "self"; (ii) the UN excluded from the plebiscite the status option of emergence into sovereign statehood: that meant there was made available only the option of continuing dependent status rather than the full scope of status options to choose from; (iii) the UN and the UK Government excluded the option of separate independence for the Southern Cameroons on the ground of the territory's supposed non-economic viability: that meant it was the territory to determine the destiny of the people rather than the people determining the destiny of the territory; and (iv) the UN requested Nigeria and Cameroun Republic to each offer the terms and conditions under which they might accept joinder with the Southern Cameroons: that meant the decision on the future of the people of the Southern Cameroons was not entirely in their own hands but decisively in the hands of outsiders.

In the result there was no determination by the "self", no free choice from all the internationally recognised political status options, no determination by the people of the destiny of their territory, and no decision wholly by the people themselves on their own future.

Notes

1. These rights are mentioned expressly in Articles 1(2) and 55, and impliedly in Articles 73b and 76b, of the Charter of the United Nations. See also, Articles 19 and 20 of the African Charter on Human and Peoples' Rights.

2. UN Resolution 1514 (XV) of 14 December 1960, also known as the Declaration on Decolonisation.

3. VR Nanda, 'Self-Determination in International Law,' (1972) 66 *AJIL* 321; R Emerson, 'Self-Determination,' (1971) *AJIL* 459; M Nowak, 'The Right of Self-determination and the Protection of Minorities in Central and Eastern Europe in the Light of the Case Law of the Human Rights Committee,' 1 *International Journal on Group Rights* (1993), p.7; BG Ramcharan, 'Individual, Collective and Group Rights: History, Theory, Practice and Contemporary Evolution,' 1 *International Journal on Group Rights* (1993), p.27. (Dates in parentheses as in the journals).

4. G Wasserman, 'The Politics of Consensual Decolonization,' *The African Review Journal*, vol. 5, no. 1, 1975, p. 1.

5. M Merle, 'Les Plébiscites Organisés par les Nations Unies,' 7 *Annuaire Français du Droit International* (1961) 426.

6. M Pomerance, 'Methods of Self-Determination and the Argument of "Primitiveness",' *Canadian Yearbook of International Law*, Vol. XII (1974), p. 34.

7. Ibid; Merle, op. cit.

8. UN General Assembly Resolutions 648 and 742 of 1952, Resolution 1541 (XV) of 1960 and Resolution 2625 (XXV) of 1970 (Declaration on Principles of International Law Concerning Friendly Relations and Cooperation Among States in Accordance with the Charter of the United Nations). The more authoritative Resolution 1541 (XV) defines the three legitimate political status options offering full self-government as free association with an independent state, integration into an independent state, or independence. Resolution 2625 (XXV), also known as the Declaration on Friendly Relations declares that the 'establishment of a sovereign and independent state, the free association or integration with an independent state, or the emergence into any other political status freely determined by a people constitute modes of implementing the right of self-determination by the people.'

9. UNGA Resolution 1541 (XV) of 15 December 1960.

10. J Percival, *The 1961 Cameroon Plebiscite: Choice or Betrayal*, Langaa Research & Publishing, Bamenda, 2008, p. 78.

11. In the event, the so-called "two alternatives" imposed by the UN meant that the people of the Southern Cameroons were in fact never allowed to say *freely* what their wishes were as to their future.

12. Statement of the British Secretary of State for the Colonies, Mr. Alan Lennox-Boyd at the conclusion of the May-June 1957 London conference on the Nigerian constitution. Emphasis added.

13. *Yearbook of the United Nations* 1958, pp. 346-349; Report of the United Nations Plebiscite Commissioner for the Cameroons under United Kingdom Administration on the Plebiscites in the Northern and Southern Cameroons, 15th Session, 1961, Addendum to Agenda Item 13, UN Doc. A/4727, paragraphs 5 - 12, and also UN Doc. T/1556 of 3 April 1961.

14. "76. The basic objectives of the trusteeship system, in accordance with the purposes of the United Nations laid down in Article 1 of the present Charter, shall be: [...] b. to promote the political, economic, social, and education advancement of the inhabitants of the trust territories, and their progressive development towards self-government or independence as may be appropriate to the particular circumstances of each territory and its peoples and the freely expressed wishes of the peoples concerned, and as may be provided by the terms of each trusteeship agreement."

15. See, *Report of Visiting Mission to the Cameroons under United Kingdom Administration*, 1958, 23rd Session, 1959, Suppl. 2, UN Doc. T/1426.

16. Ibid.

17. Ibid.

18. Ibid. It was not made clear from whose perspective these 'practicable choices' were to be assessed.

19. Ibid.

20. *Report of the Plebiscite Commissioner*, paragraphs 13, 15 – 17.

21. The Report of the Plebiscite Commissioner captures in paragraph 19 the differing points of view of the Southern Cameroons' political leadership on the alternative questions to be asked at the impending plebiscite and on the qualifications to vote thereat: 'Mr. Foncha considered that the alternatives should be regional status within an independent Nigeria or separation from Nigeria and continued Trusteeship for a limited period after which a decision could be made. Dr Endeley, Mr. Mbile and Mr. Ntumazah agree with Mr. Foncha on the first alternative but favoured unification with an independent French Cameroun as the second alternative. On the question of qualifications, Mr. Foncha believed that only

those born in the Southern Cameroons should be entitled to vote in the plebiscite and in this he was supported by Mr. Ntumazah. Dr Endeley and Mr. Mbile, however, felt that the register should include certain residents not born in the Territory.' It is ironical that Endeley and Mbile who first suggested 'unification' with independent French Cameroun later vigorously opposed that option, while Foncha who initially opposed it later became its exponent! The Endeley-Mbile thesis on voter qualification would have given the vote to resident Nigerians and to the large Camerounese émigré community that had sought and obtained refuge in the Southern Cameroons in order to escape repression, *travaux forcés*, and *indigénat* in their native French Cameroun.

22. See Chem-Langhee & Njeuma, 'The Pan-Kamerun Movement 1949-1961,' in Kale (ed.), *An African Experiment in Nation-Building: The Bilingual Cameroon Republic since Reunification*, Westview Press, 1980, p. 54.

23. See *Agreed Statement by Mr. JN Foncha, Premier of the Southern Cameroons, and Dr EML Endeley, Leader of the Opposition in the Southern Cameroons House of Assembly*, 14th Session, 1959, Annexes, Agenda Item 41, UN Doc. A/C.4/414.

24. In French Cameroun, for example, when it was to achieve independence it was only the position of Ahidjo as Premier of the territory that counted; that of the various opposition groups was ignored. That country, of course has never known democracy, before or after independence.

25. United Nations General Assembly Resolution 224(III) of 18 November 1948.

26. The Declaration is emphatic that colonial powers must take immediate steps to transfer all powers to the colonised peoples without any reservation and that economic non-viability cannot be invoked as an excuse for delaying independence. It proclaims "the necessity of bringing to a speedy and unconditional end colonialism in all its forms and manifestations" and declares that immediate steps must be taken in all territories which have not yet attained independence "to transfer all powers to the peoples of those territories without any conditions or reservations in accordance with their freely expressed will and desire [...] in order to enable them to enjoy complete independence and freedom."

27. Cameroun Republic has since sought, vainly, to anchor its colonisation of the Southern Cameroons on a concept of 'colonisation by consent', which consent is said to have been given at the plebiscite, and which colonisation is claimed to have been facilitated and sanctioned by the United Nations in Resolution 1608.

28. E Ardener, in *West Africa*, 1961, pp. 878-879. Emphasis added.

29. Doc. No. 25/A.P.A/11 of 28 October 1960, report on the First Enlightenment Campaign from Assistant Plebiscite Administrator Wum to the Deputy Plebiscite Administrator, Buea.

30. J Percival, op. cit., p. 41.

31. Ibid.

32. Ibid.

33. Ibid.

34. The Communiqué issued after the British/Southern Cameroons talks in London from 10 - 13 October 1960 stated as follows: 'Mr. Foncha, the Premier of the Southern Cameroons expressed the hope that the United Nations would be prepared, if the vote went in favour of the Cameroun Republic, to agree to a period of independence for the Southern Cameroons during which preparations would be made for the unification of the Southern Cameroons with the Cameroun Republic on a federal basis.' *Report of the Plebiscite Commissioner*, paragraph 68.

35. See, Statement of the British Secretary of State for the Colonies, Mr. Alan Lennox-Boyd at the conclusion of the May-June 1957 London Conference on the Nigerian Constitution.

36. A confidential despatch dated 7 June 1960, from Sir Andrew Cohen, the UK Representative at the United Nations, to Mr. Eastwood at the Colonial Office in London, stated: 'I believe a firm attitude on this now may save us a great deal of trouble later and I think that H.M.G.'s position should be made abundantly clear to Foncha in an effort to scotch tendencies towards the third question [...] I think it may be necessary to tell Field [Commissioner of the Southern Cameroons] firmly that the policy of H.M.G. is to discourage any tendency towards a third question very strongly.' Four months later, on 11 October 1960, the same Sir Andrew sent to the Secretary of State (repeated for information to the Commissioner of the Southern Cameroons) a confidential memo which read in part: 'First, [...] objections [...] to establishment of a separate Southern Cameroons State remains as strong as ever. Its intrinsic weakness would make it a constant source of possible friction between Nigeria and Cameroun, with possibility of intervention from Ghana, Guinea and other African States [...] We have always argued that separate independence [for the Southern Cameroons] would produce an entirely unviable state." *Declassified Secret Files on the Southern Cameroons*, Public Records Office, London.

37. Percival, op. cit., pp. 77-78.

38. A 'Top Secret' despatch dated 13 June 1960 from CB Boothby, British Foreign Office, to PM Johnston, UK Ambassador to Cameroun Republic, declared in part: "We are not attracted to the idea of an independent Southern Cameroons because it would certainly not be able to pay its way and, as you suggest, we are not at all anxious to have to do so on its behalf. We cannot gain any advantage

from being foster mother to an independent Southern Cameroons and it is clear that it would have to be fostered by somebody. The responsibility would only be likely to embarrass us with the Nigerian and Cameroun Governments in turn." *Declassified Secret Files on the Southern Cameroons*, Public Records Office, London.

39. On 12 October 1960, Lord Perth, Minister of State at the Colonial Office, sent a confidential memo to Sir John Martin of the Colonial Office, in which he wrote: "We discussed Mr. Eastwood's telegram Personal No. 4 and agreed that the all-important thing is to take Nigeria along with us in any action [...] What would worry me is if a sequel to the Southern Cameroon's try for independence was that the Northern Cameroons went the same way. That would really, I think, upset our relationship with Nigeria as a whole and for a long time to come, and that is something which we must at all cost avoid. *The Southern Cameroons and its inhabitants are undoubtedly expendable* in relation to this." Emphasis added. *Declassified Secret Files on the Southern Cameroons*, Public Records Office, London.

40. E Ardener, 'The Political History of Cameroon,' *The World Today*, vol. 18, no. 8. August 1962, p. 343.

41. At the Fourth Committee of the General Assembly of the UN in October 1959, the following remarks were made on the viability of the Southern Cameroons: Mr. Foncha "recognised that separation [from Nigeria] would entail economic hardship for some time to come." Mr. Mbile said the Southern Cameroons "could not achieve independence as a separate country because it was not economically viable." In reply to questions on this subject by the Representatives of Czechoslovakia and India, Sir Andrew Cohen, the British UN Representative, expressed the opinion that "an independent Southern Cameroons would have serious financial and economic problems; added difficulties concerning staff would make those problems even harder to solve." Mr. Ntumazah said the Southern Cameroons "could not of itself constitute a viable economic unit." Mr. Edmond of New Zealand said "the independence of the Southern Cameroons as a separate entity was ruled out by economic considerations." Krishna Menon, the Indian Representative said that "an independent territory which is not economically self-sufficient might in a very short time find itself under foreign economic domination." Espinosa the Mexican Representative pointed out that no satisfactory definition had ever been given of the necessary prerequisite of an independent state but that after listening to the various statements that had been made about the non-economic viability of the Southern Cameroons, his delegation had "serious doubts whether [the Southern Cameroons] was capable of existing as an independent state." Afghanistan and Guinea said that economic viability did not matter. Summarising the various statements that had been made, Miss Brooks (Liberia) said paragraph 2 of a resolution being drafted (imposing the so-called 'alternatives' at the impending

plebiscite) "would serve to allay any apprehensions that the Southern Cameroons might become independent as a separate entity, an eventuality which all agreed should be ruled out in view of the territory's limited economic potential".

42. Sir Sydney Phillipson, *Report on Financial, Economic and Administrative Consequences to the Southern Cameroons of Separation from the Federation of Nigeria*, Lagos, Federal Government Printer, 1959, pp. 9 and 42.

43. Ibid, paragraph 49 (5), p. 42.

44. Ibid, paragraph 12, p. 9. Emphasis added.

45. See J Benjamin, *Les Camerounais Occidentaux*. Cf. also this admission by the British contained in a confidential memo dated 7 October 1960 to Sir John Martin of the Colonial Office from Mr. CB Eastwood on his return to London after a visit to the Southern Cameroons: 'If all the political leaders unanimously demanded complete independence that, it seems to me, would be a new situation of which it would be very difficult for the United Nations not to take cognisance [...] I am at the moment disposed to think that we should be wise to support the demand. The Southern Cameroons would, of course, be a small and weak state, but with a population of at least 800,000, and perhaps nearly 1,000,000 it would be no smaller and no weaker than some of the other states in Africa. Paterson, the Financial Secretary, thinks that it would just be able to balance its Recurrent Budget.' *Declassified Secret Files on the Southern Cameroons*, Public Records Office, London.

46. A micro, mini, Lilliputian or diminutive state or territory is one that is very small spatially and demographically, that is to say, one with a population which, according to some writers, is less than 300,000 and, according to others, less than 1,000,000. See, UNITAR, *Status and Problems of Very Small States and Territories*, 1969; MH Mendelson, 'Diminutive States in the United Nations,' 21 *ICLQ* 1972, p. 609; VP Blair, *The Mini State Dilemma*, Carnegie Endowment, Geneva, 1967; J Chappez, 'Les Micro-Etats et les Nations Unies,' *AFDI*, 1974, p. 541; R Adam, 'Micro-States and United Nations,' *Indian Yearbook of International Law*, 1976, p. 80; M Gunter, 'What Happened to the United Nations Mini-State Problem?' *AJIL*, 1977, p. 110; SA de Smith, *Micro-States and Micronesia*, 1970. The UN Secretary General, in the introduction to the 1966-67 Annual Report of the work of the UN, defined (at p. 20) a mini-state as an entity "exceptionally small in area, population and human and economic resources" but which has emerged as an independent state.

47. IA Shearer (ed.), *Starke's International Law*, 11th edition, 1994, p. 88; Dinh, Daillier et Pellet, *Droit International Public*, LGDJ, Paris, 1980, p. 365; Mendelson, op. cit. Thus the island of Nauru with an area of only 8.25 sq. miles and a population

of only 3000 indigenous inhabitants achieved independence on 31 January 1968 and was admitted to membership of the UN. In 1983 the Islands of St. Kitts & Nevis (area, 262 square kilometres; pop. 40,000) gained independence from Britain. On 10 August 1998 Nevis (pop. 10,000) seceded and became a separate independent state. At the time the UN imposed the plebiscite 'choice' on the Southern Cameroons and coerced its people to vote on it. Small states like Congo-Brazzaville, Cyprus and Gabon were already members of the UN. As of late 1992 there were at least 36 UN member states each of which had a population of less than one million inhabitants. In 2001 the small Cooks Island (pop. about 20,000) became the 190th UN Member State. Republic of Palau has a population of about 15,200 inhabitants.

48. See, Declaration on Decolonisation, operative paragraph 3.

Chapter Twelve
The 'Independence by Joining' Hoax

The plebiscite questions, phrased in extremely vague and misleading terms, raised enormous problems of interpretation as to their intended meaning. Specifically, the following two expressions, *"to achieve independence"* and *"by joining"*, were not altogether clear. They called for elucidation.

Ordinarily, a territory achieves independence when it is politically free or emancipated; that is to say, when it is no longer politically dependent on or controlled by some other country. It becomes its own master, responsible for its own internal and external affairs and for its own destiny. When a territory becomes independent it is sometimes described as "independent and sovereign". The word sovereign emphasises supreme authority and means that the state, subject to the confines laid down by international law, has full competence or liberty to act within its four walls and also outside its borders in the intercourse with other states. The word independence signifies that the State is subject to no other earthly authority. Practically, independence and sovereignty mean one and the same thing because both concepts exclude dependence upon any other authority, in particular from the authority of another state.

So when the question, 'Do you wish to achieve independence?', is asked as indeed the plebiscite questions were framed, this is apt rightly to be construed as meaning, 'Do you wish to be politically free, having exclusive power to control your own affairs?' If the question had ended at that there would have been no problem of comprehension. But the matter was obfuscated by the addition of the following group of words "by joining the independent...", and by such turns of phrases as 'separate independence', 'full independence' and 'full measure of self-government' frequently used at the UN at the time.

What does "by joining" mean? A colonial territory may choose to unite with another colonial territory to form one country and to achieve independence as such. For example, the Trust Territory of Togoland under British Administration united with the Gold Coast, a Non-Self

Governing Territory also under British rule, in May 1956, and ten months later, in March 1957, the united entity achieved independence under the name Ghana. The Trust Territory of New Guinea, administered by Australia, united with the Non-Self Governing Territory of Papua, also administered by Australia, and in 1975 the united entity achieved independence as Papua New Guinea.

But how does a colonial territory achieve *independence* "by joining" a sovereign independent state? Can there be anything like *independence by dependence*? A sovereign independent state enjoys international personality. It has defined borders. The borders of a colonial territory ossify at the moment of its attainment of independence. State borders are, of course, not immutable and may be altered under circumstances permissible in international law. Nevertheless, a colonial territory that 'joins' an independent state without proper safeguards as to self-government for the territory becomes merely additional territory for that state. When that happens, the colonial territory in question could perhaps technically be described as having become 'independent' by dint of its absorption by the independent state.

Yet it is beyond doubt that the dependent status of the absorbed territory remains unchanged. In strictly legal terms there has simply been succession to territory. In fact, such a situation is hardly distinguishable from that of transfer of colonial territory. The only difference is that the classic transfer case is a unilateral act of the colonial power whereas here the act has a veneer of 'consent' by the inhabitants of the colonial territory. That is why some jurists have argued that the plebiscitary formula may be used as a method of transfer of territory.

Also, where a colonial territory opts for integration into its parent state the effect of that option is simply to confirm the *status quo*. However, constitutional adjustments are then made to accommodate the formal incorporation. In either case (whether absorption or integration) there is acquisition of territory by the independent state. For example, by act of self-determination of the people of the tiny Cocos-Keeling Island (area: 5½ sq. mi; pop: about 650 inhabitants) in December 1984, duly supervised by a UN mission, and later approved by the General Assembly, the people voted for formal integration with (that is, to become part of) Australia, which hitherto was that Island's parent State. Australia thereby gained additional territory and population, however small.

Arguably, when a colonial territory joins an independent state, it becomes *ipso facto* independent. But the argument has only a superficial attraction and is hardly persuasive. In the first place, when a dependent territory joins an independent state it does so from a position of legal inequality of status, a position of subordination. It retains that dependent status within the independent state. It does not, whether in law or fact, become independent as all matters in relation to the territory, internal or external, are outside its control.

Second, when a dependent territory joins an independent state, the international personality of the independent state does not change; it is in no way modified; there is no state succession. The dependent territory upon being absorbed, fused or integrated simply becomes additional territory for the independent state. That state simply continues albeit with increased territory and population, and consequential border adjustments.

Third, if it necessarily follows that by joining an independent state, without more, a colonial territory is thereby automatically invested with the quality of independence, the UN in framing the plebiscite questions would have left out the very significant phrase 'to achieve independence'. The questions would simply have read: 'Do you wish to join the independent Republic of Nigeria?' 'Do you wish to join the independent Republic of Cameroun?' The word "join" would then be capable of being understood as "fusing with" and automatically resulting in independence.

But the plebiscite questions included the key words "achieve independence." So what does one make of the plebiscite questions as framed, containing as they did the two antithetical ideas, "achieve independence" and "by joining"? It is submitted that in order to give meaning to the legitimate aspirations and expectations of the Southern Cameroons to statehood and in order not to make a complete nonsense of the plebiscite intended by the UN as a method of decolonising the Southern Cameroons, those two phrases must be construed as two separate requirements to be pronounced upon at one vote but giving rise to two distinct processes. Achieving independence was the basic and the first and foremost matter. Joining was a secondary matter which was to take place only after achievement of independence; so joining was not feasible without the prior achievement of independence. It is submitted that those words emphasised the fact that the Southern Cameroons had first of all to attain statehood before "joining". Upon "joining", however, and because of the vagueness of that term its new emergent status remained nebulous.

There is one situation in which a dependent territory may achieve independence with full sovereignty by 'joining' an independent state. This is when the joinder takes the form of a "free association" between the dependent territory and the independent state. In cases of free association the independent state does not acquire the freely associating dependent territory. On the contrary, a dependent territory achieving independence by 'freely associating' with an independent state *ipso facto* becomes a sovereign independent state, and is eligible for UN membership.

A classic example is the case of the four parts of the Trust Territory of the Pacific Islands. The first and second parts of that Trust Territory, the Federated States of Micronesia, and the Marshall Islands, opted in 1990 to become fully self-governing in 'free association' with the USA, and in 1991 both were admitted to membership of the UN. The fourth part of the said Trust Territory, known as Palau (about 15,200 inhabitants), also became fully self-governing in 'free association' with the USA in 1994 and was admitted (as the Republic of Palau) to membership of the UN that same year. The third part, known as the Commonwealth of the Northern Mariana Islands (about 43,500 inhabitants), became fully self-governing as a commonwealth of the USA (i.e., as an independent country that is strongly connected to the US) in 1990; but like Puerto Rico, it is not a sovereign state.

Given the unattractiveness of the so-called "two alternatives" and the ambiguous phraseology of the plebiscite questions, one would have thought that the UN would take the initiative to offer an authoritative clarification. After all, it had authored those two questions. The UN, however, chose to shift this responsibility to the Administering Authority, which in turn shifted it to Nigeria and Cameroun Republic, individually.

Trusteeship Council Resolution 2013 (XXVI) of 31 May 1960 had requested the United Kingdom:

to take *appropriate* steps, *in consultation with the authorities concerned*, to ensure that the people of the Territory are *fully informed, before the plebiscite*, of the *constitutional arrangements* that would have to be made, at the appropriate time, for the implementation of the decisions taken at the plebiscite.[1]

The Resolution clearly imposed an obligation on the UK as Administering Authority. In a more concrete way, it was the responsibility of the UK Government to ascertain from both Nigeria and Cameroun Republic the firm and clear terms and conditions, made in the utmost good faith, under which British Southern Cameroons might be expected 'to join' either of them. The terms and conditions of 'joining', once ascertained, were to be made fully known to the people of the territory well before the day of the plebiscite.

Much of the problem arose from the nebulous and most unfortunate word 'join'. Did it mean 'federate', 'in free association with', 'absorb', 'annex', 'assimilate', 'fuse', 'incorporate', 'integrate', or 'unite'? No one knew for sure. It was therefore left to the various concerned parties, acting jointly or severally, to put whatever meaning they wished on that rather woolly word. Their individual or collective understanding of that term influenced the constitutional terms and conditions of joinder offered, separately by Nigeria and Cameroun Republic, to the people of the Southern Cameroons.

The Nigerian bait

Nigeria made to British Southern Cameroons the constitutional offer of integration as a 'fully self-governing Region equal in all respects with the other Regions in an independent Nigeria.'[2] This offer was first made at the Resumed Nigerian Constitutional Conference held in London in 1958. It was confirmed in a Final Communiqué issued at the end of the constitutional discussions between Nigeria and the United Kingdom in London in May 1960[3] and was reconfirmed by the Nigerian Prime Minister, Sir Abubakar Tafawa Balewa, in a radio broadcast on 21 January 1961.[4] Details of the constitutional status of the Southern Cameroons, in the event of it electing to become a part of the Federation of Nigeria, was published, with the approval of the Nigerian Government, in an official publication, *The Two Alternatives*, issued by the Administering Authority.

The implication for the Southern Cameroons of Nigeria's offer was that the territory would become one of the component-federated states of Nigeria. It would have its own state government and control as much of its own domestic affairs as the Nigerian Federal Constitution conceded to state jurisdiction under the exclusive and concurrent lists. However, this also meant that the Southern Cameroons would be completely and permanently fused as part and parcel of Nigeria. It meant the Southern Cameroons would be incorporated into Nigeria thereby loosing its identity and specificity, with the real possibility of being overwhelmed by especially the overbearing Ibos of the contiguous Eastern Region of Nigeria.

This was not an alluring prospect for the Southern Cameroons. Despite being administered by Britain for nearly half a century as an integral part of Nigeria, the territory had fought doggedly to maintain its distinct identity and individuality. It had purposefully adopted a policy of benevolent neutrality in Nigerian politics. It had secured its separation from that country. Still, so far as the implication for British Southern Cameroons of "joining" Nigeria was concerned, the matter was abundantly clear.

British Government's perfidy and Cameroun Republic's 'pis-aller'

While the implication of 'joining' Nigeria was crystals clear, that of 'joining' Cameroun Republic remained ambiguous until the very eve of the plebiscite. It was incumbent upon the Administering Authority to take appropriate steps, as it had done regarding Nigeria, to ensure that Cameroun Republic fully disclosed the precise constitutional terms and conditions under which the Southern Cameroons could be expected to 'join' that country.

Unfortunately, Britain did not betray diligence and enthusiasm in discharging its international obligation of prising the implication of the second plebiscite question out of Cameroun Republic. Under the Constitution of the Southern Cameroons, the *Southern Cameroons (Constitution) Order in Council, 1960,*[5] the Administering Authority was responsible for the territory's external affairs and in terms of resolution 2013 (XXVI) the primary responsibility lay with the Administering Authority to "consult with the authorities concerned".

Earlier in the year, on 25 January 1960, a meeting had been held in the Colonial Office in London at which the Southern Cameroons question was discussed.[6] The meeting was presided over by the Assistant Under-Secretary of State at the Colonial Office, Mr. Christopher G. Eastwood. In the course of the meeting Mr. Emanuel of the Colonial Office pointed out, correctly, that it was the responsibility of Her Majesty's Government to ensure that there were firm and clear terms for union with either Nigeria or Cameroun Republic and that the negotiations therefore had to be between the United Kingdom which, in any case, was responsible for the external relations of the British Cameroons, and Cameroun Republic.

This pertinent and critical observation was peremptorily dismissed by Mr. Eastwood who declared imperiously that it was not the objective of the Government of the United Kingdom to obtain the best terms possible from Mr. Ahidjo, but simply to obtain from him a clear statement of his intentions and that there was no question of the United Kingdom negotiating an agreement with Mr. Ahidjo. The British Government even objected to UN participation in discussions with Cameroun Republic and, in fact, the meeting at the Colonial Office resolved that UN participation "should be avoided" for "there was no point in the UN taking part." The Government of Her Britannic Majesty had of course decided, in the eternally shameful words of Lord Perth, Minister of State at the Colonial Office, that 'the Southern Cameroons and its inhabitants are expendable.'

Britain therefore adopted a nonchalant attitude in this matter. On 17 October 1960, the UN Plebiscite Commissioner, Ambassador Djalal Abdoh, arrived in Buea, capital of the Southern Cameroons. He was surprised to find that the Administering Authority had so far taken no steps towards ascertaining from Cameroun Republic the terms under which the Southern Cameroons could be expected to 'join' that country. Rather than assume its responsibility in this matter, the Administering Authority informed the Premier of the Southern Cameroons and certain of his colleagues that a duty clearly rested upon them to work out, in consultation with Cameroun Republic, the terms upon which the Southern Cameroons would join that country if the plebiscite favoured that choice.

The Administering Authority had not taken this same lackadaisical approach regarding Nigeria. It had not required the Southern Cameroons to enter into consultation with Nigeria regarding the terms of 'joining' that country. Why this shift in attitude on the part of the Administering Authority?[7] This attitudinal shift was all the more strange because the responsibility for consulting with Nigeria and with Cameroun Republic lay fully with the Administering Authority and not with the Southern Cameroons itself which enjoyed only internal self-government, its external affairs being controlled by the Administering Authority.

In the face of the stated hands off attitude adopted by the Administering Authority and given the fact that the date of the impending plebiscite was not too far off, the Premier of the Southern Cameroons, Mr. J. N. Foncha, took up the challenge of holding talks with the political leaders of Cameroun Republic. Fortunately, as early as January 1960 Mr. Foncha had initiated some exploratory contacts with Mr. Ahidjo, President of Cameroun Republic, on the issue of possible political association. Foncha had been invited to that country's Independence Day celebrations on 1st January 1960, and he had seized the opportunity to hold private talks with Ahidjo on the subject of what was, in a fit of infantile sentimentalism, politically referred to as 'unification'.

It was only after Foncha had made these preliminary contacts with Ahidjo that the Administering Authority then invited the Government of Cameroun Republic to enter, officially, into discussions with Premier Foncha with a view to clarifying the issues involved. On 10 February 1960, the UK Chargé d'Affaires in Yaoundé saw President Ahidjo and informed him that the UK Government would welcome *informal* discussions between him and Premier Foncha on problems of 'unification'. Ahidjo replied that such talks would merely be exploratory and that in any event they could not be held before May 1960 as elections were scheduled to take place in that country in April. The following month, in March, the Minister of Foreign Affairs of Cameroun Republic reiterated this point to the UK Ambassador in Yaoundé.

That same month the Administering Authority surprisingly appointed Sir Sydney Phillipson as 'constitutional and economic adviser' to assist Premier Foncha and his Ministerial colleagues in an examination of the constitutional, fiscal and economic problems likely to arise out of 'joining' Cameroun Republic and to help them formulate any proposals they might wish to put forward.

This Sir Sydney seemed always ready to act as spoiler. He was the very person the Administering Authority had appointed two years earlier to report on the economic viability of the Southern Cameroons. He was the one who made the erroneous but very damaging statement in his 1959 Report that British Southern Cameroons was not economically viable to stand on its own as a separate independent state. He was also the very person who had been appointed by the British as 'independent' chairman of the Mamfe Plebiscite Conference and who had hurriedly closed it, declaring that the delegates had failed to agree on the plebiscite questions to be put to the people. Since he had taken such a jaundiced view on all these issues it was most unlikely that he would counsel (and in fact he did not counsel) the taking of a robust and business-like attitude in discussions with Cameroun Republic.

In June 1960 Foncha sent an outline of his constitutional proposal to Ahidjo and suggested that an early opportunity be found to discuss it. When Ahidjo paid a state visit to the Southern Cameroons from 15-17 July 1960, he and certain members of his Government seized the occasion to hold discussions with Foncha and certain members of his Government as well. A communiqué issued afterwards stated that at the end of the discussions the two sides 'unanimously adopted' a resolution by which they, inter alia, "agreed to reunification on a federal basis adapted to the conditions peculiar to all sections of Kamerun." In August 1960, three Ministers of the Southern Cameroons' Government took with them to Yaoundé, capital of Cameroun Republic, outline proposals for a federal constitution and held further discussions with the representatives of Cameroun Republic.[8]

In early October 1960, the Secretary of State for the Colonies, at the request of Premier Foncha, held talks in London with a delegation of Ministers from the Southern Cameroons and members of the Opposition parties.[9] The talks revealed considerable differences of view on the implications of the second plebiscite question. Her Majesty's Government stated categorically that the United Nations in adopting the 'two alternatives' of 'joining' Nigeria or 'joining' Cameroun Republic, clearly ruled out a period of continuing Trusteeship or separate independence for the Southern Cameroons. This could hardly have been true. But this was a piece of British *Realpolitik* and an act of brinkmanship on the part of the British Secretary of State for the Colonies. Her Britannic Majesty's Government offered no explanation for this alleged UN attitude which, to say the least, was rationally inexplicable, morally unjustifiable and legally indefensible.

In the opinion of the UK Government, if the plebiscite went in favour of the second choice, arrangements would have to be made 'for the early termination of Trusteeship *and the transfer of sovereignty to the Republic*.'[10] The latter part of this statement was indeed strange, unless it was intended as a bogey to scare the Southern Cameroons out of voting for the 'alternative' of 'joining' Cameroun Republic. The Secretary of State went on to put forward the following interpretation of the second plebiscite question:

> A vote for attaining independence by joining the Republic would mean that, by an early date to be decided by the United Nations after consultations with the Governments of the Southern Cameroons, the Cameroun Republic and the United Kingdom as Administering Authority, the Southern Cameroons and the Cameroun Republic would unite in a Federal United Cameroon Republic. The arrangements would be worked out after the plebiscite by a conference consisting of representative delegations of equal status from the Republic and the Southern Cameroons. The United Nations and the United Kingdom would also be associated with this conference.[11]

In view of the fact that all the delegates of the Southern Cameroons agreed to this interpretation presented by the Secretary of State on the meaning of the second question, and in the absence of a new and authoritative definition of the question by the United Nations, it was recognized that the next step was to obtain the concurrence of the President of Cameroun Republic with this interpretation.

Accordingly, a third meeting between Premier Foncha and his delegation, and President Ahidjo and his delegation, was held in Yaoundé in mid-October 1960. A resolution was adopted and an outline of a draft proposal for a federal constitution in the event of a vote in favour of the second plebiscite question. The resolution took the form of a communiqué. It recalled the decision taken at the 14th session of the UN General Assembly concerning the plebiscite to be held in the Southern Cameroons. It declared that in the event of a vote in favour of the Southern Cameroons 'joining' Cameroun Republic 'the implementation of "reunification" on the federal basis adaptable to conditions peculiar to all sections of the Cameroons cannot be automatic but gradual.' It further recalled that 'the political heads have already met twice to examine the broad outlines of the constitution of the two federated states' and that 'they have, at the conclusion of their third meeting of 10-13 October 1960, decided to adopt the broad outlines of the Constitution which they will adopt in the event of the plebiscite vote being favourable to them.'

The second document, entitled 'Outline Proposals for a Draft Constitution for a Federal United Kamerun Republic', was in the form of a Joint Declaration. It declared, inter alia, that the two sides 'wish to create a federal State' outside the British Commonwealth and the French Community; that 'nationals of the federated states will enjoy Cameroon nationality'; that the Federal Legislature will consist of a Federal Assembly and a Federal Senate; that federal laws will only be enacted in such a way that no measures contrary to the interests of one State will be imposed upon it by the majority; that the Federation will be created by the Southern Cameroons and Cameroun Republic; and that if the vote went in favour of "unification" those entrusted with the affairs of the unified Cameroon would put the Federal Constitution to the people to pronounce themselves on it.

These two documents, the *Communiqué* and the *Joint Declaration* were signed by the Premier of the Southern Cameroons (Mr. J. N. Foncha) and by the President and the Prime Minister of Cameroun Republic (Messrs Ahmadou Ahidjo and Charles Assalé). Both documents were published in a Press Release issued by the Information Service of the Southern Cameroons Government on

17 October 1960, the very day the UN Plebiscite Commissioner arrived in Buea. The Deputy Commissioner of the Southern Cameroons, Mr. Milne, also forwarded copies of the documents to the UN Plebiscite Commissioner.

Inasmuch as these documents purported to have been signed by Hon. J. N. Foncha, Premier of the Southern Cameroons for and on behalf of the Government of the Southern Cameroons, the Plebiscite Commissioner felt it necessary to ascertain whether the agreements contained therein had the official endorsement of the Administering Authority and could be construed as providing a basis for an official explanation of the second alternative in the plebiscite, in compliance with the request addressed to the Administering Authority under operative paragraph 3 of Trusteeship Council Resolution 2013 (XXVI). The Plebiscite Commissioner needed to satisfy himself on this matter because the Premier was dealing here with a matter relating to foreign affairs, a subject still controlled by the Administering Authority. Despite repeated inquiries from the Plebiscite Commissioner, the Administering Authority chose to be evasive on the question of whether the Foncha-Ahidjo Agreements enjoyed the official sanction of the British Government and whether they made the implications of the second choice sufficiently clear.

On 26 October 1960, a meeting took place between Mr. J. O. Field, Commissioner of the Southern Cameroons, and Ambassador Djalal Abdoh, the UN Plebiscite Commissioner. At that meeting Mr. Field stated that Foncha had signed the Agreement with Ahidjo as Leader of the Government Party and not on behalf of the Southern Cameroons Government. He said that Foncha signed the agreement in his personal capacity and issued it as a statement of the intentions of the party he headed. He went on to say that the Government of the Southern Cameroons was not a party to the said Agreements and was in no way committed to them. Finally, he stated that the Press Release containing the outline proposals of the proposed federal constitution was not an authoritative statement made on behalf of the Southern Cameroons Government.[12]

In short, therefore, the Commissioner of the Southern Cameroons was saying that the Foncha-Ahidjo Agreements neither constituted the official position of the Southern Cameroons Government, nor had the endorsement of the Administering Authority. This in effect meant that those Agreements were invalid and could not possibly be used as a basis for the enlightenment campaign that the Plebiscite Commissioner had planned. It was already the end of October.

The plebiscite was barely three months away. There was still no authoritative statement on the meaning of the second plebiscite question. The people of the Southern Cameroons remained in the dark as to the precise terms under which they might be expected to 'join' Cameroun Republic. The Administering Authority had still not fully fulfilled its obligations under Resolution 2013 (XXVI). Time was of the essence in this matter.

On 29 October 1960, therefore, the Plebiscite Commissioner wrote again to the Commissioner of the Southern Cameroons seeking clarification on this matter. The Commissioner made no reply. Foncha then decided on an appearance before the General Assembly.

But prior to doing so, he sought a meeting with Mr. Ahidjo, which meeting was held in Yaoundé from 1-2 December 1960. After this meeting, the fourth to be held between both leaders, the two parties issued a signed communiqué stating their *"full agreement"*: (i) that the General Assembly had clearly put the two questions in the plebiscite to be held on February 11, 1961; (ii) that 'the two delegations [...] endors[e] the interpretation of the second question arrived at [during] the London Conference'; and, (iii) that the post-plebiscite Conference, 'in which representatives from the United Nations Organization and the Administering Authority will take part, shall have to determine the period and terms of the transfer of sovereignty to a body representing the future federation.'[13]

Mr. Ahidjo having concurred (as did the Southern Cameroons All Party Delegation to the London talks earlier in October) with the interpretation put forward by the British Secretary of State for the Colonies, Mr. Foncha evidently saw no further need for taking the matter to the General Assembly.

By 5 December 1960, the Commissioner of the Southern Cameroons had not replied to the letter addressed to him five weeks earlier by the UN Plebiscite Commissioner. So, on 6 December 1960, the Plebiscite Commissioner addressed another letter on the same subject to the Acting Commissioner of the Southern Cameroons, the substantive office-holder being absent. On 9 December 1960, the Acting Commissioner sent the following evasive reply:

1. I am directed by the Secretary of State for the Colonies (Mr. Iain Macleod) to reply to your letter of 29th October, 1960 [...]
3. As regards the implications of [...] joining the Republic of the Cameroun, Her Majesty's Government approached the Government of the Republic early in 1960, and on a number of subsequent occasions, with a view to promoting negotiations on this point. Her Majesty's Government has also repeatedly expressed to the Premier of the Southern Cameroons its view that the terms on which the Territory might be united with the Cameroun Republic should be discussed between him and the Government of the Republic. [...] Her Majesty's Government considered it appropriate for Mr. Foncha to consult directly with the President of the Cameroun Republic.
4. As you are aware, a number of meetings have taken place both in Yaounde and in Buea at which Mr. Foncha and his colleagues have discussed this question with President Ahidjo and members of his Government. These meetings resulted finally in a communiqué, which was issued after the meeting held in Yaoundé early in October, a copy of which has already been supplied to you.
5. Subsequently, and as you are also aware, the Secretary of State for the Colonies (Mr. Iain Macleod) agreed at the request of Mr. Foncha to receive a delegation representing government and other parties in the Southern Cameroons. Discussions were held during November when this matter was reviewed. A communiqué setting out the results of these discussions was issued on 17th November, and a copy of this communiqué has been supplied to you. As the communiqué says, Her Majesty's Government took the view that *a period of independence for the Southern Cameroons before union with the Cameroun Republic such as was sought by Mr. Foncha* was not consistent with the questions which had been decided upon by the General Assembly and that in view of the interpretation which Mr. Foncha wished to place upon the question of joining the Cameroun Republic

the matter would have to be put before the General Assembly once again for an authoritative ruling. They have conveyed this statement, of which a copy is attached, from which it will be seen that he now agrees with Mr. Macleod's interpretation of this question.[14]

This letter indicated the role played by the UK Government merely as facilitator to 'promote negotiations' between Foncha and Ahidjo. It also outlined the efforts made by Mr. Foncha to clarify the terms under which the Southern Cameroons might 'join' Cameroun Republic. But it studiously expressed no view as to the status of the Foncha-Ahidjo Agreement and on the question of whether the Agreement had made the implications of the second choice sufficiently clear. The Plebiscite Commissioner was not satisfied with the contents of the letter from the Acting Commissioner of the Southern Cameroons. So he addressed yet another letter to him. The letter was dated 12 December 1960, and four days later, on 16 December, the Acting Commissioner replied as follows:

> I am directed by the Secretary of State for the Colonies [...] to inform you that Her Majesty's Government believe that they are in a position to fulfil this request in respect of the plebiscite question relating to Nigeria. Her Majesty's Government hope that they will be in a position to fulfil the request in respect of the question relating to the Republic of Cameroun as soon as the President of the Republic of Cameroun returns from his present absence abroad [...][15]

By mid-December of 1960 the UK Government, as this reply admits, was only still hoping it would be in a position to fulfil the request in respect of the plebiscite question relating to Cameroun Republic. Once again, the reply refused to confront the nub of the problem. The British were purposefully prevaricating. On 16 December 1960, the same day on which the Acting Commissioner of the Southern Cameroons replied to the letter of the UN Plebiscite Commissioner, the Government of the United Kingdom, through its Embassy in Yaoundé, requested from the Government of

Cameroun Republic an official statement setting forth the conditions under which, in the view of Cameroun Republic, the Southern Cameroons might 'join' that country. It was envisaged that such a statement would, together with the terms of the understanding already given by the Federation of Nigeria on the implications of the first question, form the basis of the campaign of enlightenment to be carried out in the Southern Cameroons before the plebiscite.

The reply from Cameroun Republic came a week later. It was sent through its Ministry of Foreign Affairs and was contained in a *Note Verbale* dated 24 December 1960 addressed to the British Embassy in Yaounde. The *Note* stated as follows:

> The Ministry of Foreign Affairs presents its compliments to the British Embassy to Cameroun at Yaoundé and with reference to its *note verbale* No. F.M. 68 (1041/60) dated 16 December 1960, has the honour to state that, following the conversations which have just taken place at Douala between the President of the Republic of Cameroun and Mr. Foncha, the Premier of the Southern Cameroons, it has been decided that, in connexion with the plebiscite organised in the Southern Cameroons on the question of whether that country should join the Federation of Nigeria or the Republic of Cameroun, the Government of the Republic of Cameroun has announced that it adheres to the spirit of the attached joint communiques, which indicate its desire for unification with the Cameroons under British Administration *on the basis of a federation*. The Government of the Republic of Cameroun requests the British Embassy to consider the attached communiqués as an expression of the official views of the Republic and further request that they be published for the purposes prescribed by Trusteeship Council resolution 2013 (XXVI), referred to in its *note verbale* quoted above.[16]

Attached to this *Note* were the texts, in French, of the *Communiqué* and the *Joint Declaration* issued by Messrs Foncha and Ahidjo at the conclusion of their third meeting of 10-13 October 1960, as well as the *Joint Communiqué* signed by both leaders at the conclusion of their meetings of 1-3 December 1960. The *Note*, it would be observed, reiterated the announcement already made by Cameroun

Republic that 'it adheres to the spirit of the attached joint communiqués', which communiqués 'indicate its desire for unification [...] on the basis of a Federation' and are 'an expression of the official views of the Republic.'

The contents of the three attached documents formed the basis of a possible political association between the Southern Cameroons and Cameroun Republic. The documents provided, inter alia, for: (i) a federation of two states, equal in status; (ii) a post-plebiscite conference consisting of representative delegations of equal status from the two countries; (iii) the association of the UN and the United Kingdom with this conference; and (iv) the transfer of sovereign powers to an organization representing the future Federation.

Southern Cameroons and Cameroun Republic were thus clearly in agreement that the term 'to join' meant 'to federate', in other words, both countries would form a federal union. The statement contained in the *Note* and publicised in *The Two Alternatives* evidenced a clear intention on the part of Cameroun Republic to be bound by the contents of the three instruments attached thereto and to accept binding legal obligations vis-à-vis the Southern Cameroons.[17]

Moreover, in international law, the *Note* constituted a unilateral act of a 'heteronormative character',[18] giving rise to an international legal obligation.[19] The statements contained in the above documents from Cameroun Republic to the UK Government through its Embassy in Yaounde were therefore taken as constituting the undertaking given by that country regarding the second plebiscite question.

Throughout this episode the Administering Authority did not betray diligence and enthusiasm in discharging the duty clearly incumbent upon it to ascertain from Cameroun Republic the conditions under which, in its view, the Southern Cameroons might 'join' it. And yet under *The Southern Cameroons (Constitution) Order in Council, 1960*, the Administering Authority was responsible for the territory's external affairs and in terms of resolution 2013 (XXVI) the primary responsibility lay with the Administering Authority to "consult with the authorities concerned."

Nigeria had given its undertaking much earlier. By contrast it was not until Christmas Eve 1960 that Cameroun Republic at last officially transmitted its own undertaking – characteristically nebulous in phraseology and most economical in content. The undertaking was far less precise than that given by Nigeria.

The Administering Authority issued both undertakings in a booklet deceptively entitled *The Two Alternatives*, produced for the plebiscite enlightenment campaign.[20] One hundred thousand copies were distributed widely throughout the territory. But it needs little imagination to see that given the high level of illiteracy in the territory at the time, not many people accessed the document; and that even the few who did may not have understood its content and the meaning of the questions put to them. It may therefore be said, without fear of serious contradiction, that the people did not understand the implications of the outcome of their vote, that is, the political consequences of what they were being forced and rushed to vote for.

The publication and distribution of *The Two Alternatives* marked the official launch of the enlightenment campaign. It was only at this late hour, towards the end of January 1961, that there was an informed campaign, backed by official documentation, to explain to the people the meaning of each of the 'two alternatives', as distinct from the political implications or consequences of each, a matter about which the Plebiscite Supervisory Officers were under strict orders from the British to maintain total silence. Meanwhile, various actors, already on the ground much earlier, were on their soapbox giving what were for the most part garbled and truncated accounts of the stakes involved. The scheduled plebiscite date was barely two weeks away. This was hardly enough time to mount any serious and meaningful campaign of explanation and so-called enlightenment.

Moreover, *The Two Alternatives* was, as the report of the first enlightenment campaign importantly observed, of 'little use with an illiterate population'. Furthermore, it was extremely "difficult to get the matter over by interpreters, who themselves had not a wide command of English"[21] or knowledge of what was at issue. The UN Plebiscite Commissioner was thus able to observe in his Report that, 'It may be said that the campaign did not come up to expectations.'[22]

Chief Nyenti's fledgling Cameroons Commoners' Congress (CCC) was thus obliged to address, towards the end of January 1961, a letter to the UN Secretary General informing him of the following grave failings regarding the plebiscite: (i) 'There was confusion in the territory with a majority of the people believing that voting for the white box[23] means the Southern Cameroons will break away from Nigeria in order to be a separate sovereign state; very many villagers imagine this separate state to be called Cameroons Republic'; (ii) 'The plebiscite has dishonoured the Trusteeship Agreement, Article 3, and the United Nations Charter, Article 76b, which say our territory should be promoted towards self-government or independence'; and (iii) 'Only a handful of people registered themselves for the plebiscite.'[24]

The Plebiscite Poll

The plebiscite was supervised by the United Nations and conducted by a staff of United Kingdom Plebiscite Administrators selected by the Colonial Office, from amongst candidates with wide experience in overseas territories. There was a Plebiscite Administrator (Mr. Hubert Childs), a Deputy Plebiscite Administrator (Mr. J. Dixon), five Assistant Plebiscite Administrators[25] and twenty-six Plebiscite Supervisory Officers.[26] A total of 349,652 people (181,711 women and 167,941 men) registered for the plebiscite, representing roughly 90% of the potential electorate.

Seven political parties took part in the campaigns. Two parties campaigned for 'joining' Nigeria,[27] two for 'joining' Cameroun Republic,[28] and three stood for separate independence for the Southern Cameroons.[29] The latter parties were not satisfied with either of the plebiscite 'alternatives'. They favoured separate independence for the Southern Cameroons. They clearly represented a strong and identifiable body of opinion in the Southern Cameroons. They would certainly have carried the day had the people of the territory been given the status option of independence. With the UK Government staunchly opposed to that option all three pro-independence political parties gave up, by mid-January 1961, their valiant fight for that option. Those parties gave up in understandable utter frustration and absolute disgust at the absurdity of the plebiscite exercise.

Mr. Foncha, as leader of the movement in favour of joinder with Cameroun Republic, centred his campaign on an appeal to a so-called 'unification of "brothers" separated by colonial boundaries.' The weakness of that argument was patent. The boundaries of the 'unified' entity he was campaigning in favour of would still be 'colonial boundaries'. The thesis about 'unification of brothers' applied more to the proposition for 'joining' Nigeria. The whole length of the common frontier between the Southern Cameroons and Nigeria cuts through communities belonging to the same tribal groups. Because the Southern Cameroons was jointly administered with Nigeria for nearly half a century, the two peoples got to know each other well. They lived and worked together, intermarried and shared a common official language and a common educational, legal, constitutional and administrative system. The period of the Nigerian connection was 46 years, far longer, far more involved and more intense, and far more meaningful than the brief spell from 1887-1914 when the area that subsequently became the Southern Cameroons was part of German *Kamerun*.

In any event, the Nigerian constitutional offer of a federal self-governing region was honest, concrete and detailed. By contrast, Cameroun Republic's federal offer was wishy-washy. That country itself remained an unknown land to the generality of the people of the Southern Cameroons. There were, of course, citizens of Cameroun Republic who had fled terrorism, repression and slavery-like labour in their native land and sought sanctuary in the safe haven of the Southern Cameroons either as refugees or political exiles. But France and Mr. Ahidjo, 'the French puppet President of that French neo-colonial state', had succeeded in demonising the whole lot of them as robbers and *maquisards* (terrorists), and that was the ordinary man's perception of these Cameroun Republic émigrés.

The plebiscite campaign was in general a negative campaign. Each side concentrated its fire not on why the people should vote for the 'alternative' it espoused but on why they should not vote for the other 'alternative'. Endeley conjured the fear of Cameroun Republic as *terra incognita* and, moreover, as land awash with blood and steep in a culture of despotism, repression and barbarism. Foncha countered by raising the spectre of Ibo (Nigerian) conceit, arrogance and domination. Since this was a lived reality of many a Southern Cameroons citizen, the Ibo bogey or 'Ibophobia' proved to be the main determinant of the plebiscite outcome.

But in fact, rationally, Endeley's case was stronger than Foncha's. Cameroun Republic was definitely an unknown land. The enduring dictatorship, violence and lack of basic human rights in that country are not such factors as likely to have induced a rational person to vote for 'joining' that country. During the campaigns, Endeley made the following Daniel-like prophesy:

> If you vote for Cameroun Republic, you will invite a new system under which everyone lives in fear of the Police and the Army. You will not be free to move about; you cannot lecture freely or discuss your political views in public; you must carry your tax receipt round your neck like a dog; and you can be arrested and flogged by the Police and even imprisoned without a fair trial. [...] Anyone accused of an offence in Cameroun Republic is manhandled and flogged and is generally treated as a guilty criminal. Even the most junior policeman there seems to have the power of life and death over the common people. [...] A vote for Cameroun Republic will be the signal for new economic troubles in the Southern Cameroons. [...] Cameroun Republic is still a colony of France. French troops are still stationed in Douala and Yaounde [...] to prevent Mr. Ahidjo's Government from being overthrown, and to protect the interests of the many thousands of Frenchmen who have settled there! [...] Frenchmen are reliably understood to be planning to take over the CDC plantations. It is no use for the Southern Cameroons to move from the British colony system to the French colony system. [...]
>
> Who amongst you would like to live in a country where your life and property are constantly in danger? Who amongst you, peaceful citizens of the Southern Cameroons, will like to live in a country where you may be shot at as you move along the street, or your wife killed as she toils on the farm? Who amongst you would like to live in French Cameroun, a country red with the blood of thousands of innocent victims killed by terrorists and the Ahidjo regime? Who amongst you, good citizens of the Southern Cameroons, will like to live in

a land where people's houses and shops are burnt every day and looted; where you can be arrested without cause, beaten, searched and imprisoned without a fair trial? Who amongst you will like to live in a country, which lacks complete respect for human dignity and where you cannot speak out your mind freely or pursue your business in peace? Surely none of you! Who of you will like your children to grow up in servitude? Surely none of you! That is what will be our lot if we join French Cameroun. If you wish to save yourself from the aforementioned indignities make sure you vote for the Southern Cameroons to remain as it has been for the past forty years. [...] A vote for the white box [representing the proposition for joining Republique du Cameroun] will mean a complete change in our language, system of government and way of life. Progress will be stopped. [...] In the Southern Cameroons [...] political differences are settled by arguments and by the ballot box. In French Cameroun, political differences are settled by guns and poison. If you want to avert the impending confusion that will befall the Southern Cameroons, and if you want the territory to develop into a country where all will be fairly treated and adequately catered for; where there will be equal opportunities for everyone, irrespective of tribe, creed, race or political association, then cast your vote in the GREEN BOX [representing the proposition for joining Nigeria] during the plebiscite on February 11.[30]

This was a powerful and factual appeal. Voting in favour of the proposition to join Cameroun Republic amounted to foolishly and dangerously taking a plunge into an abyss. Time has proved this to be the case. But in February 1961 the force of Endeley's compelling argument was lost in the throes of an anti-Ibo feeling that proved just too strong. The plebiscite results were therefore reflective of an anti-Ibo vote (a desire to escape Ibo overbearing character and Ibo hegemony) rather than of a desire positively to 'join' Cameroun Republic; a vote prompted by emotion rather than reflection, irrationality rather than rationality.

On polling day 94.75% of all registered voters turned out to cast their ballots. When the votes were counted the result showed that 97,741 (29.51% of the valid votes) were cast in favour of 'joining' Nigeria, while 233,571 (70.49% of the valid votes) were cast seemingly for 'joining' Cameroun Republic. The results for each of the six divisions of the Territory were as follows:[31]

DIVISION: Registered Voters / Vote for Joining Nigeria / Vote for Joining Cameroun Republic
VICTORIA: 36,302 / 11,916 / 22,082
KUMBA: 63,173 / 32,733 / 27,600
MAMFE: 46,372 / 10,050 / 33,267
BAMENDA: 126,299 / 12,341 / 108,486
WUM: 38,599 / 8,784 / 27,115
NKAMBE: 38,907 / 21,917 / 15,022
Totals: 349,652 / 97,741 / 233,571

In his Report to the UN General Assembly, the Plebiscite Commissioner pronounced the plebiscite 'efficiently organised and conducted.' He paid glowing tribute to the people of the Southern Cameroons for the 'remarkable calm which prevailed' during the poll and for 'the respect they showed for law and order.'[32] He felt 'satisfied that the people of the Southern Cameroons had the opportunity to express their wishes freely and secretly at the polls *concerning the alternatives offered in the plebiscite'.*[33]

He made no pronouncement as to fairness of the very plebiscite exercise itself in light of the fact that the people were not offered the status option of independence. He was however of the well informed view that although the majority of the people were aware that the decision they were called upon to make meant "joining" one of the two neighbouring countries, *'they may not have grasped the detailed implications of the alternatives at the plebiscite'.*[34]

In conclusion, the Plebiscite Commissioner deemed it useful to recall and to remind the General Assembly of the formula advanced by the British Secretary of State for the Colonies at the London Conference with political leaders of the Southern Cameroons. He also recalled that the formula was endorsed by representatives of the Government Party of the Southern Cameroons, led by Premier

Foncha, and by a delegation of the Government of Cameroun Republic, led by President Ahidjo, at their meeting in Yaoundé on 1 and 2 December 1960. Finally, the Commissioner pointed out that it was agreed at the Yaoundé meeting that the post-plebiscite conference would have as its aim the fixing of time limits and conditions for the transfer of sovereign powers (evidently by independent Southern Cameroons) to an organisation representing the future federation.

Notes

1. *Report of the Plebiscite Commissioner*, paragraph 48. Emphasis added.

2. *Southern Cameroons Plebiscite 1961: The Two Alternatives*, Buea, Southern Cameroons Gazette, no. 4 vol. 7, 27 January 1961, pp. 7-12.

3. See White Paper, *Nigerian Constitutional Discussions, May 1960*, London, Her Majesty Stationery Office, June 1960, Cmnd. 1063.

4. *Report of the Plebiscite Commissioner*, paragraphs 57-59.

5. See, Statutory Instrument No. 1654 of 1960 (West Africa). The Constitution was made on 12 September, laid before the British Parliament on 16 September and entered into force on 1 October 1960.

6. '*Note of a Meeting Held in the Colonial Office on Friday Morning the 25th January, 1960*.' Present at the Meeting were: Mr. Eastwood (in the chair); Sir Andrew Cohen and Mr. Caston (UK Mission, New York); Messrs Jerrom, Emanuel, Ryrie, Burr and Browning (Colonial Office); Mr. Boothby (Head of the African Department at the Foreign Office); Mr. Johnson (Ambassadors-designate to Cameroun Republic); and Messrs Mitchell and Hale (Foreign Office). *Declassified Secret Files on the Southern Cameroons*, Public Records Office, London.

7. The behaviour of the Administering Authority in this matter smacked of dereliction of responsibility and betrayed a certain bias in favour of the 'alternative' for 'joining' Nigeria.

8. *Report of the Plebiscite Commissioner*, paragraph 61.

9. The delegation comprised: Hon. JN Foncha, Premier; Hon. ST Muna, Minister of Commerce and Industries; Hon. AN Jua, Minister of Social Services; Hon. WNO Effiom, Minister of Works and Transport; Hon. EML Endeley, OBE, Leader of the Opposition; Hon. PN Motomby-Woleta, Opposition Chief Whip; Hon. Rev. JC Kangsen, CPNC Member for Wum Central; Hon. SE Ncha, CPNC Member for Mamfe North; Hon. PM Kale, Leader of the C.U.P. party; HRH Galega II, Fon of Bali; and HRH Chief Oben of Mamfe.

10. *Report of the Plebiscite Commissioner*, paragraph 68. Emphasis added.
11. Ibid.
12. *Report of the Plebiscite Commissioner*, paragraph 66.
13. Ibid., paragraph 71.
14. Ibid., paragraph 74. Emphasis added.
15. Ibid., paragraph 76.
16. Ibid., paragraph 79. Emphasis added.
17. In the *Eastern Greenland Case* (1933) PCIJ, Ser. A/B, No. 53, p.71, the Court declared that a statement of that nature, including even a unilateral oral declaration in the nature of a promise, given by a Foreign Minister, in reply to a request by the diplomatic agent of a foreign power in regard to a question falling within his province is binding upon the State to which the Minister belongs.
18. Dinh et al., op. cit., p. 329.
19. In the *Nuclear Tests Case* (Australia v. France), Judgment, ICJ Rep. 1974, 253, the ICJ stated that a declaration may be made by way of unilateral act by a state concerning a legal or factual situation under such circumstances as to have the effect of creating a legal obligation on that state.
20. *Southern Cameroons Gazette*, No. 4, vol. 7 of 27 January 1961, Legal Notice No. 36.
21. See *Report of First Enlightenment Campaign*, op. cit.
22. Ibid., paragraph 205.
23. White was the agreed colour for the proposition favouring 'joining' République du Cameroun.
24. Letter Ref. CCC/58 dated 26 January 1961, from the CCC political party and signed by Chief Nyenti, to the Secretary General of the United Nations. Declassified Secret Files on the Southern Cameroons, Public Records Office, London.
25. These were Mr. RB Allen (Finance and Supply Services, Buea); Mr. PL Allpress (Victoria and Kumba); Mr. CS Grisman (Mamfe); Mr. ARPPK Cameron (Bamenda); and Mr. JD Tallantire (Wum and Nkambe). See *Plebiscite Commissioner's Report*, paragraphs 101 to 109.
26. There was one PSO in each of the 26 parliamentary constituencies (referred to for the purposes of the plebiscite as plebiscite districts) into which the Southern Cameroons had been carved pursuant to s.12 of the Southern Cameroons (Constitution) Order in Council, 1960. With one exception, all the PSO were

graduates of universities in the United Kingdom and the majority of them had done National Service in the British Armed Forces. *Plebiscite Commissioner's Report*, paragraphs 101 to 109.

27. Those that campaigned for integration with Nigeria were: the Cameroons Moslem Congress (CMC) of Mr. Malam Sale; and the Cameroons People's National Convention (CPNC), a merger in June 1960 of Dr. E.M.L. Endeley's Kamerun National Congress (KNC) and Mr. N.N. Mbile's Kamerun People's Party (KPP).

28. The parties that campaigned for 'joining' République du Cameroun were: the Kamerun National Democratic Party (KNDP) of Mr. J.N. Foncha, and the One Kamerun party (OK) of Mr. Ndeh Ntumazah, a 'party' fronting for the UPC party in République du Cameroun, banned in that country on account of its 'terrorist' activities.

29. These were: the Kamerun United Party (KUP) of Mr. P.M. Kale, the Cameroons Commoners' Congress (CCC) of Chief Nyenti, and the Cameroons Indigenes Party (CIP) of Mr. Jesco Manga-Williams.

30. CPNC Strategic Committee, *Plebiscite Message*, Buea, 1961, pp. 3-5, 7-8.

31. Data compiled from Plebiscite Commissioner's Report, 11 April 1961. The total number of valid votes cast was 331 312. This does not tally with the total number of registered voters (349 652). The difference of 18 341 can be ascribed to cases of spoilt votes and/or voter abstention. Still, these figures differ by as much as 24 864 from those provided by the Southern Cameroons Information Service in 1961 (a total of 306 448 valid votes, 209 444 for "joining" Cameroun Republic and 97 004 for "joining" Nigeria) and reproduced in C Atang, *A Breach of Trust*, p. 25 [date, publisher and place of publication not given].

32. *Report of the Plebiscite Commissioner*, paragraphs 312-313.

33. Ibid., paragraph 313. Emphasis added.

34. Idem. Emphasis added.

Chapter Thirteen
Was the Southern Cameroons Ever Decolonised?

Termination of Trusteeship: the Wheeling and Dealing at the United Nations

At the plebiscite the people of the Southern Cameroons voted affirmatively for independence and also pronounced themselves in "favour" of the alternative to "join" Cameroun Republic. Two months after that vote, on 21 April, the UN adopted Resolution 1608 (XV) by which it noted that the Southern Cameroons had voted to achieve independence and also to "join" Cameroun Republic, and that accordingly the Trusteeship Agreement concerning the territory would be terminated in accordance with Article 76b of its Charter. Infelicitously, however, the UN appointed 1 October 1961 as the date for the occurrence of all those three events, namely, independence of the Southern Cameroons, political association of the Southern Cameroons and Cameroun Republic, and termination of the Trusteeship Agreement concerning the Southern Cameroons.

What status then did the Southern Cameroons emerge into after 1 October 1961, considering the concomitance of its independence and its "joining" with Cameroun Republic? This inquiry is important for the purpose of determining whether it can be said that the basic objective of the trusteeship system, in regard to the Southern Cameroons, was achieved, bearing in mind Article 76b of the UN Charter and Article 3 of the Trusteeship Agreement for the Cameroons under United Kingdom Administration.

The plebiscite having gone the way it did, it was then for the General Assembly to evaluate the result and take appropriate decisions in the light of the recommendations of the Fourth Committee. Two months after the plebiscite, on 13 April 1961, the Fourth Committee decided to consider the Trusteeship Council's Report on the Future of the Cameroons under United Kingdom Administration, and the Plebiscite Commissioner's Report.[1] The Fourth Committee also granted requests for oral hearings from 23 petitioners, 9 of them from the Southern Cameroons. Of the 9, two expressed dissatisfaction with the plebiscite results in the

Northern Cameroons, while seven contested the plebiscite results in the Southern Cameroons and urged the UN to partition the Territory conformable with the result for each division.²

Throughout that fateful month of April 1961, the handling of the Southern Cameroons question at the UN was characterised by much wheeling and dealing, and bad faith on the part of many players. On 15 April 1961, a draft resolution, sponsored by ten Francophone African States,³ was submitted to the Fourth Committee. In terms of that draft resolution, a six-member commission elected by the General Assembly was to visit the British Northern Cameroons and the British Southern Cameroons to ascertain in particular whether the basic objectives of the Trusteeship system could be regarded as achieved throughout the territory of the Cameroons under United Kingdom Administration.

Four days later, on 19 April 1961, that draft resolution was revised, at the instigation of France and Cameroun Republic. In the revised draft, the proposed commission was only 'to ascertain whether the separation of the administration of the Northern Cameroons from that of Nigeria [had] been effectively carried out.'

Cameroun Republic was evidently satisfied with the result in the Southern Cameroons and did not want it revisited. But it was disappointed with the result in the Northern Cameroons. Arithmetically, if the results for both Southern and Northern Cameroons were computed for the whole of the British Cameroons the alternative at the plebiscite of "joining" Cameroun Republic would have carried the day. Realizing this Cameroun Republic tried, but unsuccessfully, to get France to push for the computation of the results for the British Cameroons (Southern and Northern) taken as a whole. France had just a few years earlier opposed such a procedure in Togo and was thus morally unqualified to push now for a unitary plebiscite result in the British Cameroons.

Having thus failed to secure French support for a unitary plebiscite result Cameroun Republic then claimed that the poll in the Northern Cameroons was tainted with irregularities and called for the ballot there to be retaken in the hope that the vote would go in its favour. Cameroun Republic had to tread carefully as in a minefield because if the whole plebiscite issue were to be re-opened, the pro-independence-as-a-sovereign-state voice was going to resurface and prevail.

Meanwhile, on 18 April 1961, another draft resolution was submitted by Ethiopia, India, Iran, Ireland, Jordan, Libya, Morocco, Nepal, New Zealand, Pakistan, Saudi Arabia and Sudan joined by the Federation of Malaya and Liberia as co-sponsors. This draft resolution [A/C.4/L.685] was adopted as a whole by a roll-call vote of 59 to 2, with 9 abstentions. The Fourth Committee recommended it to the General Assembly for adoption. In that draft resolution the General Assembly:

> 5. Invites the Administering Authority, the Government of the Southern Cameroons and the Republic of Cameroun to initiate urgent discussions with a view to formalizing, before 1 October 1961, the arrangements by which the agreed and declared policies of the concerned parties for a union of the Southern Cameroons with the Republic of Cameroun into a Federal United Cameroun Republic will be implemented;
>
> 6. Appoints a Commission of three constitutional and administrative experts to be nominated one each by three Member States designated by the General Assembly to assist at the request of the parties concerned in the discussions referred to in paragraph 5 above.

It was clear that draft resolution A/C.4/L.685 had financial implications. The Fourth Committee was fully alive to this fact. In its report on this matter on 20 April 1961, the Committee pointed out that the adoption of the recommended draft resolution 'would give rise to additional expenditures in 1961 of some US$46,000 which would be included in the supplementary estimates for 1961 to be submitted to the General Assembly at its 16th session.' On the same day the UN Secretary General noted that:

> Should the draft resolution as recommended by the Fourth Committee be adopted by the General Assembly, financial commitments up to $46,000 will have to be made for which no budgetary provision is included in the 1961 budget. In

that event the Secretary General would propose to meet these requirements as unforeseen expenses for the financial year 1961, and will submit supplementary estimates to the General Assembly in its sixteenth session in this regard.[4]

The following day, on 21 April 1961, the General Assembly adopted Resolution 1608 (XV) on *The Future of the Trust Territory of the Cameroons under United Kingdom Administration*. This resolution was a dangerously watered-down version of resolution A/C.4/L.685, which the Fourth Committee had earlier adopted and recommended for adoption by the General Assembly as well.

In Resolution 1608 (XV) operative paragraph 6 in the Fourth Committee's resolution A/C.4/L.685 disappears altogether, seemingly because of financial constraints. The removal of this paragraph was highly prejudicial to the interest of the people of the Southern Cameroons. Furthermore, the following critical group of words 'for a union of the Southern Cameroons with the Republic of Cameroun into a Federal United Cameroun Republic' which appears in operative paragraph 5 of the Fourth Committee's resolution were excised from operative paragraph 5 of Resolution 1608 as adopted by the General Assembly. The excision of those words was again highly prejudicial to the interest of the Southern Cameroons.

Aided by France and supported by member States of the Francophone *Union Africaine et Malgache*, Cameroun Republic successfully opposed the inclusion of those words in the final resolution. Cameroun Republic, ill advisedly, even voted against Resolution 1608. In sharp contrast, every initiative in the interest of the Southern Cameroons was vigorously impeded or smothered by Britain's autocratic UN Representative, Sir Andrew Cohen, whose demonstrated antipathy towards the Southern Cameroons bordered on the pathological. As it turned out the Southern Cameroon's faith in the UN was misplaced and its reliance on the Organisation detrimental.

By Resolution 1608 (XV), the General Assembly:

> 2. Endorses the results of the plebiscite that: [...] (b) *The people of the Southern Cameroons have decided to achieve independence by joining the independent Republic of Cameroun*;

3. Considers that, [...] the decisions made by them through a democratic process under the supervision of the United Nations should be immediately implemented;
4. Decides that, [...] the Trusteeship Agreement of 13 December 1946 concerning the Cameroons under United Kingdom administration shall be terminated, *in accordance with Article 76b of the Charter of the United Nations* and in agreement with the Administering Authority, in the following manner: [...] (b) With respect to the Southern Cameroons, on 1 October 1961, *upon its joining the Republic of Cameroun*;
5. Invites the Administering Authority, the Government of the Southern Cameroons and the Republic of Cameroun *to initiate urgent discussions with a view to finalizing, before 1 October 1961, the arrangements by which the agreed and declared policies of the parties concerned will be implemented.*[5]

Once more the money factor plagued the Southern Cameroons "decolonisation" saga. Money was the convenient excuse invoked by the UN in 1959 in ruling out the option of separate independence for the Southern Cameroons. Now when it came to the effective implementation of the result of the truncated plebiscite it had imposed on the Southern Cameroons, money once more entered the calculus in working out the future of the territory and its people. The UN considered the paltry sum of $46 000 too large an amount to spend in order to secure and safeguard the Southern Cameroons and the dignity and worth of its people. One wonders what happened to the much vaunted principle of human dignity and worth, and the principle of the equality of all peoples and nations, small and large.

Had the UN provided the much needed constitutional and administrative experts[6] the Southern Cameroons would have at least been an internationally guaranteed independent self-governing state within an overarching federal system and would have been admitted to UN membership. It would today not be the dependent territory it is, under the colonial yoke of Cameroun Republic. Given these facts, the question that arises is whether the Trusteeship concerning the Southern Cameroons was terminated in accordance with Article 76b of the UN Charter as the General Assembly asserts in operative paragraph 4 of Resolution 1608 (XV).

Termination of Trusteeship and Article 76b of the UN Charter

The Charter of the United Nations contains provisions bearing on the terms of trusteeship agreements and their alteration or amendment, but nothing on termination of the same.[7] However, the United Nations took the view that termination of each trusteeship agreement was necessarily implied in the achievement of the basic objectives of the trusteeship. This view was informed by the consideration that the International Trusteeship System is based on the concept of a trust reposing on the trustee authority.[8] Moreover, since the United Nations approved the terms and alterations or amendments of all trusteeship agreements it necessarily followed that it also had power to terminate such agreements. Indeed, just as the General Assembly decided in 1946 to approve each trusteeship agreement, subsequently it also decided to terminate each such appropriate trusteeship in agreement with the administering authority.[9]

Furthermore, Article 76b of the Charter strongly suggests that eventual termination of a trusteeship agreement is inherent in the declared goal of the Trust, namely, 'progressive development towards self-government or independence.' Admittedly, neither the Charter nor the individual trusteeship agreements gave any timeframe within which the ultimate goal of self-government or independence was to be achieved.[10] Nevertheless, it was understood that upon attainment, by each trust territory, of the basic objectives of the trusteeship system, the Trust in respect of the territory concerned would be terminated.

The basic objectives of the trusteeship system are set out in Article 76 of the Charter.[11] The primary purpose of the system, and the paramount obligation of the administering authority, was 'to promote the political, economic, social and educational advancement of the inhabitants of the trust territories.' Another objective of the system, and also an idea which runs throughout the Charter, was 'to encourage respect for human rights and fundamental freedoms for all without distinction as to race, sex, language, or religion.' Fundamental human rights evidently include the right to freedom from colonial domination and the eventual right of every human being to a share in the political independence of his or her country.

Article 76b therefore recognises, in language of some elasticity, as one of the objectives of the trusteeship system the promotion of the progressive development of the inhabitants of the trust territory 'towards self-government or independence as may be appropriate to the particular circumstances of each territory and its peoples and the freely expressed wishes of the peoples concerned and as may be provided by the terms of each trusteeship agreement.' Progressive development towards 'self-government or independence' appeared as the ultimate objective of the system. But the attainment of that final goal depended upon the particular circumstances of each territory and its peoples, the freely expressed wishes of the peoples concerned, and the terms of each trusteeship agreement.

The expression "self-government or independence" lent itself to an interpretative difficulty. Apparently, it was a compromise formulation between two opposing views expressed at the founding conference of the United Nations. One view was in favour of a phraseology referring to "independence" *tout court,* while another view preferred a reference to "self-government" alone as adequate.[12] The "or" (in the phrase "self-government or independence") is therefore capable of being construed as conjunctive or disjunctive. Construed disjunctively the compromise formulation means that independence was not assumed to be the proper goal for all trust territories – some could achieve independence while others could achieve merely self-government. The problem with this interpretation was the difficulty of determining the criteria for entitlement to independence. Construed conjunctively, however, the formulation means ascribing the same meaning to both terms, in effect saying that "self-government" is merely shorthand for "full self-government" and means the same thing as "independence". In practice, self-government was considered the penultimate stage in the political evolution towards independence. It was considered a stage indicative of ripeness for independence, the ultimate goal of the trusteeship system.

In Article 3 of the Trusteeship Agreement for the British Cameroons the Administering Authority undertook to administer the territory in such a manner 'as to achieve the basic objectives of the International Trusteeship System laid down in Article 76 of the United Nations Charter.' Article 6 of the Agreement obliged the

Administering Authority to 'promote the development of free political institutions suited to the territory' and to give the inhabitants 'a progressively increasing share' in the government of the territory with a view to their political advancement 'in accordance with Article 76b of the United Nations Charter.' Under the said Article 76b administering authorities assume an obligation to ensure the progressive development of the inhabitants of trust territories towards 'self-government or independence'.

The political sentiment of the majority of the United Nations Members was always in favour of early independence for colonial peoples. However, there was no agreed definition of the status of 'self-government or independence', the attainment of which warranted termination of trusteeship.[13] In other words, although the ultimate objective of the trusteeship system was 'self-government or independence', it was not altogether clear at what point in time or at what stage in the process of political advancement of a trust territory it could be said that the ultimate objective had been attained. And yet until the attainment of the status of 'self-government or independence' the ultimate objective of the system would not have been fulfilled and the trusteeship would not be terminated. In order to address this intractable problem, the General Assembly, on 20 December 1952, adopted Resolution 648 (VII) listing factors to be taken into account in deciding whether a territory is or is not a territory whose people have yet attained a full measure of self-government. Annexed to the Resolution was a list of *'Factors Indicative of the Attainment of Independence or Other Separate Systems of Self-Government'*.[14]

The administering authorities never accepted these factors as an exhaustive binding definition.[15] Their attitude did not however deter the General Assembly from going ahead to assume competence to evaluate and decide, on the basis of the listed factors, whether or not a territory was self-governing. Although a decision on the matter was, in principle, not binding on the administering authorities, each eventually cooperated with the United Nations on this issue.[16] Indeed, between 1948 and 1955 the Trusteeship Council and the General Assembly adopted a series of special resolutions for the administering authorities to carry out.[17] These resolutions were adopted for the purpose of achieving as early as possible the basic objectives of the trust. The administering authority of each trust territory was called upon to faithfully discharge its obligations under the particular trusteeship agreement and in conformity with these special resolutions. Consistent with these resolutions, the General Assembly recommended, on 26 February 1957, that the administering authorities concerned take the necessary measures for the early attainment of self-government or independence by five named trust territories, including the British Cameroons.[18]

In spite of its administrative union with Nigeria since 1924, the Southern Cameroons was, from 1954, administered as a separate and distinct unit of the Nigerian Federation, possessing some local executive and legislative autonomy, and responsible for its own budget. In 1958 a Premier of the Southern Cameroons was designated. An unofficial majority in the Executive Council became the principal instrument of policy in the territory. The elected Membership of the House of Assembly was enlarged from 13 to 26 elected members. A House of Chiefs was set up as the upper house of the legislature, with powers similar to those of the House of Lords in London. Improvements were made in the electoral system and by the time of the 1961 plebiscite there was universal franchise, every person of age, both male and female, being able to vote. The training of Southern Cameroons' citizens was still very slow but was grudgingly accelerated by the Administering Authority. There was thus a steady though slow increase in the number of technically qualified citizens of Southern Cameroons in positions of higher responsibility in the civil service, including the Administration.[19]

By October 1961, the Southern Cameroons had more graduates from universities and specialised secondary education than many an African state at the time of their independence.[20] The Southern Cameroons had become responsible for its own budget since 1955. The cooperative movement in the territory was developed and expanded. Appropriate measures were undertaken to enable the Cameroons Development Corporation (CDC), the territory's largest agro-industry, to make an increasingly important contribution to the territory's development. An indigenous press was established and medical services were improved.[21]

Given these hard facts, in December 1958, the Government of the United Kingdom, as Administering Authority, felt able to certify in the UN General Assembly that the Southern Cameroons was expected to achieve, in 1960, the objectives set forth in Article 76b of the United Nations Charter. A General Assembly resolution of the same month noted that by the measures already taken or to be taken by some administering authorities in consultation with the United Nations and the peoples of the territories concerned, five named trust territories,[22] among them the British Cameroons, were expected to achieve in 1960 the ultimate objective of the trusteeship system (i.e. independence) laid down in Article 76b of the United Nations Charter.

Following the results of the plebiscite in the Southern Cameroons , the General Assembly, on 21 April 1961, adopted Resolution 1608 (XV) by which it decided to terminate, in accordance with Article 76b of the UN Charter and in agreement with the Administering Authority, the Trusteeship Agreement of 13 December 1946 concerning the Southern Cameroons. The manner of termination stipulated by the Assembly consisted of two aspects: (i) an effective date of termination, the set date being 1 October 1961; and (ii) a specified event expected to take place on that same date, namely, '*upon* the Southern Cameroons joining' Cameroun Republic. The Resolution went on to invite the United Kingdom, the Governments of the Southern Cameroons and Cameroun Republic 'to initiate urgent discussions with a view to *finalising*, before 1 October 1961, the *arrangements* by which the *agreed and declared policies* of the parties concerned will be *implemented*.' [23] It is worthy of note that the same Resolution had in an earlier paragraph endorsed the decision by the Southern Cameroons to achieve independence and had set the very 1st October 1961 as the effective date of that independence.

On 25 September 1961, the British Queen gave at Buckingham Palace a Proclamation 'signifying Her Majesty's agreement to the termination with respect to the Southern Cameroons of the Trusteeship Agreement of 13th December, 1946.'

Whereas by virtue of an Agreement approved by the General Assembly of the United Nations on the thirteenth day of December, 1946, We are the Administering Authority for the territory known as the Southern Cameroons and the responsibility for the administration of the said territory is vested in Our Government of the United Kingdom of Great Britain and Northern Ireland :

And whereas the General Assembly of the United Nations on the twenty-first day of April, 1961, resolved that the said Agreement should in agreement with the Administering Authority be terminated with respect to the Southern Cameroons on the first day of October, 1961, upon its joining the Republic of Cameroun:

Now, therefore, We do hereby, by and with the advice of the Our Privy Council, proclaim and declare Our agreement to the termination of the said Agreement with respect to the Southern Cameroons on the first day of October, 1961, and accordingly that Our said Government shall as from that date cease to be responsible for the administration of the Southern Cameroons.[24]

It would seem to be the case that the General Assembly's termination of trusteeship over the Southern Cameroons *ipso facto* meant that the ultimate objective of the system as spelt out in Article 76b of the United Nations Charter had been attained. It is doubtful that the UN would have terminated the trusteeship if it had not come to the settled conclusion that the objective set out in Article 76b of its Charter had been attained. The termination was a legally valid act of the competent body: the termination did not offend against the provisions of the Charter and it was the decision of the appropriate UN organ. The Southern Cameroons' plebiscite result was endorsed as the decision of the people of the territory 'to achieve independence',[25] that decision being, in the words of the General Assembly, "the freely expressed wishes" of the people.

Resolution 1608 (XV) had a definitive legal effect, but only in the sense that the Trust ceased to exist and disappeared, and that the United Kingdom as trustee became *functus officio*. In other respects serious legitimate doubts still remained, giving rise to many nagging questions. Did the disappearance of the Trust necessarily mean that the dependent status of the territory also disappeared? Did the

Southern Cameroons ever achieve other than paper or nominal independence, given that the United Nations itself had ruled out independence on the ground of a purported economic non-viability?

Was Resolution 1608 (XV) in reality no more than the UN's stamp of approval of the colonial transfer of the Southern Cameroons as a non-self-governing territory from Britain to a successor colonialist, namely, Cameroun Republic? In the circumstances, can it credibly be argued that Resolution 1608 (XV) is *res judicata* and cannot be revisited by the UN General Assembly? Can the international community divest itself of the right to concern itself with the status of a territory that was under international tutelage so long as the territory in question has not achieved independence as declared by the 1960 Declaration on Decolonisation?

The decisions of the General Assembly embodied in Resolution 1608 were only partially implemented. The Trust was terminated, but the arrangements as to joinder were never finalised, and the independence achieved was immediately suppressed as, upon the hurried departure of the British, Cameroun Republic forcibly took possession of the Southern Cameroons (its forces were moved into the territory in mid-September 1961) and assumed a colonial sovereignty over the territory (in October 1961 it appointed one of its citizens as viceroy, called '*inspecteur fédéral d'administration*', to take administrative control of the territory). That colonisation was camouflaged, first with a thin veneer of a *de facto* federation that lasted from 1 October 1961 to May 1972 and second with a counterfeit "united republic" that lasted from June 1972 to February 1984, on which date 'Cameroun Republic' (French Cameroun having achieved independence from France on 1 January 1960 by that name and style) was by law revived as a political and legal expression.

Political Status of the Southern Cameroons after Termination of the Trusteeship

Resolution 1608 was adopted on 21 April 1961. It 'endorse[d] the results of the plebiscite that [...] the people of the Southern Cameroons have [...] decided to achieve independence *by* joining the independent Republic of Cameroun.' It 'decide[d] that [...] the Trusteeship Agreement [...] shall be terminated [...] with respect to the Southern Cameroons, on 1 October 1961, *upon* its joining the Republic of Cameroun'. It invited the United Kingdom, the Southern Cameroons and Cameroun Republic 'to initiate urgent discussions with a view to *finalising* before 1 October, 1961, the arrangements by which the agreed and declared policies of the parties concerned will be implemented.'[26]

The "parties concerned" were obviously the Southern Cameroons and Cameroun Republic, and their "agreed and declared policies" were clearly those set out in the signed and published pre-plebiscite agreements for a federation of the two countries, and the transfer, on 1 October 1961, of the sovereignty of each country to the nascent Cameroon Federal Republic.

It follows that joinder was conditional upon the fulfilment of certain prior conditions. In terms of resolution 1608 the Trusteeship Agreement with respect to the Southern Cameroons was to be terminated on 1 October 1961 *"upon"* the Southern Cameroons "joining" Cameroun Republic, that is, *when* (and not *after*), the Southern Cameroons "joined" Cameroun Republic. However, the Southern Cameroons was to "join" Cameroun Republic only *after* the arrangements regarding the agreed and published policies of the two parties would have been *finalised*. The sequence of events was to be: finalisation of the pre-plebiscite agreement on a federal form of political association between the two countries; thereafter, *when* the Southern Cameroons "joins" Cameroun Republic on 1 October 1961 the trusteeship would then be terminated on that same date.

In May 1961, there was held in Buea, capital of the Southern Cameroons, the first of two main rounds of discussions[27] apparently aimed at finalising before the appointed date of 1 October 1961, arrangements for the implementation of the agreement on a federal union.[28] High on the agenda of the *Buea Tripartite Talks*, as the discussions were known, were matters regarding the security of the Southern Cameroons, the citizenship of the people of the Southern Cameroons, and the transfer of sovereignty over the Southern Cameroons. These matters were critical for the status of the Southern Cameroons in the proposed federation.

The delegation of Cameroun Republic argued that since the Southern Cameroons had no army of its own, the *armée, gendarmerie* and *sûreté* of Cameroun Republic would become the security forces of the would-be federation as well as of each of its two component states. It also argued that Cameroun Republic citizenship would be extended, collectively, to the people of the Southern Cameroons who, it was claimed, had no citizenship. Finally, Cameroun Republic claimed that United Nations Resolution 1608 (XV) required sovereignty over the Southern Cameroons to be transferred to Cameroun Republic which, so went the reasoning, was already a sovereign independent State enjoying international personality.[29]

These views could not have contrasted more with the position taken by the Southern Cameroons delegation.[30] On the matter of *security* the delegation let it be known that the Southern Cameroons was committed to raising and maintaining its own army and police to ensure the territory's security. The delegation argued that to allow Cameroun Republic security forces into the Southern Cameroons would smack of countenancing an army of occupation in the territory. It was pointed out that such would be all the more unacceptable because of the suspect level of education and training of those forces and their well known culture of violence, barbarism and incivility.[31]

In taking this understandable stand the Southern Cameroons had hoped it would be supported by the delegation of the United Kingdom and, indeed, that the Government of the United Kingdom would accede to its long-standing request to assist in the provision of training for, and the secondment of trained personnel to, a future Southern Cameroons army and police. In the course of the discussions however, the British, typically, were very evasive and it later became clear they were not prepared to accede to such a request pleading, as usual, financial constraints. Whereupon the Southern Cameroons accused the British of betrayal and of collusion with Cameroun Republic to bring it under the latter's yoke, an accusation they of course denied.[32]

After lengthy arguments on this point, a compromise was eventually reached. The Southern Cameroons would raise and maintain its own police force. Citizens of the Southern Cameroons serving in the Nigerian Army would be voluntarily repatriated to the Southern Cameroons and would eventually join Cameroun Republic soldiers in what would then become, in the deceptive words of Cameroun Republic's President, a "federal bilingual army".[33] There was thus going to be a common "bilingual" Army for the envisaged Cameroon federation, while each of the two member states of the would-be federation was to establish its own police force.[34] But there was no indication what the concept of a "bilingual army" meant and as it turned out there was never any such army. Cameroun Republic's military is a French-monolingual and French-trained and equipped force.

On the point of *transfer of sovereignty*, the Southern Cameroons delegation pointed out, correctly, that there was nothing even remotely implied in Resolution 1608 that sovereignty over the Southern Cameroons was to be transferred to Cameroun Republic. The delegation maintained that on 1 October 1961, sovereignty over both the Southern Cameroons and Cameroun Republic would have to be transferred to and vested in an "organisation representing" the would-be Cameroon federal republic, that is to say, the Federation as such.

The Attorney General of the Southern Cameroons, Mr. G. B. Smith, marshalled, in a memorandum to the Premier, a compelling line of argument against the transfer of the sovereignty of the Southern Cameroons to Cameroun Republic. If on 1 October 1961, sovereignty over the Southern Cameroons was to be transferred to Cameroun Republic, he submitted, the people of the Southern Cameroons would not at that moment be said to have achieved independence. Their dependent status would continue. Their land would become an annexed territory. The people would simply have passed from British colonial rule to Cameroun Republic colonial subjugation. They would become mere subjects of Cameroun Republic. They would loose their identity. Such a result would be highly incompatible with the dignity and the freely determined status (independence) of the people of the Southern Cameroons.

The cogency of this line of reasoning was unassailable. The plebiscite vote was first and foremost a vote *to achieve independence*; "joining" Cameroun Republic was subsidiary to it. The plebiscite was not a procedure by which the Southern Cameroons offered itself for annexation by, or integration into, Cameroun Republic.[35] The phraseology of the plebiscite questions and the provisions of Resolution 1608 did not in any way suggest that achievement of independence by the Southern Cameroons would occur *after* it had federated with Cameroun Republic.

The people of the Southern Cameroons "achieved independence" following their decision to that effect at the plebiscite on 11 February 1961. However, the UN postponed the effective date of that independence to 1 October 1961. The UN also stipulated the selfsame date as that on which the "joining" was to take place. Three separate and distinct events, namely, achievement of independence by the Southern Cameroons, formation of a federal political association between the Southern Cameroons and Cameroun Republic, and termination of the Trusteeship Agreement with respect to the Southern Cameroons, were all to take place contemporaneously. On the same date and at one and the same moment (i) the Trusteeship Agreement was to be terminated; (ii) there was to be born the independent Republic of the Southern Cameroons; and (iii) there was to emerge a Cameroon Federal Republic consisting of two states juridically equal in status, independent Southern Cameroons and independent Cameroun Republic.

The future federation could not be anything else other than a free association of independent and equal States, the Republic of the Southern Cameroons and Cameroun Republic. Both States would voluntarily limit their respective sovereignty by constituting themselves into a federal republic. Both states would also transfer sovereign powers to the nascent Cameroon Federation and become extinct as international persons, making way for the emergence of the said Federation as the new subject of international law.

While there was agreement on the formation of a federation, the detailed contents of the federal constitution however remained to be worked out and finalised. That was the object of the Foumban Meeting in July 1961. The President of Cameroun Republic, Mr. Ahidjo, who chaired the meeting, scuttled it. He had his ubiquitous French advisers to privately draw up for him a document he got the legislature of Cameroun Republic to enact on 1 September 1961 as the so-called "federal constitution" supposedly binding on the Southern Cameroons.

The document did not have the concurrence of the Southern Cameroons, whether the Government or its Parliament or its people. This was a clear case of the unlawful assumption by Cameroun Republic of sovereignty over foreign territory; the theft of territory. Mr. Ahidjo was a foreign prince, and the legislature of Cameroun Republic a foreign parliament. They had no constituent or any other powers over the Southern Cameroons. The British were still the Administering Authority in the territory.

As if the illegality of Cameroun Republic purporting to exercise constituent powers over the Southern Cameroons was not enough, the UK Government, in an act of treachery, invited Ahidjo to Buea, the capital of the Southern Cameroons, purported to hand power to him on 30 September 1961 and hurriedly left town. What then came into existence on 1 October 1961 was a mere *de facto* federation.

On that day the British Head of State, Her Majesty Queen Elizabeth II, sent a message 'on the occasion of the ending of United Kingdom Trusteeship over West Cameroon State (formerly Southern Cameroons)'. Paradoxically, the message was not addressed to Mr. J. N. Foncha, the political leader of the territory over which Britain was ending its rule after nearly half a century. The message was instead addressed to Mr. Ahidjo, the President of Cameroun Republic, territory over which the British never exercised any authority. The message read:

> On the occasion of the ending of United Kingdom trusteeship in the Southern Cameroons I send your Excellency my sincere good wishes for the future of the united territories over which you now preside. I am glad that friendly cooperation between our two countries should have made it possible for the Southern Cameroons *to attain independence* in accordance with the results of the February plebiscite. I look forward to the continuation of our cordial relations in the future.

On the same day, the British Secretary of State for the Colonies, Mr. Iain Macleod, addressed a message of "best wishes" to Mr. J. N. Foncha, Premier of the Southern Cameroons. The Colonial Secretary wrote:

As the period of our trusteeship comes to an end and *your country* takes its place with the Republic of Cameroun in the new Federation, I should like to send my best wishes for the future to yourself and your countrymen. We look forward to maintaining with the Federation of Cameroon the happy ties of friendship which have linked us with the Southern Cameroons now for over 40 years.

Earlier, in a farewell speech on the eve of the *de facto* federal, Mr. Malcolm Milne, Deputy Commissioner of the Southern Cameroons and the outgoing Officer Administering Government, observed that the Southern Cameroons had "a million souls". He concluded his speech by declaring that 'our task is done, the Southern Cameroons *emerges into nationhood'*.[36] For eleven years, from 1 October 1961, until May 1972 when the political leaders of Cameroun Republic overthrew the informal Federation through the trickery of a pretended referendum, 1 October of each year was celebrated in the Southern Cameroons as Independence Day, the day the Southern Cameroons voted to emerge into nationhood.[37]

On the matter of *nationality and citizenship* the Southern Cameroons delegation refused to gratify the ambition of Cameroun Republic to extend its citizenship to the people of the Southern Cameroons. The delegation pointed out that the people of the Southern Cameroons were nationals of the Southern Cameroons. During the colonial period, since they were merely "British protected persons" and not British subjects or citizens they could only have been nationals of the Southern Cameroons. To have denied them both British and Southern Cameroons citizenship would mean they were stateless persons – an absurd result of a territory with an indigenous population and yet without citizens.

The absence of citizenship *qua* internal law of the Administering Authority, and the absence of citizenship *eo nomine* conferred by some other source did not render the people of the Southern Cameroons stateless. Their nationality was for various purposes of the law attributable to the territory itself. Admittedly, the Southern Cameroons was still under international tutelage and consequently did not constitute a nation of any recognised state in international law. But that only meant the national status of its people lay in abeyance. That status surfaced, by operation of law, at the precise moment of its independence on 1 October 1961. The people of the Southern Cameroons have thus always been nationals of the Southern Cameroons.[38]

It follows from the above analysis that as from 1 October 1961, when United Kingdom trusteeship over the Southern Cameroons was terminated, up to May 1972 when the informal Cameroon federation was overthrown, the Southern Cameroons, as a federated state, was arguably a half-sovereign independent state on account of its internal independence, and arguably also a qualified subject of international law.

By associating with Cameroun Republic in a federal union, be it merely informal (for even such factual situations do produce legal effects), it voluntarily limited its sovereignty and submerged its international personality. Its external relations with other states were absorbed entirely by the federal Government. But being a federated state, it enjoyed internal government status within an overarching two-state federal arrangement. It had legal personality under municipal law. It exercised such measure of territorial competence within the state as conceded by what passed for the federal constitution and controlled much of its internal affairs. It had authority over, and the allegiance of, its citizens. It had a constitution with detailed provisions on the various facets of government. There was a Head of Government (the Prime Minister),[39] an Executive Council (the Cabinet), a bicameral legislature (House of Assembly and House of Chiefs) with power to make laws for the peace, order and good government of the State, a Police Force with responsibility for maintaining and securing public safety and public order, a Public Service, and so on.

The overthrow of the *de facto* federation destroyed all of this. The Southern Cameroons state was abolished. Its constitution was also abolished. Its institutions were dissolved. Its political and territorial unity was impaired. Cameroun Republic now took complete control of the territory. It imposed its pro-consuls as the new rulers of the territory. It decreed French the language of administration. It imposed French value systems and the French system of administration.

The very basis of the political association between the Southern Cameroons and Cameroun Republic was thus completely destroyed. The opinion of the people of the Southern Cameroons, freely expressed by informed and democratic processes, as to whether they desired a detrimental change in their political status, was never properly sought and was lacking. Even if such opinion were properly sought it would evidently never have been given because no people ever voted for a detrimental change in their political status. With the forcible takeover of the Southern Cameroons it effectively became an occupied territory and a dependency of Cameroun Republic.

Notes

1. In addition to these two Reports, documentation before the Fourth Committee included two cables addressed to the UN Secretary General, one dated 14 February 1961, from Cameroun Republic's Permanent Representative at the UN, and the other dated 19 February 1961, directly from the Government of Cameroun Republic. There were also two letters addressed to the Chairperson of the Fourth Committee, one dated 10 April 1961, from the UK Representative on the Fourth Committee, and the other dated 12 April 1961, from the Permanent Representative of Nigeria to the UN. The cables from Cameroun Republic in substance contested the plebiscite results in the Northern Cameroons.

2. The two petitioners who expressed dissatisfaction with the plebiscite results in the Northern Cameroons were Mr. JN Foncha (KNDP) and Mr. Ndeh Ntumazah (OK). The seven petitioners who urged a partition of the Southern Cameroons conformable with the plebiscite results for each Division of the Southern Cameroons were: Dr EML Endeley, Mr. Nerius Mbile, Mr. Samuel Endeley, Mr. Samuel Andoh Seh, Mr. Ajebe Sone, Chief Bokwe Sakwe, and Chief Martin of Bakweri Molongo. These seven petitioners were echoing a signed resolution of the Victoria Divisional Council dated 21 March 1961, and addressed to the UN Secretary General. The resolution reiterated that 'the people of Victoria Division... are determined to continue their association with the Federation of Nigeria' and called for a nullification of the plebiscite because:

'(a) the Administering Authority had failed [...] to ensure that the people of the Territory were fully informed, before the plebiscite, of constitutional relations with the Cameroun Republic [...];

(b) the so-called "enlightenment campaign" decided upon by the Administering Authority was put in motion only a few weeks before the plebiscite and could hardly have any appreciable effect on the outcome of the plebiscite;

(c) the grasslanders both in their own homes in the Bamenda Area and in the plantations on the coast voted on a tribal basis paying little or no regard to the merits of the constitutional arrangements proffered respectively by the Federation of Nigeria and the Cameroun Republic as recorded in the Administering Authority's pamphlet entitled "The Two Alternatives";

(d) it is now an open secret in this Territory that both the KNDP and OK had brought a large number of men and women from the Cameroun Republic to swell their votes, and that these thugs actually voted for the White Box at the plebiscite.' The resolution then concluded: 'We, the indigenous people of the Victoria Division, have clearly demonstrated by our vote at the plebiscite that we wish to continue our association with the Federation of Nigeria as a full-fledged and self-governing Region in that Federation. Since the tribes in Bamenda Division and their associates have opted blindly to join the Cameroun Republic, we have decided to urge the United Nations Organisation to partition the Territory conformable to the results of the plebiscite.' See, Letter dated 21 March 1961 signed by the Chairman of the Victoria Divisional Council to the Secretary General of the United Nations, New York. *Declassified Secret Files on the Southern Cameroons*, Public Records Office, London.

3. Central African Republic, Chad, Congo-Brazzaville, Dahomey [Benin], Gabon, Ivory Coast, Madagascar, Niger, Senegal, and Upper Volta [Burkina Faso].

4. UN General Assembly Fifteenth session, Doc. A/C.5/866 Financial Implications of the Draft Resolution presented by the Fourth Committee in Doc. A/4737: Note by the Secretary General. Agenda Item 13. See page 32 of Annexes to the Plebiscite Commissioner's Report for the Cameroons under United Kingdom Administration, UN General Assembly Doc. A/4727 of 11 April 1961.

5. Emphasis added.

6. Which it had done in the case of the Ethiopia-Eritrea federation in 1950: UNGA Res. 390(V) A of 2 Dec. 1950.

7. Article 79 of the Charter provides that the terms of trusteeship for each territory, including any alteration or amendment, shall be agreed upon by the "states directly concerned" and shall be approved by the General Assembly or the Security Council as appropriate. In respect of the Trusteeship for the British Cameroons, the UK Government considered and regarded France as the 'state directly concerned', obviously because of the geographical propinquity of the British Cameroons to French Cameroun.

8. The administering authority did not enjoy exclusive advantage or an unrestricted plenitude of power in the trust territory. From the very idea of a trust (tutelage or *fideicommissum*) the administering authority enjoyed only delegated and a fundamentally limited authority.

9. Under Article 85 of the Charter, the General Assembly with the cooperation and assistance of the Trusteeship Council exercises all the functions of the United Nations with regard to trusteeship agreements for all territories not designated as strategic areas.

10. Only the Trusteeship Agreement for Somaliland, submitted by Italy and approved by the General Assembly in 1950, included a termination date – ten years from the signing of the Agreement. This exceptional case apart, the various administering authorities stubbornly refused, in spite of constant pressure within the UN for early independence, to be tied down to a specific timeframe within which trusteeship would be terminated. However, between November 1948 and December 1955, the General Assembly adopted a number of resolutions dealing with various questions of legal as well as political and administrative character, always with a view to the speedy achievement of the basic objectives of the trusteeship and its early termination. See, Resolutions 226 (III) of 18 November 1948, 320 (IV) of 15 November 1949, 558 (VI) of 18 January 1952, 648 (VII) of 20 December 1952, 742 (VIII) of 1953, and 858 (IX) of 15 December 1955.

11. See Article 76 as supplemented by Article 73 (Declaration regarding non-self-governing territories) and Article 84 (contribution of the trusteeship system to international peace and security).

12. Bowett, DW, *The Law of International Institutions*, Stevens & Sons, London, 1982, pp. 76-86; see also, Sands & Klein, *Bowett's Law of International Institutions*, Sweet & Maxwell, London, 2001, pp. 66-67.

13. Ibid.

14. Yearbook of the United Nations, 1952, pp. 564-565.

15. Bowett, op. cit.

16. Ibid.

17. Res. 226 (III) recommended that administering authorities take all possible steps to accelerate the progressive development towards self-government or independence of the trust territories they administer. Res. 320 (IV) expressed the General Assembly's full support of the Trusteeship Council's recommendations to administering authorities for the adoption by them of measures which would hasten the advancement of the trust territories towards self-government or independence in accordance with the objectives laid down in Art.76b of the Charter. Res. 558 (VI) called for information concerning measures taken or contemplated towards self-government or independence, and, *inter*

alia, the estimated period of time required for such measures and for the attainment of the ultimate objective. Res. 648 (VII) listed factors that should be taken into account in deciding whether a territory is or is not one whose people have yet attained a full measure of self-government. Res. 858 (IX) re-affirmed Resolution 558 (VI).

18. Others were French Cameroun, French Togoland, Ruanda-Urundi and Tanganyika.

19. *United Nations Yearbook*, 1958, pp. 347-349.

20. For example, by 1 October 1961 there were at least five Barristers-at-Law from the Southern Cameroons, having been called to the Bar in one or other of the four Inns of Court in England (Sabum, ET Egbe, SML Endeley, PB Engo, and Mensah), two of them appointed First Grade Magistrates (Egbe and Engo). There were also medical doctors (e.g. Abba, Diboue, EML Endeley, VA Ngu, AB Yongbang), engineers (e.g. Tamanjong Ndumu, Sendze), a number of qualified pharmacists (such as HN Elangwe and SML Endeley) and senior nurses. In addition there were a number of others who held graduate and/or postgraduate degrees in various disciplines: ST Muna (education), BT Sakah (social anthropology), JC Kangkolo (veterinary science and general agriculture), Nzo Ekangaki (arts and diplomacy), JC Awunti (forestry), WB Ntuba (commerce and economics), BN Fonlon (letters, languages, education and philosophy), Fon Angwafor III (agriculture), VC Nchami (public administration and political science), PEN Malafa (journalism), BTB Foretia (education, and later law), Chief VE Mukete (botany), Mrs. G Endeley née Silo Steane (sociology), Mrs. D Atabong (education), Njoh Litumbe (accountancy), Rev. MA Fondo (theology), FN Ndang (public administration), MO Oyebog (agriculture), WM Moutchia (languages). These graduates from Southern Cameroons and others not mentioned here studied in various universities around the world: Ibadan, Nigeria; Yaba College, Nigeria; Legon, Ghana; Fourah Bay, Sierra Leone; London, England; Durham, England; Edinburgh, Scotland; Oxford, England; Delhi, India; Cambridge, England; Paris-Sorbonne, France; Iowa, USA; New York, USA; Manchester, England; Leeds, England; Nagpur, India; Virginia, USA; Reading, England; Dublin, Ireland; Trinidad, West Indies. Within three years, by 1964, the number of Southern Cameroons university graduates in all fields of learning and from various universities around the world had increased exponentially to over two hundred.

21. *United Nations Yearbook*, 1958, pp. 346-349.

22. The named countries were: British Cameroons, French Cameroun, French Togoland, Italian Somaliland, and Western Samoa (under New Zealand administration. United Nations Yearbook, 1958, p. 331.

23. Emphasis added.

24. *Southern Cameroons Gazette*, No. 50, vol. 7, Buea, 30 September 1961, p. 273.

25. Indubitably, the plebiscite vote was primarily a vote for independence, the matter of joining being subsidiary. Had the joinder not taken place the Southern Cameroons would not have reverted to the status of a colonial territory! Its independence decision would have remained valid, although, conceivably, termination of the trusteeship would probably not have taken place on the appointed date of 1 October 1961. In light of Cameroun Republic's foot dragging and truancy regarding the finalisation, before 1 October 1961, of the agreed policies of the two countries, the Southern Cameroons could legitimately have backed off from the joinder, the plebiscite results notwithstanding.

26. Emphasis added.

27. The other round of discussions was the inconclusive talks at Foumban in Cameroun Republic, at which the British and the United Nations were conspicuously absent!

28. 'Record of the Tripartite Conference between Representatives of the République of Cameroun, of the Southern Cameroons, and of the United Kingdom, held in the House of Assembly at Buea from 15-17 June 1961, under the chairmanship of His Honour the Commissioner of the Southern Cameroons, Mr. J.O. Field, CMG'. *Declassified Secret Files on the Southern Cameroons*, P.R.O., London.

29. Ibid.

30. Representing *Cameroun Republic*: Messrs Ahmadou Ahidjo, President of that country; Charles Okala, Foreign Minister; Christian Tobie Kuoh, Secretary General of the Presidency; Jean-Faustin Betayene, Secretary General of the Ministry of Foreign Affairs; Owono, Ambassador to Liberia; Missomba, Sureté Nationale; Louis Domissy, Technical Adviser to the President; and Col. Blanc, Technical Adviser. Representing the *United Kingdom*: Sir Roger Stevens, Foreign Office; Mr. C.G. Eastwood, Colonial Office; Mr. A.G.H. Gardner-Brown, Colonial Office; Mr. P.M. Johnston, Her Majesty's Ambassador at Yaounde; Mr. P.M. River, British Embassy at Yaounde. Representing the *Southern Cameroons*: Messrs J.N. Foncha, Premier of that country; A.N. Jua, Minister of Social Services; S.T. Muna, Minister of Commerce and Industry; P.M. Kemcha, Minister of Natural Resources. Also present were: Mr. M. Milne, Deputy Commissioner of the Southern Cameroons; Mr. B.G. Smith, Attorney-General of the Southern Cameroons; and Sir Sydney Phillipson, Financial Secretary (i.e. minister of finance) of the Southern Cameroons. As these last three were British they were not strictly speaking considered as part of the Southern Cameroons delegation. See 'Record of Tripartite Conference', op. cit., *Declassified Secret Files on the Southern Cameroons*, Public Records Office, London.

31. Ibid.

32. Ibid.

33. Ibid.

34. Chapter IV of the Constitution of the Federated State of West Cameroon (as the Southern Cameroons was designated under the federal constitution) therefore made provision for the establishment of the State's Police Force. That Force was raised and placed under the command of the State's Commissioner of Police. It was charged with maintaining and securing public safety and public order in the federated state.

35. That generation of Southern Cameroons voters could not have validly done so even if they had wanted. For that would have been like condemning future generations to slavery.

36. The two messages and the speech are reproduced in Press Release No. 1562, Bulletin No. 1, West Cameroon Information Service, Buea, 9 October 1961, pp. 3 and 8. Emphasis added.

37. Article 56 of the 'Federal Constitution' enacted as follows: 'On 1st October 1961 the Government of the *Republic of Southern Cameroon* [...] and the Government of the Republic of Cameroun shall become the Governments of the two Federated States respectively.' (Emphasis added.) This telling provision has always escaped the attention of commentators, in part because Articles 48-60 (Title XI, the Transitional and Special Provisions) were later excised from the Constitution. These Articles contained very revealing information. From them we also learn, for example, that the 'Federal Constitution' was, strangely enough, signed on 1 September 1961 by Ahmadou Ahidjo when there was no federation in existence and when he had no capacity to sign any such document. He was at the material time still President of a foreign state, République du Cameroun, and had no competence to legislate either for the Southern Cameroons or for the future Federation. We also learn that Ahidjo gave himself absolute powers to rule by decree during the first six months of the Federation (Article 50); that the Federal National Assembly was composed of deputies in proportion to the number of inhabitants of each Federated State in the studious ratio of one deputy to 80,000 inhabitants (Article 54); that the Government of the Republic of Southern Cameroons and the Government of République du Cameroun were the Governments of the two federated States respectively (Article 56); that the French text of the Federal Constitution was the authoritative version (Article 59); that the population of the Southern Cameroons was put at 800,000 (arbitrarily, since this was its population as it stood some five years previously and by the end of 1961 its population was at least 1,100,000) and that of République du Cameroun

(inflated) at 3,200,000 so as to yield, following Article 54, an allotment of 10 deputies for West Cameroon and 40 for East Cameroun, in the Federal National Assembly.

38. On 1 October 1961, they also became *de facto* citizens of the *de facto* federal Republic. In a federation, member-state nationality automatically carries Union citizenship. Article 1 paragraph 9 of the 'federal constitution' provided that 'nationals of the Federated States shall be citizens of the federal Republic and shall possess Cameroonian nationality.' Thus, during the *de facto* federation, every Cameroonian owed a double allegiance, one to the federation by dint of their *federal Republic of Cameroon citizenship or nationality* (often written in shorthand as "Cameroonian nationality", that is, shorn of the qualifying adjectival phrase 'Federal Republic' as is the case in all federations). The other allegiance was owed to the federated State of their origin by virtue of their State nationality. Correlatively they also had two levels of protection, one at State level and the other at Federal level.

39. Before entering upon the duties of his office the Prime Minister took and subscribed the following *Oath of Allegiance*, and *Oath of Office:* "I [...] do swear (or solemnly declare and affirm) that I will be faithful and bear true allegiance to the people of the Federal Republic of Cameroon *and particularly to the People of the Federated State of West Cameroon*. (So help me God). [...] I [...] do swear (or solemnly declare and affirm) that I will *well and truly serve the People of West Cameroon* in the office of Prime Minister and Head of Government of the Federated State of West Cameroon and that I will observe the Constitution of the Federal Republic of Cameroon and of the Federated State of West Cameroon. (So help me God)." Schedules to the Constitution of West Cameroon. Emphasis added.

Chapter Fourteen
A Historical Injustice Crying Out to be Set Right

In all its dealings with the Southern Cameroons, Cameroun Republic has always appealed to fraud, tricks and lies as methods of statecraft. This disgraceful method of conducting public affairs has resulted in one critical consequence never anticipated by that country: Cameroun Republic's frontier with the Southern Cameroons continues as unchanged in character. The frontier line between both countries has thus always remained, *de jure*, an international boundary, notwithstanding the informal federation and Cameroun Republic's assumption of a colonial sovereignty over the Southern Cameroons.

During the period of the *de facto* federation that frontier line merely had the *appearance* of an internal boundary. By voting against UN Resolution 1608 (XV), which endorsed the plebiscite result and decided to terminate the Trusteeship concerning the Southern Cameroons, Cameroun Republic thereby continued its international boundary with the Southern Cameroons as unchanged in character.

Furthermore, the so-called 'federal republic' and 'united republic' were not genuine and enduring constitutional arrangements but merely stratagems and spurious contraptions designed to whitewash Cameroun Republic's colonial occupation of the Southern Cameroons. That being the case the international boundary between the two countries never legally acquired an internal character.

Further still, in 1984 the President of the so-called 'united republic of Cameroon', acting at his whim, revived Cameroun Republic as a legal and political expression. That action *ipso facto* confirmed Cameroun Republic's frontier line with the Southern Cameroons as an international boundary.

Finally, the confirmation of the international character of the boundary line between the Southern Cameroons and Cameroun Republic is further evidenced by the fact that Cameroun Republic has always maintained along the frontier line the military, police and customs barriers existing before independence. These barriers exist to control the movement of persons, goods and services between both countries, and up to the 1970s any Southern Cameroons citizen intending to travel to Cameroun Republic needed a *laissez-passer* to be able to enter that country.

Today, the people of the Southern Cameroons do not enjoy even a modicum of local self-government, their territory being administered by nationals of Cameroun Republic appointed by Cameroun Republic. They are denied basic human rights and are daily the object of the highhandedness of, and ruthless repression by, Cameroun Republic security forces. They have no voice in or control over any matter affecting their lives, their future, and their territory.

Cameroun Republic has assumed suzerainty in the territory. That is an unwarranted privileged status, politically, economically, culturally and socially. That status is highly prejudicial to the general interests, the dignity and the self-worth of the people of the territory. By all accounts this is far worse than anything experienced under British colonial administration.

Like all colonial territories the Southern Cameroons is entitled, as a matter of law and justice, to enter into its inheritance by emerging into sovereign statehood. Sadly, the UN and the Administering Authority failed to honour their moral and legal obligations to the people of the Southern Cameroons. Procedurally the conduct of the plebiscite may have been free. Substantively, however, it was neither full nor fair. No political status options were offered as required by the 1960 Declaration on decolonisation. By denying the Southern Cameroons the option of separate independence the UN and Britain violated the inalienable right of the people of the Southern Cameroons to emerge from colonial yoke by choosing to establish a sovereign independent state.

As a global political organisation of sovereign states, the UN is massive, bureaucratic and slow. It is government-led and being a creation of humans, it is as human in its ambitions and failings as any other human product. A critical element about that Organisation is its susceptibility to geo-political factors. States appeal to it to serve their perceived political interests. The history of the UN shows that states readily accept its deliberations when such are not in conflict with their interests, but tend to reject or question them if they are perceived not to be in their interest or that of their "friends."

Take the case of the Southern Cameroons, for example. Britain took the view that it would not have anything to gain by being at least morally required, even if only a contingent requirement, to provide a future sovereign independent Southern Cameroons with development assistance. It also took the view that the Southern Cameroons was good only as infilling material at the border of Nigeria. Having, in its perceived national interest, come to these conclusions, Britain was able to get its "friends" at the UN to join forces with her in opposing the emergence of the Southern Cameroons as a sovereign independent state. The success of Britain's UN "diplomacy" in ensuring the defeat of Southern Cameroons' rightful claim to sovereign statehood enabled Britain to save a few pennies and also enabled it to pass in the eyes of Nigeria as champion of Nigerian interest, for what that was worth.

No one, not even the political rulership of Cameroun Republic, has ever argued, or can credibly argue, that before the *de facto* federation on 1 October 1961, the Southern Cameroons was a part of Cameroun Republic. The view in some quarters is that on that date the Southern Cameroons became incorporated into and formed part of Cameroun Republic. The latter itself while subscribing to the incorporation theory, contends that it did no more than recover people and territory it had lost (it has been unable to say when these became part of Cameroun Republic and when it lost before claiming to be recovering them). This is an incongruous contention in view of its subsequent averments in the Bakassi case that on 11 February 1961 the Southern Cameroons voted for its incorporation, and was incorporated, into Cameroun Republic. There is no evidence whatsoever that the Southern Cameroons was, on 1 October 1961, incorporated into Cameroun Republic. There is also no evidence as to when and how Cameroun Republic acquired and then lost the Southern Cameroons territory and people it claims to have simply recovered on 1 October 1961.

The plebiscite vote was not a mandate for incorporation. It was essentially a vote for independence, "joining" to form a federal union being only an eventuality to which, certainly, there was a conditional political commitment, but only a political commitment. After all, Cameroun Republic rejected UN Resolution 1608 (XV) which called on her and the Southern Cameroons to finalise the agreement on a federal union before the appointed date of joinder. The Southern Cameroons was in fact not bound to accept the UN imposition. It could have legitimately insisted on full, not nominal, independence. Even after the plebiscite it could have rejected joinder with Cameroun Republic, especially in light of the latter's vote against UN Resolution 1608 (XV) of 21 April 1961 and its continuing chicanery, lies and duplicity, failings that are called diplomacy and political astuteness in that country.

The plebiscite vote was also not a mandate for transfer of the territory. There is not a single instance of decolonisation by the UN in which the plebiscite has been used as a method of transfer of territory; not even the case of the plebiscite in the Northern Cameroons which resulted in that territory becoming a part of Nigeria; that was an informed choice by the people in exercise of the right to self-determination. At any rate, the plebiscite in the Southern Cameroons was not about transfer of territory. The possibly anecdotal claim attributed to Charles de Gaulle, then President of France, that the Southern Cameroons was *'un petit cadeau de la reine d'Angleterre'* has no substance in law. The 'gift', if there was ever such a thing, was ineffectual. The Southern Cameroons was not the property of either the UN or Britain. Neither could therefore validly transfer the territory, gratuitously or for value. Admittedly, it is not beyond the realm of possibility that there could have been an odious Anglo-French *entente cordiale* on this matter. However outlandish it may sound, the two Powers could conceivably have reached a secret package deal in terms of which Britain was to grab the Northern Cameroons for Nigeria and France the Southern Cameroons for Cameroun Republic.[1] Only in such an uncanny context would de Gaulle's cryptic remark make sense. In any case, there does not seem to be in existence any instrument, duly signed by the UN or the UK Government, attesting to the claimed transfer of the Southern Cameroons to Cameroun Republic.

Either the Southern Cameroons achieved independence or it did not. In one view, it never did. This is highly improbable. To accept such a view would mean that the plebiscite was a pretended decolonisation exercise and that the Southern Cameroons situation is a classic case of a colonial territory still to be actually decolonised by the United Nations. It would also mean that there was a

Mephistophelean conspiracy at the United Nations to play a confidence trick on the people of the Southern Cameroons. Indeed, if the non-independence thesis is correct it would mean the plebiscite was a gigantic political fraud by the UN. And if it was a fraud, then the poll was a complete nullity with all what that would entail in law. This scenario is improbable. More likely, however, is the thesis that the Southern Cameroons achieved independence, though admittedly not as a separate sovereign state (given its federal association with Cameroun Republic), and that independence was suppressed. The UN itself maintains that the Southern Cameroons achieved independence consistent with Article 76b of the UN Charter as evidenced by the valid termination of trusteeship over the territory. It also maintains that it has no residual responsibility for the territory.[2] The inescapable conclusion is that the Southern Cameroons/Cameroun Republic federation was a political association of two independent states, and not the case of a colonial territory fusing into an independent state, which then transformed itself into a federation.

Cameroun Republic violated the Constitution of the Federal Republic of Cameroon and violated the constitutional rights of the Southern Cameroons under that Constitution. The *raison d'être* of Article 47(1) of the Federal Constitution was the maintenance of the territorial integrity of, and political balance in, the Federation. The article sought to obviate three major dangers: Southern Cameroons asserting the right to withdraw from the Federation (the Southern Cameroons had considered calling for a secession clause to be included in the Constitution); annexation of the Southern Cameroons to Cameroun Republic; and the legal hegemony and political imperialism of Cameroun Republic. The objective of the 1972 coup was to procure the complete fusion of the Southern Cameroons into Cameroun Republic (under the thin disguise of a unitary state), the very danger Article 47(1) sought to prevent. Because every territory has a fundamental right of self-preservation, it would be unreasonable to expect the Southern Cameroons to permit, suffer, or endure the suppression of its self-determination and submit to colonialism and oppression by Cameroun Republic.

Few unions between states have worked anywhere in the world. Africa is no exception to this reality, though since the late 1950s a variety of unions have been tried. The Tanzanian union apart, all union attempts in the continent in the name of an increasingly elusive African brotherhood have failed.[3] Any union involving real surrender of power to a central authority is unlikely to succeed. In part this is because of the despotic and totalitarian tendency of African political leadership. In part also it is because such a surrender of power rightly excites legitimate fears of absolutism and a new imperialism indistinguishable from the much decried colonialism by the "white man." The colonisation of the Southern Cameroons and the resultant struggle for liberation, like slaves fighting to be manumitted, has put the final nail on attempts at political unions between African states.

Cameroun Republic has by fraudulent manoeuvres and unremitting violence, for almost half a century already, managed to control and still seeks to control, the response of the Southern Cameroons to annexation, oppression, repression, exploitation and colonial domination. It has systematically unleashed violence in the territory and presumes to give the people of the territory harmful lectures on how to react to that sickening violence. It tosses the people back and forth like flotsam and jetsam. Whenever they have cried aloud about their intolerable condition as a colonised people, they have been told to endure the situation in the name of an indefinable fetish called "unity." With painful slowness the people of the Southern Cameroons have realised that it is their right and duty to respond to the ceaseless violence sadistically and consistently visited upon them by Cameroun Republic.

By its colonisation and terrorisation of the Southern Cameroons, Cameroun Republic violated and continues to violate: (i) the principle of sovereignty and equal rights of all peoples; (ii) the right of the people of the Southern Cameroons to self-determination; (iii) the right of the people of the Southern Cameroons to identity and a nationality; (iv) the psychological integrity and mental health of the people of the Southern Cameroons; (v) applicable Security Council Resolutions prohibiting territorial changes brought about by illegal means, contrary to the UN Charter; (vi) the principle of *uti possidetis juris* and Article 4(b) of the Constitutive Act of the

African Union; and (vii) the inalienable right of the people of the Southern Cameroons to sovereignty over their land and natural resources.

Notes

1. Secret deals at the highest level of governments do come to light from time to time. For example, only five years previously, in 1956, the British Prime Minister Anthony Eden in collusion with France took the UK to war over the Suez Canal under false pretences. In 1914 the influential French newspaper *Le Figaro* reported that Joseph Caillaux, while in high office (as prime minister of France) had in 1911 permitted France to cede Congo Brazzaville to Germany in a transaction that had brought him advantageous financial information he used to make a fortune on the Berlin Stock Exchange.

2. Statement of UN Secretary General, Mr. Kofi Annan, made at a press interview during an official visit to Cameroun Republic in May 2000. 'If I get the import of what you are trying to say, it is if the UN has any residual responsibility for *Cameroon*, and if there is any action the UN can take if things were going wrong. First of all, *Cameroon* is an independent country. The UN *normally* does not interfere in the internal affairs of independent countries, whether the history of a country ties it with the UN or not. [...] Once a country is independent, the leaders and people of that country must run its affairs.' Emphasis added. Source: www.spm.gov.cm.

3. For example, between Gambia and Senegal, Senegal and Mali, Guinea and Ghana, Libya and Egypt, Libya and Tunisia, ex-British Somaliland and ex-Italian Somalia, Northern/Southern Rhodesia and Nyassaland, Ruanda and Urundi, Cape Verde and Guinea-Bissau.

www.ingramcontent.com/pod-product-compliance
Lightning Source LLC
Chambersburg PA
CBHW021359290426
44108CB00010B/308